Quantitative Finance

Applied Quantitative Finance series

Applied Quantitative Finance is a new series developed to bring readers the very latest market tested tools, techniques and developments in quantitative finance. Written for practitioners who need to understand how things work 'on the floor', the series will deliver the most cutting-edge applications in areas such as asset pricing, risk management and financial derivatives. Although written with practitioners in mind, this series will also appeal to researchers and students who want to see how quantitative finance is applied in practice.

Also available

Chris Kenyon, Roland Stamm
DISCOUNTING, LIBOR, CVA AND FUNDING
Interest Rate and Credit Pricing

Marc Henrard
INTEREST RATE MODELLING IN THE MULTI-CURVE FRAMEWORK
Foundations, Evolution and Implementation

Ignacio Ruiz
XVA DESKS: A NEW ERA FOR RISWK MANAGEMENT
Understanding, Building and Managing Counterparty and Funding Risk

Leo Krippner
ZERO LOWER BOUND TERM STRUCTURE MODELLING
A Practitioner's Guide

Quantitative Finance

Back to Basic Principles

Adil Reghai
NATIXIS, France

palgrave
macmillan

First published 2015 by
PALGRAVE MACMILLAN

Palgrave Macmillan in the UK is an imprint of Macmillan Publishers Limited, registered in England, company number 785998, of Houndmills, Basingstoke, Hampshire RG21 6XS.

Palgrave Macmillan in the US is a division of St Martin's Press LLC, 175 Fifth Avenue, New York, NY 10010.

Palgrave Macmillan is the global academic imprint of the above companies and has companies and representatives throughout the world.

Palgrave® and Macmillan® are registered trademarks in the United States, the United Kingdom, Europe and other countries

ISBN: 978–1–137–41449–6

This book is printed on paper suitable for recycling and made from fully managed and sustained forest sources. Logging, pulping and manufacturing processes are expected to conform to the environmental regulations of the country of origin.

A catalogue record for this book is available from the British Library.

A catalog record for this book is available from the Library of Congress.

To my parents, my spouse Raja, and my daughters Rania, Soraya, Nesma & Amira

Contents

List of Figures

List of Tables

Foreword I

The valuation of financial derivatives instruments, and to some extent the way they behave, rests on a numerous and complex set of mathematical models, grouped into what is called quantitative finance. Nowadays, it should be required that each and every one involved in financial markets has a good knowledge of quantitative finance. The problem is that the many books in this field are too theoretical, with an impressive degree of mathematical formalism, which needs a high degree of competence in mathematics and quantitative methods.

As the title suggests, from absolute basics to advanced trading techniques and P&L explanations, this book aims to explain both the theory and the practice of derivatives instruments valuation in clear and accessible terms. This is not a mathematical textbook, and long and difficult equations that are not understandable by the average person are avoided wherever possible.

Practitioners have lost faith in the ability of financial models to achieve their ultimate purpose, as those models are not at all precise in their application to the complex world of real financial markets. They need to question the hypotheses that are behind models and challenge them. The models themselves should be applied in practice only tentatively, with careful assessment of their limitations in each application and in their own validity domain, as these can vary significantly across time and place.

This is especially true after the global financial crisis. The financial world has changed a lot and witnesses a much faster pace of crisis. New regulations and their application in modeling have become a very important topic which is enforced through regulatory regimes, especially Basel III and fundamental review of the trading book for the banking industry.

This book nicely covers all these subjects from a pragmatic point of view. It shows that stochastic calculus alone is not enough for properly evaluating and hedging derivatives instruments. It insists on the importance of data analysis in parameters estimation and how this extra information can be helpful in the construction of the fair valuation and most importantly the right hedging strategy.

At first sight, this ambitious objective seems to be tough to achieve. As a matter of fact, Adil Reghai has done it and furthermore treated it in a very pedagogical way.

Finally, the reader should appreciate the overall aim of Adil's book, allowing for useful comparisons – some valuation methods appearing to be more robust and trustworthy than others – and often warning against the lack of reliability of some quantitative models, due to the hypotheses on which they are built.

For all these reasons, this book is a must have for all practitioners and should be a great success.

Cédric Dubois
Global Head of Structured Equity and Funds
Derivatives Trading Natixis SA London

Foreword II

Quantitative finance has been one of the most active research fields in the last 50 years. The initial push in mathematical finance was the 'portfolio selection' theory invented by H. Markowitz. This work was a first mathematical attempt towards trying to identify and understand the trade-offs between risks and returns that is the central problem in portfolio theory. The mathematical tools used to develop portfolio selection theory resulted in a rather elementary combination of the analysis of variance and multivariate linear regression. This model of assets price immediately leads to the optimization problem of choosing the portfolio with largest return subject to a given amount of risk (measured here rather simplistically as the variance of the portfolios, ignoring fat tails and non Gaussiannity). The work by H. Markowitz was considerably extended by W. Sharpe, who proposed using dimension reduction: instead of modeling the covariance of every pair of stocks, W. Sharpe proposed to identify only a few factors and to regress asset prices on these factors. For these pioneering works, H. Markowitz and W. Sharpe received 1990 Nobel prizes in economics, the first ever awarded to work in finance.

The work of Markowitz and Sharpe introduced mathematics into what was previously considered mainly as the 'art' of portfolio management. Since then, the mathematical sophistication of models for assets and markets increased quite rapidly. 'One-period' investment models were quickly replaced by continuous-time, Brownian-motion driven models of assets (among others, the emblematic geometric Brownian motion, soon followed by more complex diffusion models with stochastic volatilities); the quadratic risk measure was substituted by much more sophisticated increasing, concave utility functions. Most importantly, the early work of R. Merton and P. Samuelson (among others!) laid the foundations of thinking about assets prices, corporate finance, and exchange rate fluctuations with sophisticated mathematical (mostly stochastic) models.

A second revolution was triggered by the appearance in the mid 1980s of the market of derivative securities. The pioneering work in this domain is due to F. Black, R. Merton and M. Scholes, who laid down the theory and the methods to price the value of an option to buy a share of a stock at a given maturity and strike price (a European call option). The basic idea to compute the price of this derivative security (etymologically, which derives its value from the underlying asset) is to construct a hedging portfolio, defined as a combination of a (fraction) of the share on which the call is written and a riskless asset, to replicate the option. The hedging portfolio is constructed in such a way that at any time the option should be worth as much as the portfolio, to eliminate arbitrage opportunities. Based on the principle of absence of arbitrage (which is highly controversial), Black and Scholes have derived an explicit expression for the price of a European call. This work, soon extended by R. Merton, was also awarded with a Nobel prize in economics.

This initial push was immediately followed by an amazing number of works providing theoretical foundations for the financial world. Most of the early developments were based on stochastic calculus making heavy use of Itô Calculus and continuous diffusion. Later, the much more demanding theory of Levy processes and jump-diffusion enters into the scene. High-frequency trading and the modeling of market microstructure naturally draws attention to discrete-event stochastic models like interacting point processes to model, at a very fine time scale, order book dynamic. Of course, all these financial models need to be calibrated to the observed prices of assets and derivatives securities using sometimes very advanced statistical estimation methods. Derivative securities pricing and arbitrage strategy also rely on accurate and fast numerical analysis. This has naturally led to an escalation in the level of mathematics (probability, statistics, partial differential equation and numerical analysis) used in finance, to a point where research problems in mathematics are completely intertwined with the theory and the practice of finance. This has also caused a proliferation of financial instruments (barrier, binary, American options, among many others), whose complexity and sophistication sometimes defies understanding! There are only a few domains in science in which there exists such an intense cross-fertilization between theory and applications.

As masterfully pointed out by the author, despite their considerable mathematical sophistications the models used today in financial mathematics are in general fragile, being based on over-simplistic models of assets and market dynamics. For example, most financial models will still presuppose the absence of arbitrage opportunities (no trading opportunities yield profit without any downside risk), which implies the existence of an equivalent martingale measure under which discounted prices have the martingale property. These are of course the very beginning of a long list of half plausible assumptions, unverifiable axioms, which in practice have proved to be sometimes devastatingly erroneous! The book proposes novel approaches to pricing and hedging financial products safely and effectively, replacing elegant but erroneous assumptions with more realistic ones, taking into account that we live in a world of more frequent crises and fatter tail risks. Based on many years of academic research and practical trading experience, Adil Reghai convincingly assembles both proven and new approaches to answer the challenges of today's highly volatile financial markets. These models not only take their inspiration from probability and statistics, but also from physics and engineering.

This book very nicely offers an original explanation covering the field. It proposes amazing new insights and techniques and opens exciting avenues of research.

The vision developed in this book, questioning the foundations of mathematical finance, is truly unique. I have learned a lot reading this amazing book and I sincerely hope that the reader will enjoy reading these pages as much as I did!

Eric Moulines
Professor at Télécom-Paris Tech

Acknowledgments

I would like to thank Nicole El Karoui, who taught me so much, and Jean Michel Lasry, who introduced me to this fascinating field and with whom I started my career. Also I would like to thank Christophe Chazot. He was my boss back in the late 1990s in London. One day, he asked me to step in for him to give a lecture for the Masters of Finance programme in Nice. I accepted without really knowing what I was in for. This programme is unique. Most of the teachers are practitioners, while students are carefully chosen from the top engineering and business schools. The aim is to provide them with insights into the business and ensure their familiarity with the requisite tools is operative by the end of their training. I am delighted to have taken part in this unique experience, especially as this Masters is currently ranked among the top 10 in the world by the *Wall Street Journal.* I share this success with my colleagues, especially Tarek Amyuni, head of the Specialized Masters in Financial Markets, Innovations and Technologies (FMIT) at SKEMA. I would like to thank him as a friend and colleague who devotes huge energy to this programme and to working in the interest of his students.

Quant work is collaborative. Progress is achieved by talking to people, reading papers and testing. I would like to thank many of my colleagues and peers. In particular, I would like to mention here some people whom I know well and who have unconsciously shaped the way I present this book.

Nicole El Karoui: for her friendship and advice over the years. She was in favour of mixing stochastics and statistics. On my undergraduate course she insisted on avoiding the perfect fit paradigm in favour of studying errors of fit when using statistical models.

Bruno Dupire: for his friendship and timely explanations and exchanges. I always enjoy talking with Bruno. He is innovative, detail-oriented, focused on creating value, yet modest.

Jim Gatheral: for sharing ideas and concepts and his enlightening explanations on several subjects. Among other things he offers is an excellent best starting point to understand any topic.

Lorenzo Bergomi: as a friend who has brought so much to the discipline. I bear in mind one of his descriptions of a 'quant': "quants are like doctors, they need to prepare the medicine before the patient is sick. If they bring the medicine too late the patient has suffered for too long and it won't work. If the medicine is provided in advance, the patient is unconscious and will not take it. A good quant is one who has the medicine and waits until the patient suffers just a little before delivering it".

Philippe Balland: for teaching me so much when I was in his team at Merrill Lynch. He taught me how to separate technical knowledge (stochastic calculus) from transient issues (statistical nature of the knowledge). Thanks to his teaching and years of work afterwards, I have been able to reconcile the two areas of knowledge in a clear way and effectively produce models for pricing and hedging. I also learnt how to move around with my laptop and undertake fascinating work on the move (I'm not sure my wife much appreciated this!).

Alex Langnau: for a unique and timely friendship beyond description, and for sharing thoughts and exchanging ideas and concepts. His thinking, derived from his background in physics, has profoundly influenced my own. Thanks to him, I have been able to complete the bridge between derivatives quants and investment quants.

I would also like to thank Mohamed El Babsiri, Taoufik Cherif and Michel Crouhy for encouraging me to make the effort to write a book from my lecture notes.

My thanks to many who have helped me in my thinking, exchanged with me on different issues: this book is a synthesis of our common knowledge. Any errors are, however, mine.

I thank the following: M. Messaoud, E. Giraud, A. Ben Haj Yedder, J. Luu, M. Souaille, M. Lakhdar, J.M. Prevost, G. El Boury, G. Boya, L. Jacquel, A. Moulim, F. El Khyari, S. Mielnik, T. Combarel, V. Garcin, M. Irsutti, O. Aw, E Tetard, F Hihi, L. Mathieu, M. Rivaud, L. Tur and A. Ibrahim.

I would like also to express my appreciation of Gisele Masante. She has dealt with a host of administrative and logistical tasks for many years.

Finally, my thanks go to all the students over the years who have attended my classes. They asked questions and helped me progress.

1 | Financial Modeling

A Introduction

At the time of writing, the term **model** has been widely overused and misused. The US subprime financial crisis in 2008 and 2009 and its subsequent impacts on the rest of the economy have prompted some journalists and magazines to launch unfair attacks on '**quants**', that is the designers of models.

This book presents a clear and systematic approach which addresses the problems of modeling. It discusses old and new models used on an everyday basis by us as practitioners in derivatives and also in quantitative investment.

The proposed approach is incremental as in the exact sciences.

In particular, we show the added value provided by the models and their use in practice.

Each model has a domain of validity and new models, with their added complexity, are only used when absolutely necessary, that is when older models fail to explain the trader's or investor's PnL.

We insist on the philosophy of modeling in the field of derivatives and asset management and offer a valuation and estimation methodology which copes with the non-Gaussian nature of returns , generally known as the Smile.

We suggest a methodology inspired from the exact sciences, allowing students, academics, practitioners and a general readership to understand developments in this field and, more importantly, **how to adapt to new situations (new products, markets, regulations) by choosing the right model for the right task at the right time.**

Derivatives pricing can be seen as extrapolation of the present (fit existing tradable products like vanilla options to price new ones like barrier options) and that quantitative investment is an extrapolation of the past (fit past patterns to predict the future). In our approach, we argue that derivatives pricing relies on extrapolation of both the present and the past. Our method allows the correct pricing of hedging instruments, as well as control of the **PnL** due to the variability of financial markets. The fair pricing of derivatives cannot ignore so-called historical probability.

Similarly, statistical models require risk-neutral models. The latter offer a benchmark, a typical set of scenarios, which should be free of anomaly or arbitrage. They constitute essential building blocks with which we compare strategies and detect cases where there is extrapolation from the past to the future in order to identify the ones that go wrong. This detection is key as it selects sane strategies and excludes those not worth playing.

In this book, stochastic calculus is not the only modeling tool for financial practitioners. We combine it with a statistical approach to obtain models well suited to a shifting reality. We insist on this **beneficial mixture** to obtain the right model and fair pricing, the best **PnL explanation**, and the appropriate hedging strategy for different products/markets.

We mix stochastic calculus with statistics. Thanks to the interaction of these two fields, we can solve the difficult problem of 'over-fitting' in the quantitative investment area. We define a computable measure of over-fitting. This is a measure of the toxicity of over-learning.

We also propose adapted measures of **toxicity** to identify the different hidden risks in financial derivative products. These risks include the Smile and its dynamic, dividends and their variability, fat tails and stochastic interest rates among typical mono underlying risk typologies.

The predictive power of exact sciences is derived from fundamental principles, as well as the existence of fundamental constants. This is a concept that is generally absent from the world of financial modeling. Financial models lack universality in time and space but we show that we can come close to quasi-truths in modeling and modestly target the most important objective of financial modeling that is **the capacity to predict and explain the PnL for a financial derivative or strategy**. In other words, the prime property of a model is its ability to explain the PnL evolution. We are **back to basics**: the origin of the Black–Scholes model (the hedging argument), construction of the replication portfolio, and exact accounting for the various cash flows.

By accepting the limitations of financial modeling (at best we can achieve quasi- or truths) we devise complementary tools and risk monitors to capture market-regime changes.

These new monitoring tools are based on volatility and correlation. Once again, they are the result of this beneficial mixture of stochastic and statistical models.

2 About Modeling

A Philosophy of modeling

Using the term '**philosophy**' implies problems or questions with ambiguous answers. Regarding derivatives, the question that first spring to mind is the following:

Why do we need a modeling philosophy for financial products and particularly derivatives?

This is a legitimate question. The need arose from a fundamental difference between the financial sector and the field of physics. Indeed, in mathematical finance there is no universal law. Socio economic agents are rational but there is no principle, such as the principle of conservation of energy in physics, that governs them. Similarly, in the socio-economic world, which drives the financial world, we lack universal constants such as the universal constant of gravity.

So, does the lack of universal laws imply that one should abandon modeling efforts in finance all together?

The answer, fortunately, is no. Despite the absence of universal laws and universal constants, we can still observe a number of **features** that help us grasp financial phenomena at least to an extent. In addition, an understanding of how these features affect our positions has a major bearing on the way we think about financial actions. This greatly simplifies our modeling task. This is important because we are not trying to model exact movements of financial assets but rather to build effective theories that suffice for the financial problem at hand. We can concentrate and find characteristics that may impact the decisions we make and the positions we have.

Another equally legitimate question is **whether the exact sciences and their methodology can be of some help in our approach?**

The answer is yes, and in fact exact sciences contribute towards building the edifice of financial modeling.

The exact sciences offer us a wide panorama of problem-solving methods. What follows are some important examples of transfer of scientific methods to the field of mathematical finance.

- **The incremental approach:** Modern science has always started with simple models and then moved to more complex ones, following the fineness of the phenomena studied. The modern theory of modeling financial derivative transactions really started with the Black & Scholes model. Since then, several trends have emerged and been adapted to different usages.
- **Observation and data collection:** astronomy started by using this method. This has provided a huge amount of data from which the physicist conjectures laws. At present, in finance, there are huge databases. For example, about 300 gigabytes of financial series are collected every week. Today, financial engineering teams include astrophysicists, who are vital to ensuring the mastery of databases and their judicious exploitation.
- **Displaying data in a synthetic way:** the first models that emerged in science were based on the synthesis of observed data, collected in the wild or even produced in the laboratory. Similarly, in finance, despite the absence of a universal theory, several empirical laws, developed by both traders and quants, provide curves and surfaces that are relatively compact and easy to follow.
- **Lab simulation:** Simulations form part of scientific methods, with potential major impact on human society. The most prominent example in modern times is probably the Manhattan Project, which had a crucial bearing on World War II. Today, in finance, simulations greatly improve our understanding of day-to-day risks and enables us to study the behavior and reaction of portfolios to different scenarios (past and hypothetical). Tens of trillions of random numbers are generated every day (50 billion random numbers every second!) in banks to produce the valuation and risk sensitivities of assets under management. In addition, parallel computing and grid computing in farms is developed on similar scale in investment banks as in very large theoretical physics labs, like CERN or Los Alamos.

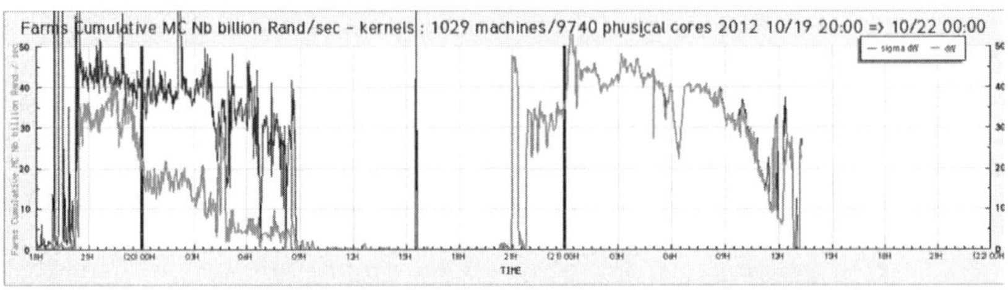

Figure 1 Number of random numbers simulated during a day for a segment of a derivative activity

In Figure 1 we show the number of random numbers simulated during the day. We observe great activity during the night to produce all scenarios and 'greeks' for the following day. We also see that during the day, real-time processing calls for a huge number of simulations to calculate real-time greeks.

- **Calibration or 'inverse problems':** in science, calibration is also known as an inverse problem. This exercise is undertaken in all disciplines, mainly to identify the model parameters that fit the measures taken in the field. In finance, this calibration exercise is not only repeated hundreds of millions of times every day, but also allows the aggregation of positions **consistently**. Indeed, in equity derivatives business for example, 90% of investment banks use the local volatility model (Dupire B., 1994) which calibrates vanilla products before valuing options. In fixed-income business, almost everyone uses the SABR (Hagan, Kumar, Lesniewski, & Woodward, 2002) model as well, to model the volatility used to price swaptions, the most liquid options in this business.
  Finally, just as crucial, if not the most important, is the question that everyone raises regarding the role of financial models in the valuation of derivatives and the asset allocation process.
- **The search for consistency:** models offer something that is essential. They provide basic building blocks and without these, **consistent decision-making** would not be possible. They make it possible to aggregate different instruments in a consistent fashion. They also create the link between the description of a financial instrument and the hedging activity (hence the daily operative activity) associated with the product. They make it possible to express assumptions in the investment area and verify the validity of assumptions a posteriori in an objective way. Models may be just an imperfect representation of reality but they are the cement with which conceptualizing across different investment activities is possible.
- **Sensitivity analysis:** scientists develop simple or complex models and calculate sensitivities with respect to all parameters. This analysis forms the backbone of any understanding. Scientists use sensitivity analysis to assess the contribution of each parameter and apply these numbers to enable optimization. In finance, we compute sensitivities and this aids the most important trading exercises that is implementation of the hedging strategy and explanation of the PnL evolution. In finance, we use several techniques to compute sensitivities:
  1. Closed form formulae: this is possible in a few analytical cases and is useful in obtaining numerical benchmarks.
  2. Finite differences: this is the most commonly used method. Thanks to the massive development of grid computing farms, the different scenarios participating in finite difference calculations are distributed. However, this can present truncation and rounding errors. In practice, this sometimes generates poor greeks and false risk alerts. For a pricing function, which takes n input

parameters, we need no fewer than 2n evaluations to compute sensitivities with respect to each of the parameters:

$$\frac{\partial f}{\partial x_i} \cong \frac{f(x_1,\ldots,x_i+h,\ldots x_n) - f(x_1,\ldots,x_i-h,\ldots x_n)}{2h} \tag{2.1}$$

3. Algorithmic and Automatic Differentiation (AAD): this technique has been used for more than five decades in other industrial areas such as aeroplane design and weather forecasting. Since the crisis, and thanks to the regulator, banks have rediscovered AAD for financial problems. It is now common for banks to use these techniques to produce the greeks on a daily basis. What is remarkable is that with the adjoint technique it is possible to produce n sensitivities of a pricing function for an algorithmic cost less than four times one total price computation. Graphs in future chapters are produced thanks to this methodology.

What is the purpose of financial models in asset allocation?

The answer is to provide a transparent methodology that is quantitative to allocate resources, assess performance and learn steadily. Science proposes hypotheses and then tests them via experimentation. Asset allocators form assumptions on future returns and risks. They then allocate their resources employing a transparent optimization technique. Subsequently, the portfolio performance is analysed and the attribution of performances to each decision can be assessed. The algorithm that links inputs (observables and assumptions) to outputs (allocations and performances) is then checked and verified to see if it is correct or not. To a certain extent, it is the trend for the treasury account, or the asset manager's equity line and its ability to **explain the evolution** that is key in the financial modeling field.

What is the purpose of financial models in derivatives?

The answer we give to this question is **pragmatic.** In our opinion, above all, models provide financial operators who manage derivative positions, with an explanation for **the shift in their profit and loss accounts.** In other words, this helps monitor their **treasury** account and risk manage it properly. We are thus **back to basics** in modeling to explain the manufacturing cost of a derivatives contract.

In this sense, the model is not universal, but adapts to the operator's situation. It is obvious that the operator is sensitive to the market in which he/she operates and that the model should include some components of the market properties, such as volatility or, more generally the market regime.

Of course, there are other objectives, such as to produce models that can predict financial time series.

In this area, we believe it is very difficult, if not impossible, to predict tomorrow's financial market outcome: nobody can predict the future with certainty. However, though this assertion is true for one single financial time series, there are some data structures that show inertia and become predictable. Typically, averages can be relatively well predicted. In other words, nobody can predict the future direction of the market with certainty but we can reasonably predict risk, the market regime and other global indicators.

Another very successful use of models is their ability to create synthetic indicators that summarize situations or business conditions. It must be remembered that the results of these models are based on certain assumptions which, unlike the situation in physics, **can change from day to day** and must always be kept in mind. Typically, in the new financial era, **liquidity, concentration** and **size**, are all important aspects in modeling.

All this will become clearer later. But first, the reader needs to bear in mind the following key points:

- In finance, there is **no universal law** as in physics.
- Like physics, though, an **incremental approach** is needed to address the problems of modeling.
- **Successful modeling principles** combine two approaches:
  - Study data (relies on statistics, with filtering approaches, averaging, estimation, and prediction).
  - Calibrate the prices of observable products (relies on stochastic calculus, algorithms and the computation of sensitivities).
- **The most important goal**, and performance standard for the valuation of a derivative or any investment algorithm is its ability **to explain the profit and loss account: explain the PnL evolution and to verify the validity of assumptions in an objective way.**

So far, we have presented elements of our modeling philosophy. It is now important to do exercises to absorb this philosophy.

In the remainder of this section we will analyse the statements, often unfounded, of some critics as to current methods of calculating the 'Value at Risk' – VaR.

We will then provide answers which validate our philosophy and the science and effectiveness of quantitative methods applied by practitioners.

What about criticism of current methods?

During the crisis, many critics have attacked the models used in practice. They have basically claimed that the industry has only used Gaussian models. First of all, many institutions, if not all, had their systems include fat-tail scenarios. Secondly, it is very important to point out that even if in the production chain some parts of the analysis rely on Gaussian returns this is the exception rather than the rule.

These exceptions were also part of an incremental approach. Another point is that it is preferable to obtain robust calculations that are not exact than to obtain sophisticated calculations and methodologies that have a lot of quirks, bugs and pitfalls.

For this particular point, the Gaussian Value At Risk (how much a bank can lose in one day with a certain confidence level based on Gaussian assumptions) provides an initial view of risk incurred. In particular, it has the merit of providing a benchmark to study the evolution for this measure. It is clearly better to have a calculation based on fat-tail returns as will be explained in Chapter 10. However, several banks, alerted by the number of exceptions (times where the daily loss exceeds the calculated VaR), have rapidly changed the way they manage risk, either by reducing some identified positions or by properly hedging their stress test scenarios.

It is for this reason that we defend the incremental approach. The results obtained by Gaussian models offer some insight, even if slightly inaccurate, into regime changes and their impact on our positions. Moreover, nothing prevents this approach from being improved to take into account the statistical properties of the time series, including the presence of fat tails as rightly advocated by Benoit Mandelbrot (Mandelbrot, 4 June 1962) half a century ago.

A few reasons for the crisis!

The crisis mainly occurred in the credit derivatives business. There was fraud and we believe this was a major aspect of the crisis. In the credit derivatives area, it is very difficult to provide a model that explains how the PnL shifts when spreads widens and the default event occurs. This is intrinsic to this area. Indeed, in many cases we have observed the default event happening with relatively low credit spreads. In such a situation, the default event represents a discontinuity and hedging does not replicate the product at hand. We can't obtain a smooth function taking the value of the contract from its price to its payoff.

We believe that the success of models lies in their ability to explain hedging cost in a smooth, regular way. And this is precisely what could not be achieved in the credit derivatives area.

In this book, we focus on the scope of financial modeling where it is possible to smoothly explain the shift in the PnL. This is notably the case in equity derivatives from which we extract all the applications in this book. We noticed that during the crisis models were able to explain the shift in strategies and positions exactly. We concentrate on the PnL explanation task.

A final word about the crisis: the regulators rightly identified as absent from the modeling of the time global interactions between different operators as materialized in counterparty, liquidity and concentration risk. These risks must be monitored as they have a major impact on the stability of the system. There were many models to describe micro-behavior but nothing to describe the full dynamic of the system, even basically. This is precisely why we advocate simple models, robust and easy to connect to each other so as to have a clear overview of the total risk.

My life as a quant

A quant's life is rich and varied. A quant adopts a multidisciplinary approach: to some extent, he/she is a doctor, physicist, mathematician, algorithmic designer, computer scientist, police inspector and commando.

- The doctor: vital for a doctor is the ability to listen. A quant needs to understand the trader and figure out the context and the problem. This requires modesty and a willingness to listen.
- The physicist: the environment of the option, market, constraints and regulations all create a particular system for the problem at hand. Like physicists in the 18th century, a quant needs to select the main drivers helping him or her to model the problem. In this exercise, laboratory experiments and simulations and back-of-the-envelope calculations are allowed and encouraged.
- The mathematician: after setting the stage, some calculations are necessary. Tractability sometime allows closed-form formulae to be obtained. At other times, commonly the case, this is not possible and we have recourse to numerical approaches.
- The creator of algorithms: The birth of the algorithm: at this stage, one needs to write a pseudo-code or a numerical code which is not indebted to any form of structure or framework. This conceptual piece is essential in order to have a clear view and to be able to develop the system in a modular way.
- The computer scientist: here comes the system and now code of a different nature needs writing. While we can describe the previous code as a part for a violinist, here the code resembles that of a conductor of the orchestra, who needs to guide the whole ensemble in a consistent way, respecting the existing pattern.
- If all the above steps go smoothly and if the model is validated by risk departments, the model goes into production and starts a second life. Now we need new skills:
- The police inspector: using models every day in a million different scenarios, for risk management, generates situations where they fail, where numerical instabilities appear, and where inconsistent results are obtained. Traders or risk managers rightfully complain and raise alerts. Quants then come onto the scene and try to understand what has happened with few clues and sometimes without being able to deal with the failure. Quants then try, like Sherlock Holmes and Doctor Watson, to understand the 'crime' and identify the guilty party in the machinery. If the problem is urgent, the quant becomes a commando.
- The commando: once the quant discovers a serious problem, he/she must act fast and correct the problem at once, to enable risk managers in the front office

and risk department to retrieve their capacity to hedge in real time and recover a clear view of the risk.

Now that we've laid out some general principles and shared some of the exciting aspects of the modeler's job, it makes sense to offer some concrete examples of what we can borrow from physics and apply to mathematical finance. Later in the book, we will apply these principles to the modeling of market data for the pricing and hedging of derivatives options, as well as in the quantitative investment area.

One important **take away** is that the philosophy behind modeling in finance is the capacity to **explain the PnL evolution**. Any time a model is developed, it is not to produce prices but strategies (hedging or investment) and the ability to explain movements in this complex combination between the stochastic or optimization model and the market structure or statistics.

In the next chapter, we will describe – referring for example to the law of universal gravitation – the impact the exact sciences have already made or may make in the future in pricing and hedging options as well as in asset allocation.

In Chapter 3, we use our 'step by step' methodology on simple products and identify the adequacy of simple models to price and hedge these products. We show the intrinsic properties of numerous smile models. We draft a list of distinguishing properties linked to pricing and hedging within these models.

In Chapter 4, we give an answer to the fair valuation problem in the presence of the smile and it's dynamic. This answer is related to the basic PnL equation, its evolution and capacity to replicate the contract given a hedging methodology. At this stage, we show how to combine stochastic calculus and statistical knowledge to produce the fair price. In this sense, we are back to basics when, for the first time, apply the Black & Scholes formula to a statistically distributed asset. The pricing and hedging volatility stems from the historical data and the pricing model is the result of the stochastic calculus and more precisely helps explain the PnL shift for a trading strategy.

In Chapter 5, we repeat the experience for mono-underlying option. We set up stochastic models and statistical estimation techniques and combine them to produce fair valuation techniques adequate for hedging purposes. On each occasion, the PnL is the means to measure the performance of such an association.

In Chapter 6, we provide a general pricing formula including all the mono-underlying type of risks.

In Chapters 4, 5 and 6, we also provide new measures of toxicity. They are useful to rank products according to their inherent difficulty to price and hedge. They also help identify where risk managers of all kinds (front office traders, quants, risk managers from the risk department) need to be cautious on the choice of model and the parameter estimation.

In Chapter 7, we look at the multi-asset case. As previously, we start from a simple model and extend it to fit the added complexity that appears in some products.

Once again, we return to basics looking closely at the PnL evolution equation. To fight the dimensionality curse, we propose a simple way to incorporate the correlation skew.

In Chapter 8, we consider the delta one business where all the previous convexities matter so little. However, the drift component and simple question of discounting are tackled. Regulations and a collateral type of contract create a new PnL evolution equation, and the miracle of linear and risk-neutral pricing is jeopardized. We show how we can simply adjust discounting curves to cope with common situations.

In Chapter 9, we present quantitative investment strategies; we introduce classical measures of performance. With the martingale modeling arsenal, we also tackle the complex evaluation of the over-fitting problem.

In Chapter 10, we propose new risk-monitoring tools. They help identify market regime changes when they occur. These occasions are moments of fragility for derivatives models and investments alike. The hidden hypotheses in the markets break down and hedging/investment strategies need to be adapted. This is an era of dynamic risk management. The innovation here is to combine two fields – stochastic calculus and statistics – to figure out the best monitoring tools.

B An example from physics and some applications in finance

Kepler, the astronomer, was the first to set out a number of laws empirically obtained by carefully studying measures of the trajectories of the planets by his predecessor, **Tycho Brahe.**

The **Aires Law** is one of these laws.

It expresses an **invariant** in the time required to travel some distance if it covers the same surface of the elliptical path.

In Figure 2, via data crunching, Kepler noticed that the time necessary to travel from P1 to P2 is the same as to travel from A1 to A2. The graph can be found on:

http://upload.wikimedia.org/wikipedia/commons/e/e9/Ellipse_Kepler_Loi2.svg.

Without understanding the reasons for the existence of this **invariant**, Kepler's law emerged from the collected data. This very elegant law has provided a simplified property of the trajectories of planets.

Newton paved the way to a theory – the theory of gravity – that could predict the shape of the trajectories. The theory also helped to make the law previously found by **Galileo** on falling bodies consistent in relation to the gravitational motion of the planets. It is of great interest in science when two apparently unconnected problems find a common root. Newton, with some constants in the model (a single constant, the gravitational constant is needed), managed to make sense of a lot of observations, to connect them to have a **predictive** capacity.

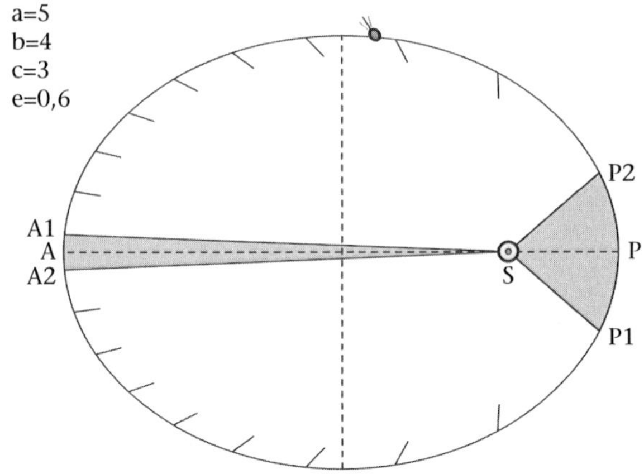

Figure 2 Kepler Aires law

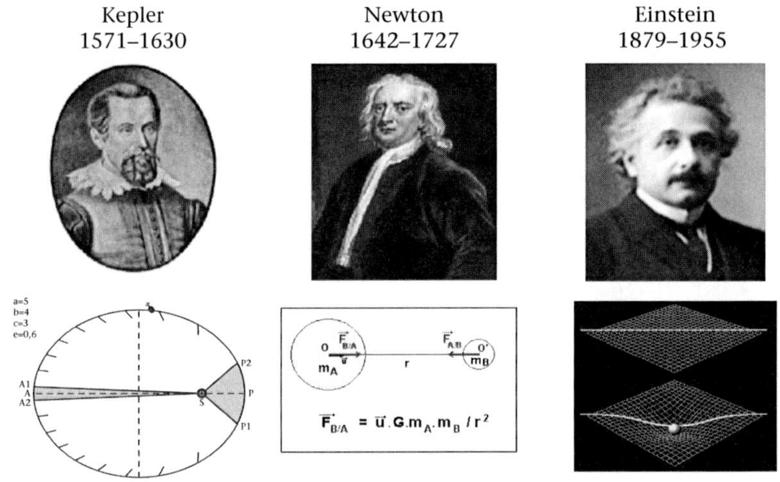

Figure 3 Incremental modeling approach from physics

This last point is very important. Indeed, knowledge of the position of different planets and conjugation with the laws of gravity, predict the existence of an elliptical trajectory and even calculate it in advance. The Keplerian laws are consequences of Newtonian theory – simple applications. He generalized the laws and found the root to match them and all the observations.

Regarding the Keplerian laws, we could also find an ellipse with certain properties, but still had to observe the system in equilibrium. A system of planets that would be disrupted by the arrival of a massive new planet could be completed, calculated and predicted by Newton's laws, even Kepler's laws would have to wait for the completion of the new balance before estimating the new parameters of ellipses.

Although the laws of gravity are sufficient to solve most problems related to the prediction of planet movements, these laws have showed some weaknesses in predicting the phenomenon of the perihelion of Mercury. It was therefore necessary to use a different model based on the curvature of space-time introduced by Einstein. His model has not only confirmed the most recent observations but also shown a stronger predictive power for many natural phenomena.

Thus the history of physics, improved by successive approaches, tells us a lot about the methodology used to build financial models more efficiently. Financial markets lack any gravitational constant or constant of nature, so we can only 'aspire', by being as clear as possible via our assumptions and the practical implementation of our models.

We will now take the methodology used in physics, as described above, and try to apply it to financial modeling.

Indeed, when it comes to valuing even the simplest type of options, a fundamental issue arises: the Smile.

Smile is a surface of points with x and y axes, representing respectively the maturity and strike of the option. For each pair (maturity, strike) we associate a point of volatility level. Practitioners classically state: *'Volatility is the wrong number to put in the wrong formula, Black & Scholes, to get the right price'.*

Behind this hides market logic that is the sufficiency of matching the market price. In the rest of the book we shall demonstrate via examples that statistics naturally complement the market photography to obtain a fair valuation, in other words the one that corresponds to the hedging cost.

That said, the Smile surface reflects vanilla options prices for different maturities and strikes. This surface is an image with very specific and conventional glasses, the price situation for vanilla options. If we take the example of a stock, we can make several observations:

- *The Smile surface is not flat*: it expresses the fact that market participants are well aware that the returns are not Gaussian.
- The level of implied volatilities for *low strikes is higher than the level of volatility for high strikes*: this is usually explained as a concept of insurance that is valued in puts with low strikes. It is a market where operators cover their downside risk. This phenomenon, known as the skew, emerged after the 1987 market crash.
- **The distance from the flat surface fades away when the maturity increases.** In other words, the slope and the Smile curvature tend to decrease as maturities increase.

The elements observed can be modeled mathematically using a Keplerian approach. The operator observes the market prices through his Black & Scholes formula glasses and obtains an implied volatility surface.

Table 1 Black & Scholes pricing formula

Black & Scholes formula	Implied volatility
$BS(S_0, r, \sigma, K, T) = S_0 N(d_1) - Ke^{-rT} N(d_2)$	
$d_{1,2} = \frac{\ln\left(\frac{S_0 e^{rT}}{K}\right) \pm \frac{1}{2}\sigma^2 T}{\sigma\sqrt{T}}$	$\text{price} = BS(S_0, r, \sum(K,T), K, T)$
$N(x) = \frac{1}{\sqrt{2\pi}} \int_{-\infty}^{x} e^{-\frac{u^2}{2}} du$	

The calculation of Black & Scholes price was made under the assumption of no dividends. It is very interesting to note that the problem of calculating implied volatilities from market option prices is commonly known as an **inverse problem.** Given the few call prices in the market, one needs to deal carefully with this issue as it represents an extrapolation problem.

Figure 4 represents a typical volatility surface in the Equity world:

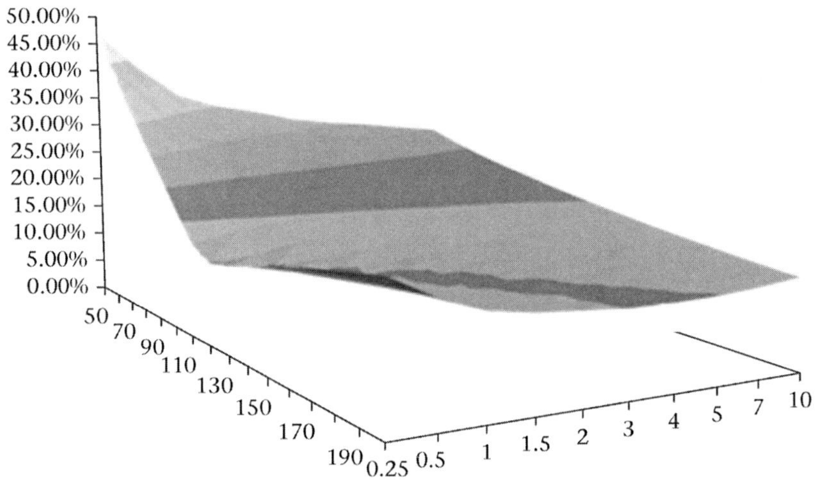

Figure 4 Sample implied volatility surface

Since we are at a turning point in financial modeling, a central question arises.

What can we do to move from the Keplerian (observation) world to the Newtonian (explanation) world?

Is it possible, in other words to establish a theory, a model that builds the entire volatility surface with some degree of explanation and prediction?

It is true that there is no universal law and therefore we face a major obstacle. Fortunately, in the socio-economic world there is the notion of **statistical invariant.** These are quantities that are stationary over long periods of time. These quantities, which vary very little in the statistical sense of the term, are fundamental **pillars for any modeling.** These numbers make it easy to follow complex data and thus give us the opportunity to provide **quasi-Newtonian** models in the physics world. We say quasi-Newtonian, and not Newtonian, because they offer predictive power under assumptions that can change in case of a change in market regime. The subprime crisis and the radical shift in paradigm have reminded us of this instability.

The fact remains that these models provide a virtually Newtonian modeling power, as well as a significant predictability that unlocks value in making, valuing and hedging products. Again, being almost Newtonian means that some modeling assumptions may change over time. This is rare a situation but it is certain to happen.

Regarding volatility, can our Keplerian observations help identify these pillars?

The answer is yes, and we can list some widely known properties in the literature which are common features to all financial markets at all times:

- *Mean Reversion*: this is an ever-present property when volatility is studied. The restoring force depends on the market we study. A highly liquid market such as the exchange rate shows a restoring force of the order of 10 days (extremely strong). This means that 5 days are enough to restore a new equilibrium if lacking. At the same time, a market such as a stock index will display mean reversion with a weaker strength of about 6 months.
- *Smile slope decreases as an inverse of the square root of time:* this property is observed in all markets. It is related to the properties of regression to the mean, as has been observed for the volatility skew. When we regress the stock returns on the volatility, the short term slope is stronger than the long term slope. Therefore the relationship between volatility and stock fades away with time.
- *Smile curvature decreases as an inverse of time:* in the same way, this property is observed in all equity markets. This is the expression that the risk on short-term volatility is greater than over the long term. To match this observation, variance at all times must be equal. This can only be achieved with a high mean reversion process and high volatility of volatility.
- *Put curvature is higher than call curvature:* this property is certainly due to the fact that puts are also used as a protection against default events.

A proposal for a Keplerian model in this case would take the following form:

We observe that the smile is a collection of slices, each of which is the sum of a slope and a curvature

This representation is purely Keplerian. It is a simplistic geometrical representation which offers geometric smoothness.

It does not necessarily offer the smoothness of the PnL and hedges.

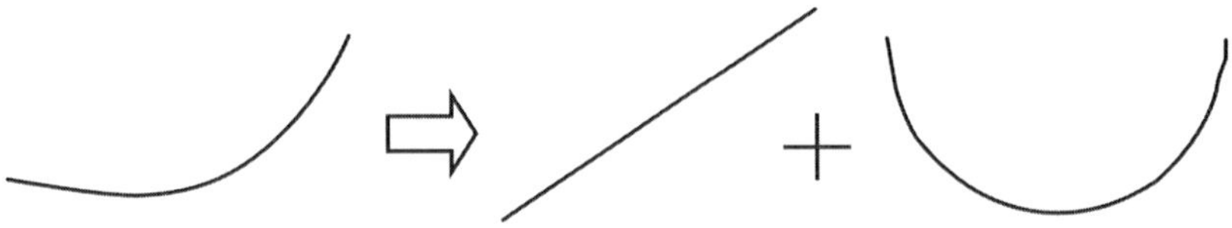

Figure 5 Smile slice observation

We start by generating the parameters of a parabolic shape with a possible functional form as follows:

$$\begin{aligned}&\text{At the money volatility: } \Sigma_{ATM}(T)\\&\text{At the money volatility slope } S(T) = a + \frac{b}{\sqrt{T}}\\&\text{Put curvature } Cp(T) = c + \frac{d}{T^{\alpha}}\\&\text{Call curvature } Cc(T) = e + \frac{f}{T^{\alpha}}\end{aligned} \tag{2.2}$$

Volatility Smile can be calculated as follows:

$$\Sigma_{ATM}(T,K) = \Sigma_{ATM}(T) + S(T)\ln\left(\frac{K}{F_T}\right) + \begin{cases}\frac{1}{2}Cp(T)\ln^2\left(\frac{K}{F_T}\right) & si \quad K \leq F_T\\ \frac{1}{2}Cc(T)\ln^2\left(\frac{K}{F_T}\right) & si \quad K \geq F_T\end{cases} \tag{2.3}$$

where F_T represents the forward at maturity T.

This formulation can certainly be improved to control not only the shape of the Smile locally but also the way the surface Smile is extrapolated on the wings.

We then obtain the following Smile, part of one of the widely employed Smile modeling practices for trading desks.

This approach is welcomed by traders for several reasons:

- *Rapidity*: the *rapid* generation of the volatility surface, given the parameters. This is obvious when we see the formulas that are used. Other models cannot generate the entire volatility surface so simply. However, caution is required so as not to fall into a 'fast mispricing' model.
- *Simplicity*: all parameters are easy to understand and their effect on the final shape of the surface is easy to anticipate, given that each parameter has an independent and orthogonal action, providing more intuition.
- *Flexibility*: the model allows the calibration of all volatility surfaces observed in practice. Indeed, four parameters per slice seem to be enough in most cases. In the case of very liquid instruments such as indices, a non-parametric approach is necessary as detailed later.

However, we encounter several problems with the use of this type of model, fundamental to their Keplerian nature:

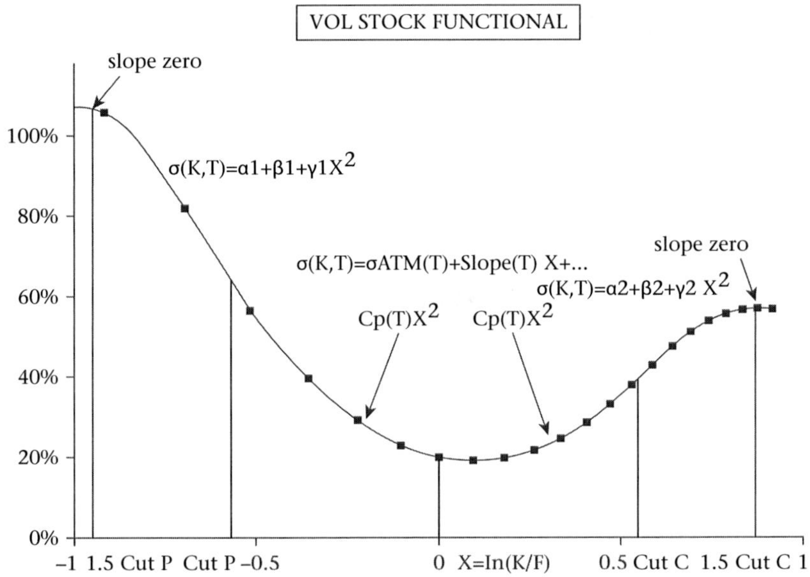

Figure 6 Implied volatility slice (Keplerian type of model)

- The parameters of the functional forms are calibrated *posteriori* once the option price equilibrium is reached – in this approach traders are market takers rather than market makers.
- The resulting surface does not guarantee the absence of arbitrage opportunity, thus creating problems not only vis-à-vis the market but also in many downstream treatments like the classical calculation of local volatility.
- The functional form changes due to the market dynamic as a response to movements of the spot and the forward. There is no specification in the current model to validate these behaviors or control them.
- The smoothness of the geometry does not offer smoothness in the valuation of positions in the book over time. Vanilla options age naturally and use different parameters when time passes and traders face difficulties explaining their PnL evolution and observe unsmooth greeks.

It is interesting to note that a recently inspired a stochastic volatility model (SVI) parameterization has become very popular.

$$\Sigma(T,K) = a + b\left(\rho\left(\ln\left(\frac{K}{F_T}\right) - m\right) + \sqrt{\left(\ln\left(\frac{K}{F_T}\right) - m\right)^2 + \sigma^2}\right) \qquad (2.4)$$

A detailed description of the topic can be found in (Gatheral, The volatilty surface, a Practitioner's guide, 2006).

Indeed, a Stochastic Volatility Inspired (SVI) approach with few parameters can be used to obtain classical forms which merge with a parabolic shape around the asset forward. Unlike the previous form, extrapolation of this functional form is less of a problem in terms of arbitrage. Finally, very effective methods exist to calibrate the parameters of the functional form. Implementation details can be found in (Martini, 2009).

A proposal for a quasi-Newtonian model is based on the specification of the dynamics of the spot, ensuring that all behaviors observed a priori are obtained through estimation or calibration parameters.

We propose to reinterpret each Kepler observation on the properties of the volatility surface as a consequence of the property of the model dynamic. – cf. Table 2 below:

Table 2 Stylized facts from data observations

Property	Description	Model
Mean Reversion	Implied volatility tends to mean revert around an average volatility level.	Orstein Uhlenbeck
Smile Slope decreases as $\approx 1/\sqrt{T}$	Volatility slope behaves as the at the money implied volatility.	Model of stochastic volatility with two factors in order to control separately at the money and the skew.
Smile curvature decreases as $\approx 1/T^{\alpha}$	Volatility curvature behaves as the At the money with a different speed of mean reversion.	A two factors stochastic volatility enables this type of control.
Put curvature is higher than the call curvature	Dissymmetry between calls and puts.	Jump model allows the generation of put prices more expensive than call prices.
Smile dynamic	When the spot vibrates, volatility at the money approximately follows the smile (we call it sticky strike).	A mixture model between local volatility and stochastic volatility allows this type of behavior.

We can propose the following model for the process. For reasons of presentation, we omit dividends.

Volatility example: Introduction

The underlying philosophy for volatility modeling is to satisfy a series of constraints:

- *Nature of the volatility*
  Volatility number has to be compared with some historical measure.
- *Shape of the At the money volatility*

Short-term volatility representation is mostly impacted by mean reversion effect. Long-term volatility representation is impacted by stochastic interest rates volatility.

- *Shape of the skew and curvature*
  Downward Slope is mainly due to volatility risk and in the case of stocks to credit risk. It decreases as a function of the inverse of the square root of maturity. Curvature decreases as the inverse of maturity.
- *Extrapolation in time*
  Long-term smile at money volatility is due to the interest rates volatility. Long-term smile is due to the cost of delta hedge and vega hedge when the volatility changes. These costs, as described later, are known to be vanna (change of delta when volatility moves) and vomma (change of vega when volatility changes, also known as vol gamma). Other effects such as jumps have little effect in the long term.
- *Dynamic of the volatility*
  The 'at the money' volatility for equities around the At the money strike behaves as a sticky strike movement. In other words, the volatility associated with a given strike does not change when the spot moves. For currencies, behavior is different, it is what is called sticky delta. In other words, the volatility associated with an option and given delta does not change when the spot changes.

All these facts and constraints must be taken into account in the volatility representation model. They include both the photography (fitting observables market prices in a shot) and the dynamic (how the volatility moves when the spot i.e. main factor moves) type of constraints. Note that practical consideration must be kept in mind due to the need to update the volatility surface in real-time.

Volatility: Methodology

The methodology is based on a building block approach where each effect is injected in the model as an independent component.

To deal with the type of volatility, which can be compared with the realized volatility, we need to compare the at the money volatility with an historical estimator.

The *first component* is to build a backbone for the at the money volatility. This includes a control on the short-term and long-term volatility. The speed at which we move from one to the other is also a model parameter (speed of mean reversion). On top of this, the interest rate volatility builds up.

$$\Sigma^2(0,T) = V_0 P(T) + V_\infty (1 - P(T)) + R(T) \tag{2.5}$$

$$P(t) = \frac{1 - e^{-\frac{t}{\lambda_S}}}{\frac{t}{\lambda_S}}, R(t) = \frac{1}{T}\int_0^T \Gamma^2(t,T)\,dt \text{ and } \Gamma(t,T)$$
$$= \lambda_r \sigma_r e^{\frac{t}{\lambda_r}} \left(e^{-\frac{T}{\lambda_r}} - e^{-\frac{t}{\lambda_r}} \right)$$

V_0: Initial variance, in practice this represents the variance at three months.

V_∞: Long term variance, in practice this represents the five years variance.

λ_s: Speed of mean reversion for the volatility expressed in time. Typically, this is around six months, that is 0.5.

λ_r: Speed of mean reversion for the interest rate volatility expressed in time. Typically, this is around ten years, that is 10.

σ_r: The interest rates normal volatility, this is typically around 1%.

$\Gamma(t,T)$: The time t bond's volatility of a zero coupon of maturity T.

We see that the volatility is the sum of three components: the first two are the result of a fast mean reverting process; the third one comes from the interest rate component. All parameters involved in this modeling are inspired from empirical observations.

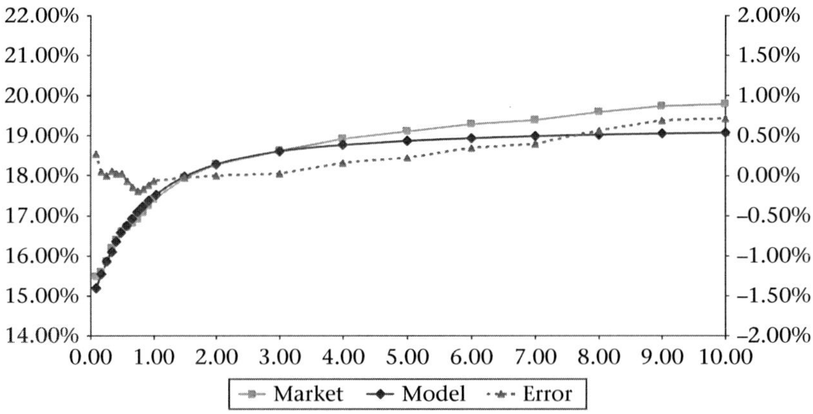

Figure 7 Fitting the backbone volatility without the interest rates contribution

In Figure 7, we observe that we have a very good fit for the global shape of the volatility. However, the error plotted is around zero on the short end but goes up in the long run. On the short end, the error is centred on zero and we can stop the modeling effort. In the long run, the error builds up. We pursue the modeling effort by introducing interest rates volatility.

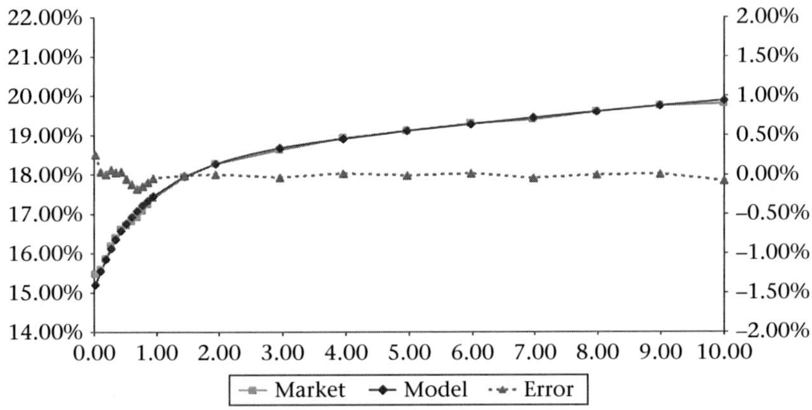

Figure 8 Fitting the backbone volatility with the interest rates contribution

In Figure 8, we observe that the fit is good both at the short end and the long end. This backbone model combines the stochastic formulation of a fast mean reverting model with stochastic interest rates. However, it gives a value for the 'at the money' volatility and needs to be complemented with features to introduce the skew, curvature and time-dependent features observed.

The *second component* will introduce these skew and curvature effects using a two-factor stochastic volatility model. One factor will be fast and the other slow.

The fast stochastic volatility factor can be modeled in the limit as a mixture of well-chosen log normal. This introduces the right shape of skew and curvature decay, in one over square root of time for the skew and one over time for the curvature. The problem with such a description is that we lose skew and curvature for the very long term. To obtain a limiting value different from zero we introduce a slow stochastic volatility (zero reversion).

One final add-on concerns the possible asymmetry between calls and puts. We introduce a jump component. The jumps are downward jumps and create a fat tail for puts. They also have an impact limited to the short end. Here is the proposed process to take into account all the previous effects:

$$\frac{dZ_t}{Z_t} = \sigma_{ShortTerm}(X)\ \sigma_t dW_t - \left(dN_t - c\sigma^X(X)\,dt\right)$$

$$d\sigma_t = \alpha_{LT}\sigma_t\left(\rho\, dW_t + \sqrt{1-\rho^2}\, dW_t^{\perp}\right)$$

$$\sigma_{ShortTerm}(X) = \exp\left(\alpha_{ST}X - \frac{1}{2}\alpha_{ST}^2\right), X \approx N(0,1) \qquad (2.6)$$

Gauss-Hermite quadrature permits a parsimonious discretization of the random centred normal variable. Thanks to the Gauss-Hermite weights and abscissae, it is possible to integrate any smooth function f with a good accuracy:

$$Ef(X) = \sum_{i=1}^{n} p_i f(x_i) + O\left(\frac{f^{(2n+1)}}{(2n+1)!}\right)$$

Using this discretization with the Pat Hagan formula, we obtain the following vanilla pricing:

$$C(K,T) = \sum_{i=1}^{Nh} p_i e^{-c(i)T} Black\left(Z_0 e^{c(i)T}, K, T, \Sigma(\sigma_0(i), \rho, \alpha_{LT}, K, T)\right)$$

With

$\{p_i, x_i\}$ — Gauss-Hermite weights and abscissa.

$\sigma_0(i) = \sigma_0 \exp\left(\alpha_{ST} x_i - \frac{1}{2}\alpha_{ST}^2\right)$ — Sampling of the initial volatility which is a result of the short term process and becomes input of the long-term process.

$c(i) = c\left(\frac{\sigma_0(i)}{\sigma_0}\right)^{\chi}$ — The credit exponent allows the increase of the credit measure of risk when the volatility risk is increased
Typically $\chi = 1$.

$$\Sigma(\sigma_0, \rho, \alpha, T, K) = \Sigma(T,F) f\left(\sigma_0, \rho, \alpha, \frac{\ln\left(\frac{F}{K}\right)}{\Sigma(T,F)}\right)$$

First part of the famous Pat Hagan formula (see Hagan, Kumar, Lesniewski, & Woodward, 2002).

$$f(\sigma_0, \rho, \alpha, x) = \frac{\alpha x}{\ln\left(\frac{\sqrt{\alpha^2 x^2 - 2\alpha x \rho + 1} - \rho + \alpha x}{1-\rho}\right)}$$

Second part of the formula.

We use the following parameters:

$$S_0 = 1, \sigma_0 = 20\%, \alpha_{ST} = 70\%, \alpha_{LT} = 30\%, \rho = -30\%, c = 1\%$$

We obtain the following implied volatility surface:

In Figure 9, we show the implied volatility calculated from the previous process. We observe large skew and curvature on the front end. On the long end, it converges to almost flat surface. We observe an asymmetry between call and put volatilities.

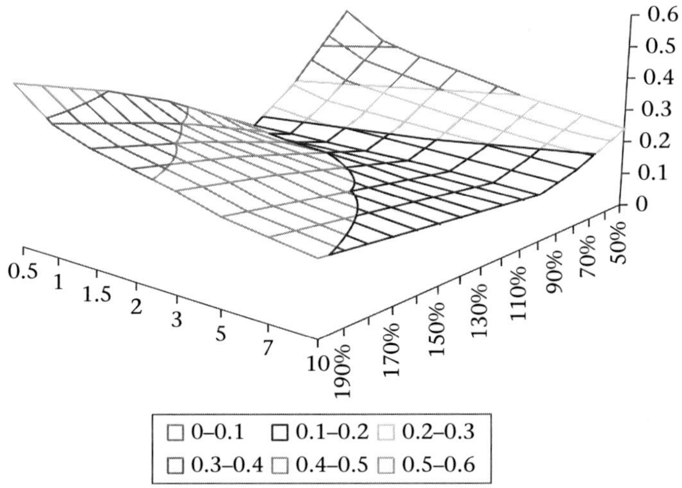

Figure 9 Implied volatility surface obtained from previous dynamic

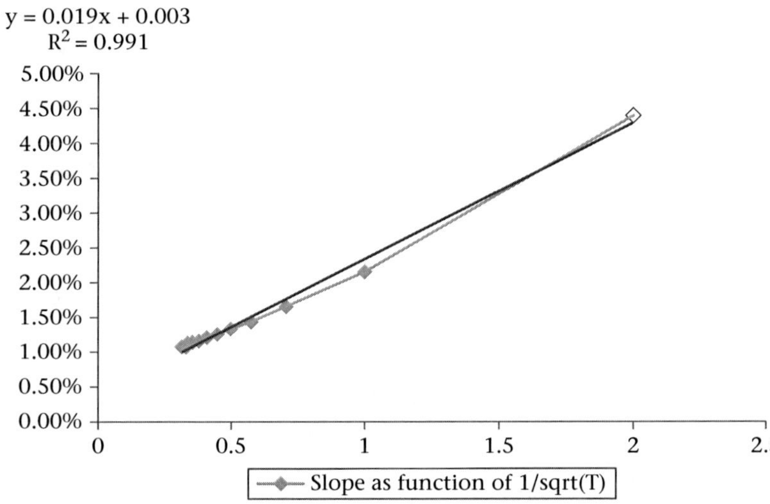

Figure 10 Slope as a function of the inverse of the square root of maturity

In Figure 10, we obtain a linear behavior of the slope as a function of the inverse of square root of maturity.

In Figure 11, we observe a linear behavior for the curvature as a function of the inverse of time.

The previous model, which builds upon the analytic tractability of the Pat Hagan formula, gets all the pre-cited features. However, we miss the perfect fit that is desirable in some liquid markets.

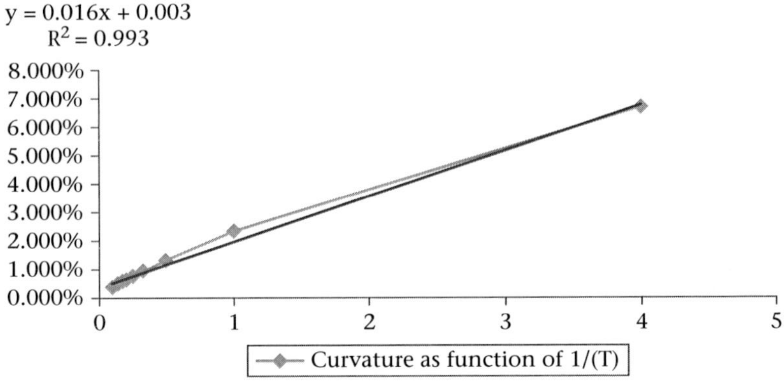

Figure 11 Curvature as a function of the inverse of time

One final *component* will introduce non-parametric function, local volatility in order to exactly fit the volatility surface in the liquid range from 50% to 200% of the spot value. We call this model *fgamma* model. It has an extra parameter called the gamma, or the mixing weight which allows control of the volatility extrapolation beyond the range of the perfect fit.

Implying the volatility from this model will be noted as follows:

$$\Sigma_{3F}(K, T)$$

Where 3F stands for the three factors within the model (two stochastic volatility factors and stochastic interest rates).

Volatility: fgamma

The previous section gives a good description of liquid points with many desirable features. However, there are two issues that are not well treated under the previous setting:

- *Perfect fit* in the case of indices: indeed parametric forms allow predictability but do not insure a perfect fit.
- *Dynamic of the volatility*: indeed, the previous model is homogeneous and it therefore will give a sticky delta type of behavior which is not what is observed in practice in the equity world.

To cope with these two issues, we apply a mixing weight (which can depend on the maturity). This has the effect of degrading the calibration, which is completed by the introduction of a local volatility process.

The process will then be given by the following equation:

$$\frac{dZ_t}{Z_t} = f(Z_t)\,\sigma_{ShortTerm}(X)\ \sigma_t dW_t - \left(dN_t - \gamma\ c\,\sigma^X(X)\,dt\right)$$
$$d\sigma_t = \gamma\alpha_{LT}\sigma_t\left(\rho\, dW_t + \sqrt{1-\rho^2}\, dW_t^{\perp}\right) \tag{2.7}$$
$$\sigma_{ShortTerm}(X) = \exp\left(\gamma\alpha_{ST}X - \frac{1}{2}\gamma^2\alpha_{ST}^2\right), X \approx N(0,1)$$

Where gamma is the mixing weight and the function f is the local volatility.

The implied volatility under this new model can be approximated as follows (see Hagan, Kumar, Lesniewski, & Woodward, 2002):

$$\Sigma_{3FLV}(K,T) \cong \Sigma_{LV}\left(f,K,T\right) * \left(\frac{\Sigma_{3F}(K,T)}{\Sigma_{3F}(F,T)}\right)^{\gamma^2}$$

This formula allows a fast, implied volatility calculation and calibration.

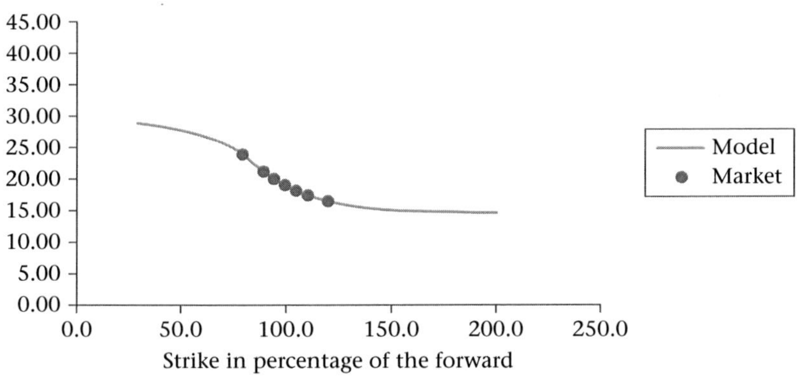

Figure 12 FGamma smile calibration with zero mixing weight

In Figure 12, we observe that the *fgamma* perfectly calibrates the market points (red points). With zero mixing weight, the smile is extrapolated almost flat.

In Figure 13, we again observe a perfect fit for the market points. With a 50% mixing weight the wings extrapolate with higher volatilities.

In Figure 14, we use a 100% mixing weight and again obtain a perfect fit on the market points. However, the smile extrapolation is different.

All the smiles generated with different mixing weights provide admissible distributions and fit market points perfectly. The mixing weight impacts the manner in which the smile extrapolates. The choice of the mixing cannot be inferred from today's data (from the market photography of today's prices). Rather it is a result of statistical inference from the volatility dynamic.

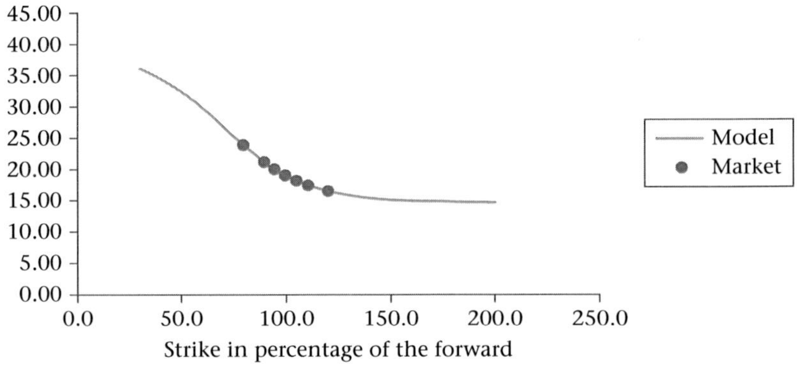

Figure 13 FGamma smile calibration with 50% mixing weight

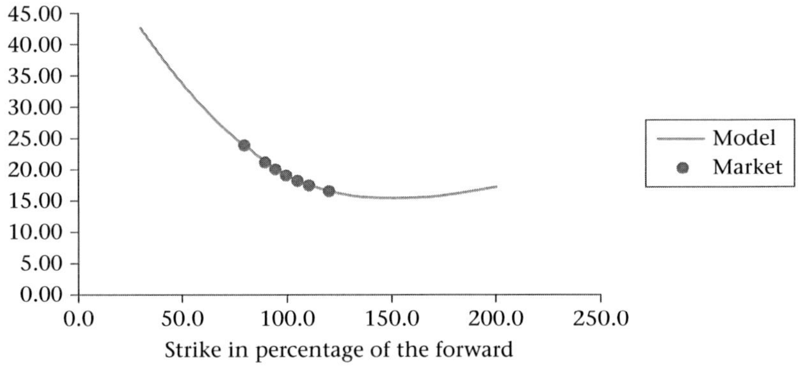

Figure 14 FGamma smile calibration with 100% mixing weight

This quasi-Newtonian approach provides a model with parameters that are estimable and historically relatively stable. After calibration data options, we have listed the model parameters in their default versions. This allows us to compare them with statistically estimated values.

With this quasi-Newtonian vision we cannot predict the future but we can predict risk. This notion is Professor Eugene Stanley's. He is a physicist who has made a huge contribution with his work on econophysics, that is physics applied to the economy. Our role as a modeler is to build models that enhance our understanding of risk and especially enable appropriate hedging.

At this stage, the confrontation of financial models with ones from physics shows that at best we can achieve quasi-Newtonian modeling. An important objective and benchmark for a model in finance is its ability to explain the Profit and Loss account. Yet, in the previous example, we can get very close to reality by capturing statistical invariants. This approach is a progressive approach and needs to be frequently confronted with data.

In the next chapter, we shall use our incremental approach to analyse classical exotic products. We shall see how we can choose the right model for the right product.

Exercise 1

1. What is the main purpose of a financial model?
2. Are financial models like universal models in physics?
3. Is Modeling the skew as a function of T of the form a + b / sqrt (T) a predictive model? Is this a Keplerian or Newtonian model?

3 From Black & Scholes to the emergence of Smile Modeling

A Study of derivatives under the Black & Scholes model

This step is crucial, as it is the first step in our incremental approach. Indeed, thanks to a relatively simple model, Black & Scholes (despite all its flaws), we are able to understand our position, the risks involved today and tomorrow, and what to put in place to perform effective hedging.

It is not just a static view of the risks, but *dynamic*. We use a simple model to explore several scenarios in spot and time. The price and hedges are explored and their dynamic is studied.

This analysis is easy to perform numerically. Implementation of the Black & Scholes model is relatively simple and robust. In many cases, we may be able to derive closed-form formulae. In other cases, it is possible to solve numerically using a partial differential equation (PDE). In general, the Monte Carlo technique offers high flexibility and can price almost any path-dependent option.

For our first analysis, we look at products where analytical formulae exist. We shall not derive them in this book. Instead we shall exploit these analytical results to explore the dynamic for risks and see under what conditions such a simple model can be used in practice for pricing and risk management.

We shall consider the following list of products: Vanilla call option, Asian, European binary option, American binary option.

We show that thanks to hedging cost estimation techniques (performing the PnL explanation exercise), and exploration of the risks dynamic, we will be able to answer important operational questions:

- When is the Black & Scholes model sufficient for pricing and hedging?
- What are the right Black & Scholes parameters (when possible?)
- What possible model extension when the Black & Scholes is not sufficient?

Methodology

Our methodology is to define a very simple dynamic for the asset. We use this simple process to price and, more importantly, hedge our product in all situations that are possible within the model, that is we explore many scenarios in spot and time.

Our simple model in the equity derivatives world is the Black & Scholes. It assumes that the equity has the following dynamic under the *real probability P*:

$$\frac{dS_t}{S_t} = \mu dt + \sigma dW_t^P$$

The asset is log normally distributed with a given volatility σ and a drift μ.

When pricing derivatives, the hedging process annihilates the dependence on the drift. If we assume a risk free rate r and a dividend yield d, the process under this hedging mechanism preserves the initial volatility but modifies the drift. The process is said to be under risk neutral probability. Its dynamic becomes:

$$\frac{dS_t}{S_t} = (r - d)\, dt + \sigma dW_t^Q \tag{3.1}$$

The model content is then summarized by the volatility number, this describes the rate at which the asset vibrates. High volatility means that the asset goes up and down very rapidly. Low volatility implies a dynamic which is principally governed by the drift. Under a zero volatility assumption, the process follows a deterministic equation for which the solution is the *forward*:

$$F_T = E^Q(S_T) = S_0 \exp((r - d)\, T)$$

With no assumption on the volatility, the resulting process is given by:

$$S_T = F_T \exp\left(\sigma W_T^Q - \frac{1}{2}\sigma^2 T\right)$$

In this model, the equity spot vibrates and evolves with time around the forward.

Valuing the payoff $\varphi\left(\left\{S_{t_1}, \ldots, S_{t_n}\right\}\right)$ at maturity T is achieved by averaging the realized payoffs under the risk neutral probability measure:

$$\pi = e^{-rT} E^Q\left(\phi\left(\left\{S_{t_1}, \ldots, S_{t_n}\right\}\right)\right) \tag{3.2}$$

But beware this price, or more exactly, the hedging cost is nothing without the replication strategy used to construct the portfolio.

In fact, this price represents the initial wealth to replicate the final payoff on all paths, provided we apply the resulting hedging strategy.

More precisely, we assume a replicating portfolio starting with the initial price.

$$C_0 = \pi$$

We apply the hedging strategy implied by the model. Its evolution equation is given by:

$$C_{t+1} - C_t = (C_t - \Delta_t S_t)\, r\Delta t + d\Delta_t S_t \Delta t + \Delta_t (S_{t+1} - S_t) \tag{3.3}$$

- The term $(C_t - \Delta_t S_t)\, r\Delta t$ represents the financing cost. For example, a call option will have a negative financing cost term. This means that anytime the financing cost increases more money is needed at inception to compensate for it. This is materialized with a higher call option price if interest rates are higher.
- The term $d\Delta_t S_t \Delta t$ corresponds to the dividend yield received from holding Δ_t stocks. For example, a call option will always have positive delta. Therefore this term generates positive inflows to the trader's PnL. This means that the price of a call option at inception must be cheaper in the presence of dividends.
- The term $\Delta_t (S_{t+1} - S_t)$ represents the amount of money generated from holding Δ_t stocks. For example, a call option will have a positive delta. However, the future spot variation can go either way. This term will permit the replication portfolio to accompany the market move in both directions but only partially.

On these assumptions, the price and hedging strategy can replicate the payoff of the option at maturity regardless of the realized path. The only requirement for this result to be true is that the unit realized volatility corresponds to the volatility used to value the option.

The most surprising fact is that this result remains true even if the process drift is arbitrary, say stochastic.

This is the Black & Scholes miracle, worth a Nobel prize.

The continuous version of the PnL evolution (3.3) is given by:

$$dC_t = (C_t - \Delta_t S_t)\, rdt + \Delta_t dS_t dt + \Delta_t dS_t$$

Rearranging the terms, gathering the replication portfolio terms on one side and the asset on the other we obtain:

$$de^{-rt} C_t = e^{-rt} \Delta_t (-(r - d)\, S_t dt + dS_t) \tag{3.4}$$

At this stage, this equation is free from probability measure. It can be compared with the physics notion 'energy conservation'. Here we are referring to cash flow conservation. The replication theory uses this equation to provide the following useful result:

If the right hand side term is a martingale, then so is the left.

Therefore, if we assume that the process is given by Equation (3.1), the left hand side of Equation (3.4) is also a martingale and we can write:

$$C_0 = E^Q\left(e^{-rT}C_T\right) \tag{3.5}$$

Note that the risk neutral valuation is simply a beautiful mathematical construct that transforms the problem of pricing and hedging into a problem of pricing by appropriately using the PnL evolution equation and making the right assumption on the process.

Unlike in physics, these equations need to be revised. The crisis and regulations have made important changes to flows exchanged during the hedging process of a derivative. Hence replication portfolio equations have evolved correspondingly.

Under the previous assumptions, the replication equation implies that under the risk neutral probability $E_Q(dC) = rCdt$. The previous equation is associated with some risk-free rate. It is then possible to compute the initial price, without accounting all intermediary hedge cost, using the equilibrium formula $E_Q\left(-C_0 + \exp(-rT)C_T\right) = 0$. However, there are other flows that can intervene. These flows have become important to include after the crisis, especially because of the scarcity of capital and importance of liquidity and capital consumption. We shall deal with the new replication portfolio in a later chapter. This will take into account margin calls due to collateral agreements (symmetric or not), CVA (counterparty risk adjustment) or DVA, FVA (funding value adjustment). In the meantime, we focus on simple hedging strategies and study their dynamic within our initial framework. Using the Black & Scholes assumptions, we pursue our exploratory journey of price and greeks for different scenarios in spot and time.

Via this model we study the price, delta and gamma according to different scenarios for the spot. We also examine the situation at the inception of the option and near the maturity of the option. These scenarios allow us to understand how our hedging strategy evolves when the spot vibrates and time passes. This study is done within the model's assumptions. However, our hedging strategy within this model can be impacted by parameters such as the repo, dividends, interest rates or any other parameter that helps define the model. If the impact of these extra parameters is linear, the trader and the practitioner will mark them in an appropriate way. When there is an important change in trading strategy and PnL evolution, the model needs to be adjusted. In an incremental way, we can detect whether a model is sufficient or not via a systematic search for convexity.

The search for convexity

The Black & Scholes model is a benchmark function that can be presented of the following form $f(t, S, \alpha_1, \ldots, \alpha_n)$. It assumes the vibration of the spot S and includes many other parameters $(\alpha_1, \ldots, \alpha_n)$ such as the rate, dividend, volatility, repo as inputs, etc. In practice, investments banks hedge these input parameters creating extra terms in their PnL evolution.

More precisely, we observe the following extra terms in the PnL equation:

$$\Delta PnL = \cdots + \frac{\partial^2 \pi}{\partial S \partial \alpha} \Delta S \Delta \alpha + \frac{\partial^2 \pi}{\partial \alpha \partial \alpha'} \Delta \alpha \Delta \alpha' + \frac{\partial^2 \pi}{\partial \alpha^2} \Delta \alpha^2 \tag{3.6}$$

These extra terms may generate a systematic loss or gain or simply have no impact on average. If there is a loss, the trader needs to adjust his/her price and lift it to compensate for this loss. The amount to be added is an estimation of the total loss in the PnL equation, represented by the following integral:

$$E_{BS} \int_0^T \left(\frac{\partial^2 \pi}{\partial S \partial \alpha} \Delta S \Delta \alpha + \frac{\partial^2 \pi}{\partial \alpha \partial \alpha'} \Delta \alpha \Delta \alpha' + \frac{\partial^2 \pi}{\partial \alpha^2} \Delta \alpha^2 \right) dt$$

This quantity is what explains the extra cost from hedging the parameters. A simple way to explore this quantity, and figure out if it is material, is to rely on the following Taylor expansion with expectation.

$$E\left(f(X)\right) \cong f(E(X)) + \frac{1}{2} Var(X) f''(E(X))$$

This result is true for any smooth function f and any random variable X. Its multidimensional version is given by:

$$E\left(f(X_1, \ldots, X_n)\right) \cong f(E(X_1), \ldots, E(X_n)) + \frac{1}{2} \sum_{i,j=1}^{n} CoVar\left(X_i, X_j\right)$$
$$\times \frac{\partial^2 f}{\partial x_i \partial x_j} (E(X_1), \ldots, E(X_n))$$

So for a n-dimensional problem, with a simple model we can explore all aspects of its convexities and cross convexities relying just on the simple model and its derivatives. It reveals the directions which could generate hedge costs during the life of the contract.

In the case of a three-dimensional problem we just calculate the value function issued from the small model for the three bi dimensional grids (3 n × n) instead of calculating a whole cube (n × n × n).

In Figure 15, we show that a convexity search for a three-dimensional function can be undertaken using three different two-dimensional projections. This is important as it makes the search for convexity a polynomial task instead of an exponential one. Once we fill these three dimensional squares, we can compute a good approximation value for the contract up to a second order expansion for every multi-dimensional scenario. Here are the details of such an approach.

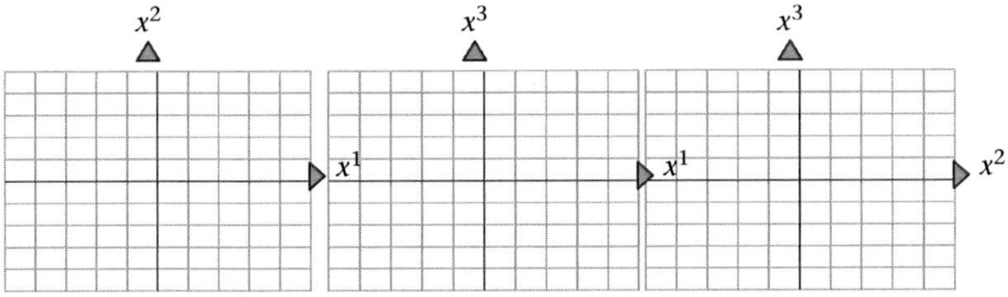

Figure 15 Convexity search for three extra parameters

- We assume that we would like to calculate the function $u(x_1,\ldots,x_n)$.
- We locate each couple of coordinates $\left(x_i,x_j\right)$ within the grid.
- We use a bi-cubic spline interpolation to value a bi-dimensional function $v_{i,j} = u\left(x_1(0),..x_i,.x_j,x_n(0)\right)$: here only two variables $\left(x_i,.x_j\right)$ have moved.
- We use a cubic spline interpolation to value a one dimensional function $u_i = u\left(x_1(0),..x_i,..x_j(0),x_n(0)\right)$: here this is a special case of the previous where just one variable has moved.

Then we perform the following calculation:

$$
\begin{aligned}
u(x_1,\ldots,x_n) &= u(0) + \sum_{i=1}^{n}(x_i - x_i(0))\partial_{x_i}u(0) \\
&\quad + \frac{1}{2}\sum_{i=1}^{n}\sum_{j=1}^{n}(x_i - x_i(0))\left(x_j - x_j(0)\right)\partial_{x_i x_j}u(0)v_{i,j} - u(0) \\
&= \sum_{i=1}^{n}\sum_{j=i+1}^{n} \begin{matrix} -(x_i - x_i(0))\,\partial_{x_i}u(0) - \left(x_j - x_j(0)\right)\partial_{x_j}u(0) \\ -\frac{1}{2}\left(x_j - x_j(0)\right)^2\partial_{x_j x_j}u(0) - \frac{1}{2}(x_i - x_i(0))^2\partial_{x_i x_i}u(0) \end{matrix} \\
&\quad + u(0) \\
&\quad + \sum_{i=1}^{n}(x_i - x_i(0))\partial_{x_i}u(0) + \frac{1}{2}\sum_{i=1}^{n}(x_i - x_i(0))^2\,\partial_{x_i x_i}u(0)
\end{aligned}
$$

Regrouping terms, we obtain the reconstruction formula:

$$
\begin{aligned}
u(x_1,\ldots,x_n) - u(0) &= \sum_{i=1}^{n}(u_i - u(0)) \\
&\quad + \sum_{i=1}^{n}\sum_{j=i+1}^{n}\left(v_{i,j} - u(0) - (u_i - u(0)) - \left(u_j - u(0)\right)\right)
\end{aligned}
$$

This methodology is very efficient and commonly used for intraday pricing and hedging. It allows the positions in a large book to be followed dynamically in turbulent times, avoiding a huge re-computation effort.

Exercise 2

1. X is a random variable and f a smooth function. Provide a method for estimating $E\left(f(X)\right)$ and generalize to a multi-asset function.

Vanilla European option

The simplest option is the Call option (or Put option). A call option is the right and not the obligation to buy the stock at maturity T for a given price, the exercise strike K. We progressively study the call option within the Black & Scholes model assumptions.

We recall the essential elements for the definition of the option and calculation of the greeks (delta and gamma) using the Black & Scholes model. We perform this analysis for a one year option at inception and one month before it expires. We do this for spot ladder scenarios (spot ranging from 50% of the initial spot to 200% of the initial spot). These are typical conditions where we expect to use the model for hedging purposes and PnL explanation exercises.

Table 3 Vanilla call payoff and pricing formula

Option's payoff	Pricing formula
$(S_T - K)^+$	$e^{-dT} S_0 N(d_1) - e^{-rT} KN(d_2)$ $d_{1/2} = \frac{\ln\left(\frac{S_0}{K}\right) + (r-d)T +/- \frac{1}{2}\sigma^2 T}{\sigma\sqrt{T}}$ $N(x) = \frac{1}{\sqrt{2\pi}} \int_{-\infty}^{x} e^{-\frac{u^2}{2}} du$

Numerical application

In the absence of interest rate and dividend yield, an 'at the money' call is given by the simple formula (usual interview question):

$$\pi\left\{(S_T - S_0)^+\right\} = 0.4\sigma\sqrt{T} S_0 \quad (3.7)$$

Now, if we apply this formula to a call option of one year maturity, with a spot equal to \$100 and a volatility of 20%, we obtain the price of \$8. This price represents the initial wealth in order to set up a hedging strategy that replicates the final payoff $(S_{1y} - 100)^+$, whatever the direction of the market (whether it goes up or down does not matter). If the spot doubles and goes to \$200, the replicating portfolio should generate \$100 starting from an initial wealth of just \$8. Similarly, if the spot in one year goes to \$50, the payoff is equal to zero and likewise for the replicating portfolio. Naturally, we can ask where the money comes from in the first case and where the money goes in the second case. In the first case, your hedging strategy as a seller tells you to buy the stock and more of it when it goes up. You become increasingly exposed to a rising stock. In the second case, when the stock falls, your hedging strategy will tell you to gradually sell your current stock position (initially you hold \$50 of stock) as the stock declines. You are basically selling low what you bought high. This has a cost. When the realized volatility is 20% uniformly over time as assumed by the pricing model, the replicating ends up at zero as predicted. In other cases, where the realized volatility exceeds 20% or is not uniformly distributed in time, the replicating portfolio could end up negative and generate a loss for the option seller.

Price scenarios

We obtain the following graph:

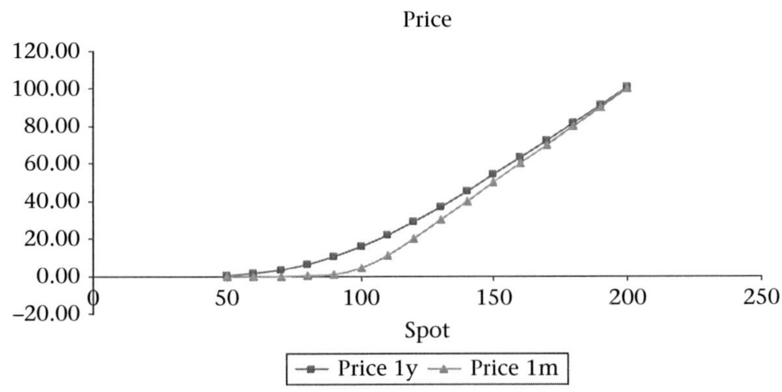

Figure 16 Vanilla call pricing graph

Delta gamma scenarios:

We can make the following comments:

- The delta takes values between 0 and 1.

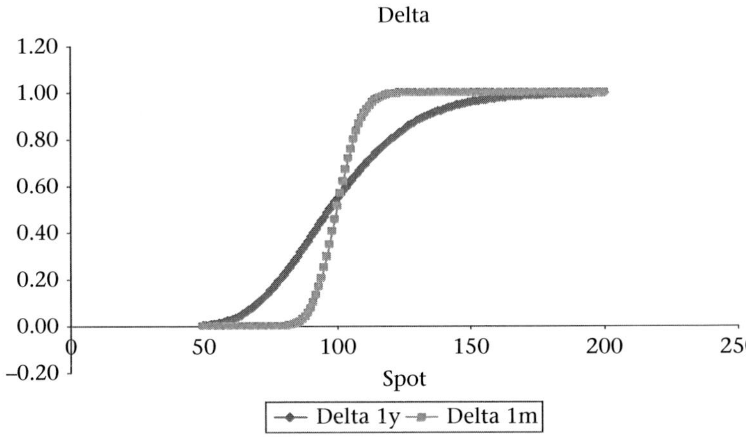

Figure 17 Vanilla call delta graph

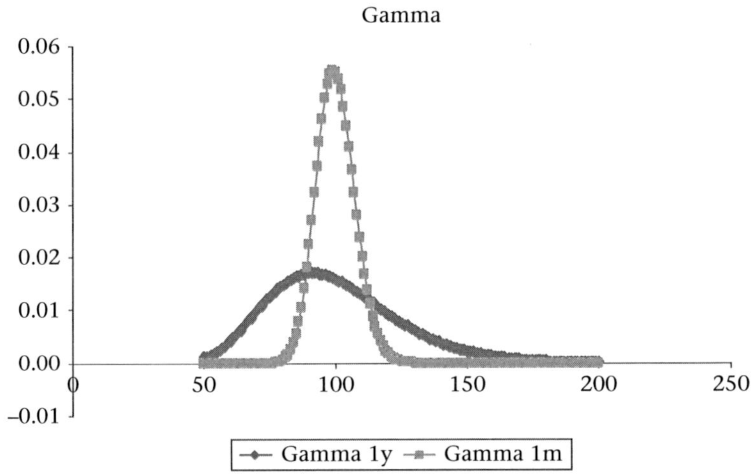

Figure 18 Vanilla call gamma graph

This remark in a good sanity check when you develop a model. In reality, the delta may vary a little when taking dividends and repo rates into account.

- Gamma is always positive.
  This is crucial. The Gamma represents the speed of change of the delta. It is not per se a hedging indicator at least within Black & Scholes assumptions, but it indicates if one needs to pay attention to the delta.
- The price of the call increases and convex with spot.
  When the spot is higher than the strike, we say that the option is in the money. When the spot is lower than the strike, the option is out of the money. When the spot is around the strike the option is at the money. Naturally, when the

spot goes up, there is a greater chance of being in the money generating more potential cash flow for the option holder. It is then expected that the price is higher. Out of the money, the option has minimum chance to pay at maturity and we observe that the price approaches zero. At the money, there is uncertainty as to the final outcome.

- The time value is maximum around the strike.
  The model price is the sum of the intrinsic value (payoff formula) plus the time value. Deep in or out of the money, we recognize the payoff formula. At the money, around the strike, the pricing formula diverges from the payoff formula, highlighting the time value of the option. There is uncertainty on the final payoff. The longer the residual maturity, the higher the time value may be.
- The valuation curve approaches the payoff when the time approaches maturity.
  All the models at maturity fit the payoff. This is a key observation, verified not only with Black & Scholes but all models. It is a classical sanity check to be made after a first implementation.

The vanilla European option needs to be known in all its details. It is a benchmark product and every other product with similar properties can be considered a vanilla product. Any product, conversely, which shows substantially different properties, needs to be more carefully studied. One has to dig deeper to fully understand the product and to be able to trade and risk-manage it.

European binary option

This option has several names: digital, discrete terminal barrier or bet option. The last name is explicit enough. The payoff of a digital call pays if the spot finishes higher than the strike, otherwise it pays zero. This option is quite common and appears either explicitly in the payoff or implicitly in many derivatives structures.

Table 4 European binary

Option's payoff	**Pricing formula**
$100\% * 1_{\{S_T \geq K\}}$	$e^{-rT} N(d_2)$ $d_2 = \frac{\ln\left(\frac{S_0}{K}\right) + (r-d)T - \frac{1}{2}\sigma^2 T}{\sigma\sqrt{T}}$ $N(x) = \frac{1}{\sqrt{2\pi}} \int_{-\infty}^{x} e^{-\frac{u^2}{2}} du$

As previously, we study this payoff using the simple valuation formula issued from the Black & Scholes model. We perform spot ladder scenarios and show price, delta and gamma at inception and one month before maturity.

Price Scenario

We obtain the following result:

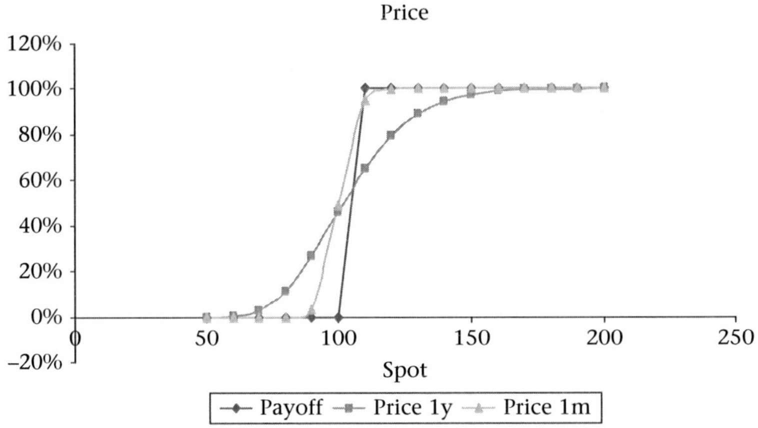

Figure 19 European binary call price graph

It is interesting to note that the pricing formula is quite simple. The pricing function increases. It looks like the delta of a call option. This is due to the following relationship:

$$\frac{\partial}{\partial K}(S_T - K)^+ = -1_{\{S_T \geq K\}} \tag{3.8}$$

Delta and gamma scenarios

We notice that the delta spot ladder of the European binary call option looks like the gamma of the European vanilla call option.

We can also make the following comments:

- As discussed earlier, the delta of the European binary is the gamma of the vanilla option.
  This means in particular that we no longer have this bounded delta from zero to one. When the spot is out of the money, the option is worth almost nothing and the delta is zero. So this means that as a hedger the replication portfolio should not be sensitive to the movements of the spot because the target to deliver remains at zero. The same thing happens when you are in the money. In this region, the option is almost worth a bond (discounted). The interesting part is at the money. Your option estends from zero to one in a small region of the spot and this needs to be captured by some hedging process. To generate this value, the hedger needs to be highly exposed to the spot. This situation makes the delta

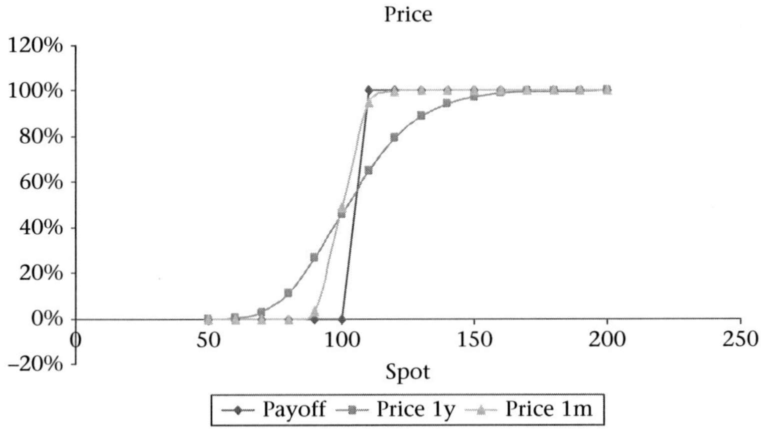

Figure 20 European binary call delta graph

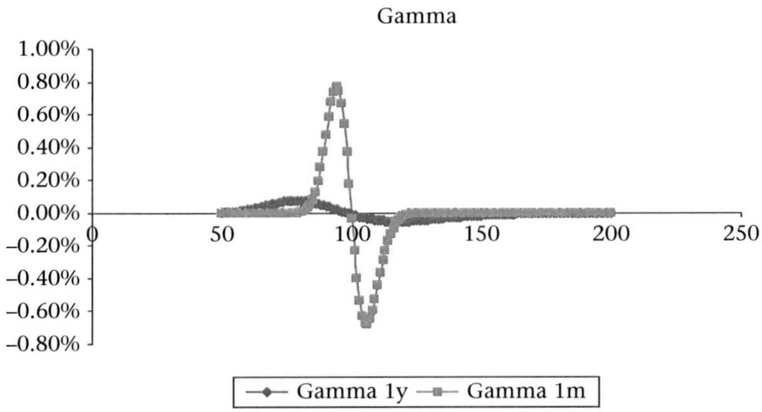

Figure 21 European binary call gamma graph

exceed one, the maximum achieved by our benchmark (call option). Just after making this amount of money we enter the out of the money region and the hedger needs to deleverage the delta just as quickly.

- Gamma of the European binary changes sign.
  The gamma is the change in the delta when the spot moves. We saw earlier that moving from out of the money with zero delta to at the money, the hedger had to have large exposure to the spot. This change of delta is fast and one needs big positive gamma. Continuing the movement up, the hedger enters the in the money region where his delta should be zero, now making the gamma highly negative to decelerate the exposure. This gamma spot ladder is substantially different from our benchmark study of the call option; it is different in terms of the magnitude of the numbers and their sign as well.

American binary option

This option pays one dollar when the share price touches the barrier level. It is also known as the American bet. This option pays whenever

Table 5 American binary

Option's payoff	**Pricing (12)**
$100\% * 1_{\{M_T \geq K\}}$ $M_T = \max_{u\in[0,T]} S_u$	$e^{-rT}\left\{\left(\frac{K}{S_0}\right)^{h_1} N(-z_1) + \left(\frac{K}{S_0}\right)^{h_2} N(-z_2)\right\}$ $h_{1,2} = \frac{\left(r-d-\frac{1}{2}\sigma^2\right)-/+\sqrt{2r\sigma^2+\left(r-d-\frac{1}{2}\sigma^2\right)^2}}{\sigma^2}$ $z_{1,2} = \frac{\ln\left(\frac{B}{S_0}\right)-/+T\sqrt{2r\sigma^2+\left(r-d-\frac{1}{2}\sigma^2\right)^2}}{\sigma\sqrt{T}}$

Numerical application

In the absence of interest rates and dividends, an American binary at the money is simply obtained from the European binary following the equation:

$$\pi\,\{\text{Binaire Américaine}\} \cong 2\pi\,\left\{\text{Binaire Européenne}\right\} \tag{3.9}$$

We perform the spot ladder analysis on the price using the previous closed form formula.

For the greeks, we use the classical finite difference schemes:

- First derivative:

$$\frac{df}{dx} \cong \frac{f(x+h)-f(x-h)}{2h}$$

- Second derivative:

$$\frac{d^2f}{dx^2} \cong \frac{f(x+h)-2f(x)+f(x-h)}{h^2}$$

Price scenario

We obtain the following graph:

The pricing formula is relatively simple.

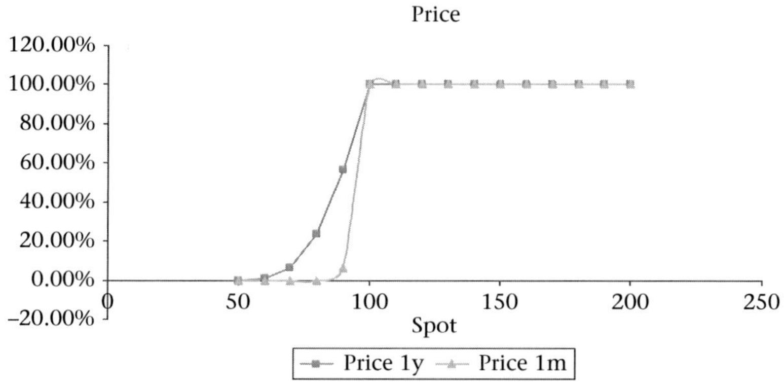

Figure 22 American binary pricing graph

Delta and gamma scenarios

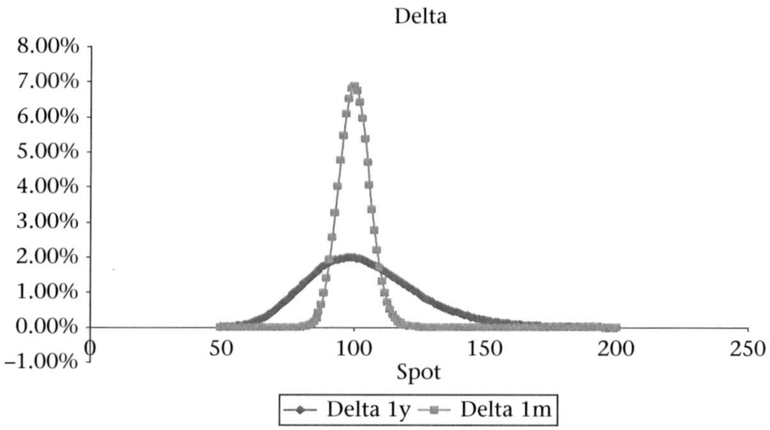

Figure 23 American binary delta graph

Looking at Figure 24, we can make the following comments:

- The delta increases while the option is alive.
  As for the European binary, when you are out of the money your delta is zero. This is because your option is almost zero and your replication portfolio must keep its value. Now, if the spot approaches the strike, the option (our replication target) approaches one. The replication portfolio must accompany this movement to generate enough money. So the delta increases rapidly. Once we hit the barrier, the option dies. This means that you need to unwind your position. If the crossing of the barrier is accompanied by an increase in the value of the asset,

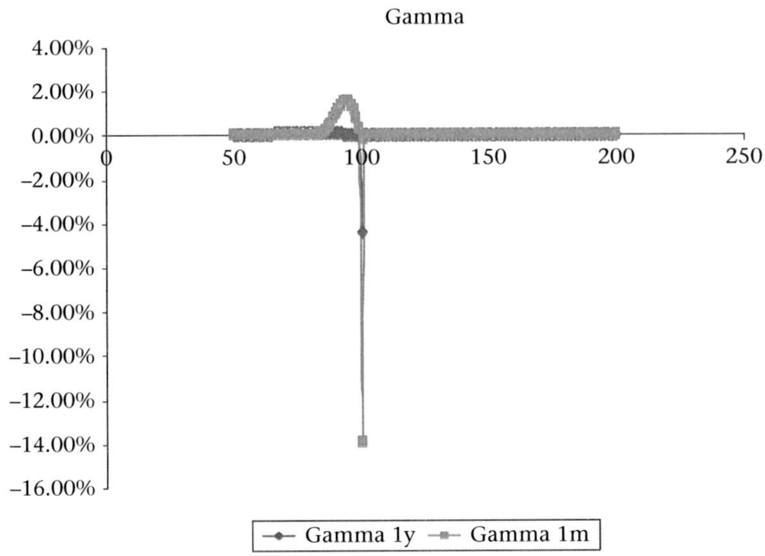

Figure 24 American binary gamma graph

there will probably be a gain for the trader to unwind. He/she will sell his/her stocks at a price that is higher than when he/she bought them. This is known as a *gap risk*. This risk costs the trader money but in this case it is positive.

- The gamma is always positive in the region where the option is alive.
  Indeed, when the spot goes up, the delta increases faster to generate the transition of the replication portfolio from zero to one. In Figure 24, we observe that some points are negative however. This is due to numerical error when calculating the second derivative. For points close to the barrier, computing an up scenario makes the spot go through the barrier and the option is no longer alive. In practice, we either make the step size smaller when moving closer to the barrier or we have recourse to derivatives that are computed using methods with no truncation error (AAD).
- The gamma profile is comparable to that of a vanilla as long as the option is alive. The delta is not bounded and the gamma has a bell shape. This shows some similarities with the European vanilla option (the call option studied above). What is clear is that the European binary option shows more differences than its American version.

Barrier option

We consider one particular barrier call Up & Out.

Table 6 Barrier option payoff and pricing formula under the Black & Scholes model

Option's payoff	Pricing formula
	$S_0 e^{-dT}\left(N(x_1)-N(x_2)\right)-Ke^{-rT}\left(N\left(x_1-\sigma\sqrt{T}\right)-N\left(x_2-\sigma\sqrt{T}\right)\right)$
$(S_T-K)^+ 1_{\{M_T<B\}}$	$-S_0 e^{-dT}\left(\frac{B}{S_0}\right)^{\frac{2(r-d)}{\sigma^2}+1}\left(N(y_1)-N(y_2)\right)$
	$+Ke^{-rT}\left(\frac{B}{S_0}\right)^{\frac{2(r-d)}{\sigma^2}-1}\left(N\left(y_1-\sigma\sqrt{T}\right)-N\left(y_2-\sigma\sqrt{T}\right)\right)$
	$x_2=\frac{\text{In}\left(\frac{S_0}{B}\right)+\left(r-d+\frac{1}{2}\sigma^2\right)T}{\sigma\sqrt{T}}$
	$x_1=\frac{\text{In}\left(\frac{S_0}{K}\right)+\left(r-d+\frac{1}{2}\sigma^2\right)T}{\sigma\sqrt{T}}$
	$y_2=\frac{\text{In}\left(\frac{B}{S_0}\right)+\left(r-d+\frac{1}{2}\sigma^2\right)T}{\sigma\sqrt{T}}$
	$y_2=\frac{\text{In}\left(\frac{B}{S_0}\right)+\left(r-d+\frac{1}{2}\sigma^2\right)T}{\sigma\sqrt{T}}$

The Barrier Up and Out is a classic equity option. If the investor believes that the stock is going up but not too much, this is a product aligned with this view. Its price as given in the formula above is lower than the call price in the Black & Scholes model.

We study its greeks in spot scenarios and here are the results.

Price scenario

We obtain the following graph:

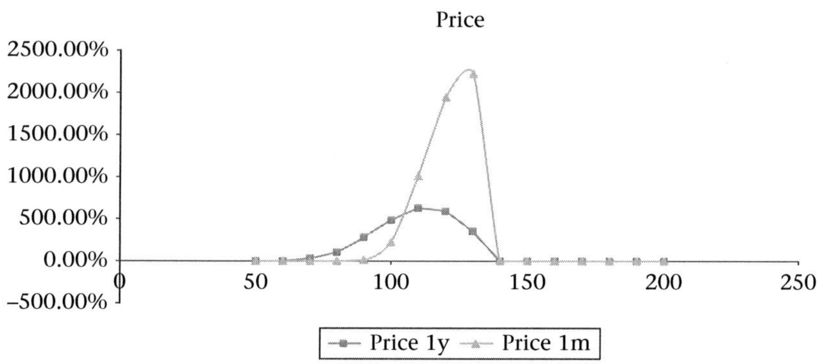

Figure 25 Barrier option pricing graph

The price of the option spot ladder varies rapidly.

Delta and gamma scenarios

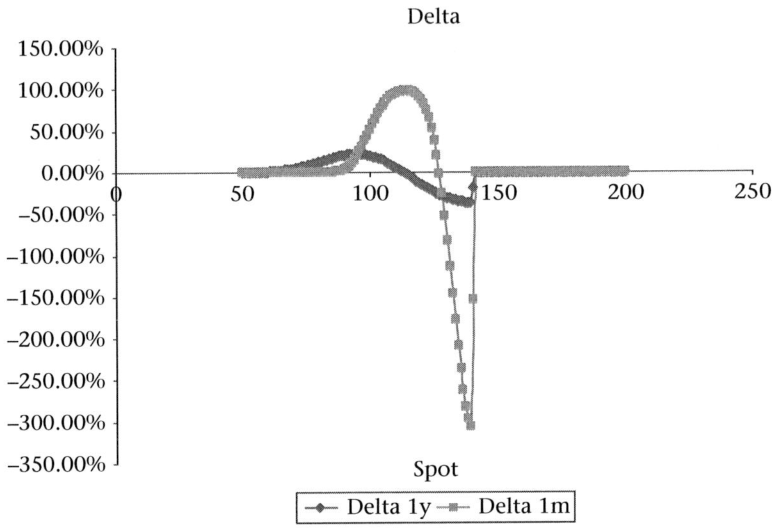

Figure 26 Barrier option delta graph

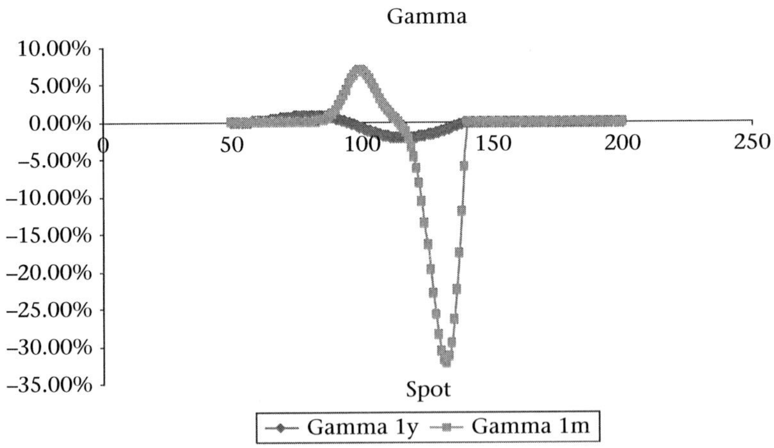

Figure 27 Barrier option gamma graph

We can make the following remarks:

- Delta is not monotonous.
  If you compare this delta spot ladder with its counterpart in the pure call option, our benchmark, we observe that in the left region (low spots), that is far from the barrier, we have the same delta profile. Intuitively, far from the barrier, the trader has to replicate a call option, so the hedging delta is the same as for the call option. When the spot moves closer to the barrier, the target to be replicated differs from a call option. To match the target (converge towards zero) the portfolio needs to destroy value as the spot moves up. So the delta in this region becomes negative.
- The absolute level of the delta can be very high.
  The region where the replication portfolio needs to take the value to zero is narrow. This is similar to what was observed for the binary option. To reach a target rapidly leverage needs to be applied. That is why we can observe high negative deltas exceeding one in absolute value.
- Gamma changes sign.
  In this product, the gamma sign is positive far from the barrier and negative close to it. In this implementation, we paid extra attention so as to have smooth greeks. They are calculated in finite differences in the interior points of the domain (making sure that the scheme does not cross the barrier). This excludes the numerical explosion observed in the American binary case.

Asian option

This option is a classical one. Compared to vanilla prices, the Asian option is characterized by cheaper prices. Low cost replication comes from the fact that the delta for this type of option is built progressively. Since the Asian option has no closed form formula, we use a moment-matching technique. This consists in calculating the exact first two moments of the Asian and then matching them, making the assumption that they are the result of a log normal. Once we have identified this particular log normal, we end up using the Black & Scholes formula.

Numerical application

In the absence of interest rates and dividends, an Asian call at the money is approximated by the following formula:

$$\pi\left\{\left(\frac{1}{T}\int_0^T S_t dt - S_0\right)^+\right\} \cong \frac{1}{\sqrt{3}} 0.4\sigma\sqrt{T}S_0 \qquad (3.10)$$

Table 7 Asian option pricing formula

Option's payoff	**Pricing(15)**
	$e^{-rT}\{M_1 N(d_1) - KN(d_2)\}$
	$M_1 = S_0 \sum_{i=1}^{n} \frac{\exp((r-d)t_i)}{n}$
$\left(\frac{1}{n}\sum_{i=1}^{n} S_{t_i} - K\right)^+$	$M_2 = \frac{S_0^2}{n^2} \sum_{i,j=1}^{n} \exp\left((r-d)\left(t_i + t_j\right) + \sigma^2 \min\left(t_i, t_j\right)\right)$
	$d_{1,2} = \frac{\ln\left(\frac{M_1}{K}\right) +/- \frac{1}{2}\sigma_A^2 t_n}{\sigma_A \sqrt{t_n}}$
	$\sigma_A^2 t_n = \ln\left(\frac{M_2}{M_1^2}\right)$

Price scenario

We obtain the following graph:

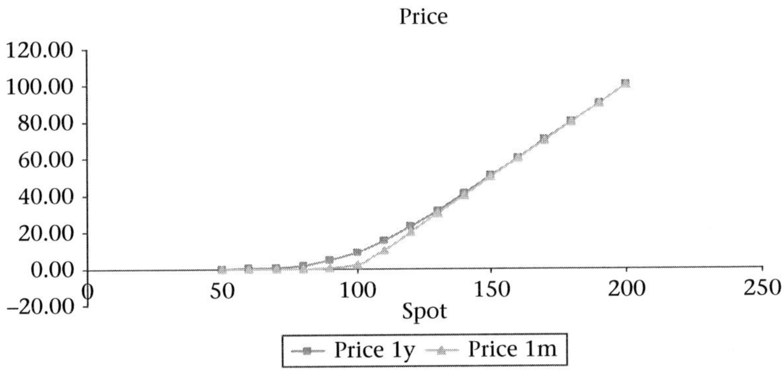

Figure 28 Asian option pricing graph

We observe high similarity with the curve for a standard vanilla option.

Delta and gamma scenarios

Once again, in Figure 28, Figure **29** and Figure **30**, we observe similarity with the curves obtained with a standard vanilla option.

However, the previous assertion should not be misunderstood. It is true that there are some limitations. Indeed, the Asian option remains path dependent. There are trajectories on which the current average exceeds the strike and the Asian optionality disappears. The Asian becomes a forward with no vega exposure. Moreover,

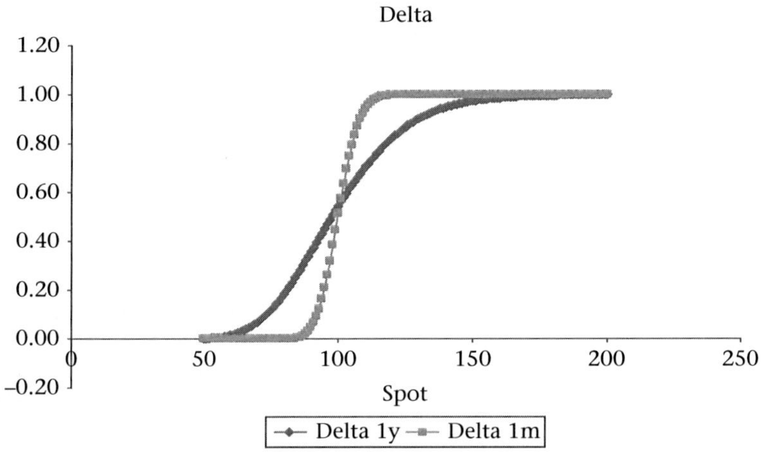

Figure 29 Asian option delta graph

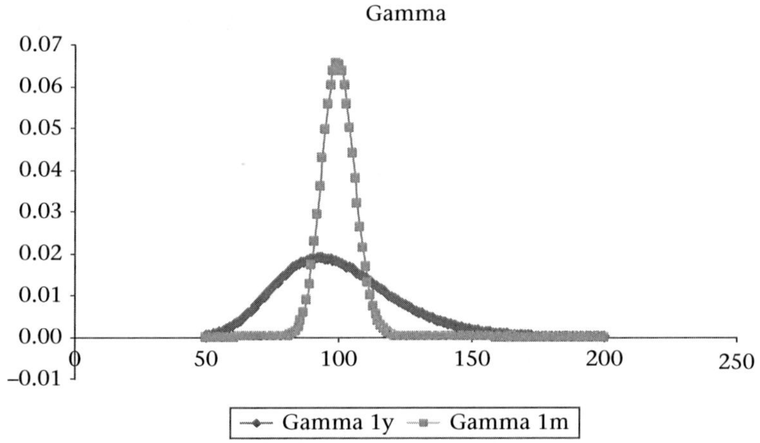

Figure 30 Asian option gamma graph

when there are similarities and when the Asian option is still alive, the proxy formula shows that the volatility of the Asian part is lower than the volatility of a pure European Call.

$$\sigma_{\text{Asian}} \cong \frac{1}{\sqrt{3}}\sigma$$

There exists another mechanism that creates a link between the terminal volatility and a path dependent version of it. This is the lookback maximum. In that case, the call option on the lookback maximum is twice as volatile as the vanilla option.

$$\sigma_{\text{Lookback Maximum}} \cong 2\sigma$$

When is it possible to use Black & Scholes

The profit and loss explanation for a delta hedging trader is expressed as follows:

$$\Delta PnL = \frac{1}{2}\Gamma S^2 \left(\left(\frac{\Delta S}{S} \right)^2 - \sigma_{BS}^2 \Delta t \right) \tag{3.11}$$

This equation is very important. It is based on the absence of transaction costs, dividends or financing costs. It summarizes the three ingredients that underlie the profit and loss explanation: (option, market and model).

These ingredients can be described as follows:

- **Option** ΓS^2: The option generates gamma, which depends on both the spot and the time. The computation of the gamma is weakly dependent on the model used. This weak dependence property emanates from experimental observations from practitioners. Unless designed on purpose, for usual products, models tend to show approximately the same gamma within a variety of models. This is because at maturity, all models share the strong constraint that is the payoff. Moving from maturity backwards to today, although using the different models making different assumptions, these gamma indicators remain close to each other. The gamma is almost the same and is a characteristic of the product.
- **Market** $\left(\frac{\Delta S}{S}\right)^2$: The market is shown by the instantaneous realized volatility. We observe that a delta hedger is able to explain his/her profit and loss evolution if he/she can predict the market realized volatility.
- **Model** σ_{BS}^2: The model used is Black & Scholes. The choice of an average volatility which balances the realized volatility ensures fair pricing.

We can go further into the question of the correctness of the pricing under the Black & Scholes model. To do so, we shall assume that **under the real probability, fair pricing corresponds to an average Profit and Loss equal to zero**. This definition of fair pricing is to the first order. A more elaborate definition, to the second order would take into account the fact that the Profit and Loss is a random variable with a given variance. Fair pricing should account for this randomness.

Therefore, the Black & Scholes Model, which ensures fair pricing to the first order, satisfies the following equation:

$$E^P(PnL) = \frac{1}{2}E^P \int_0^T \Gamma_{BS}S^2\left(\left(\frac{\Delta S}{S}\right)^2 - \sigma_{BS}^2\Delta t\right) = 0 \tag{3.12}$$

The previous equation simplifies into:

$$\sigma_{BS}^2 = \frac{E^P \int_0^T \Gamma_{BS}S^2\left(\frac{\Delta S}{S}\right)^2}{E^P \int_0^T \Gamma_{BS}S^2 dt} \tag{3.13}$$

Let us introduce some extra notations, w for a weighting function (kernel for averaging):

$$w(t,S) = \frac{\Gamma_{BS}(t,S)\,S^2}{E^P \int_0^T \Gamma_{BS}S^2 dt} \tag{3.14}$$

This kernel is based on normalization of the gamma everywhere. The **gamma map is defined everywhere, whereas the kernel can be defined all the time.** A necessary condition is to keep a constant gamma map sign.

The fair Black & Scholes volatility can be written as follows:

$$\sigma_{BS}^2 = E^P \int_0^T w(t,S)\left(\frac{\Delta S}{S}\right)^2 \tag{3.15}$$

This formula calls for many comments:

- The formula is recursive, the value of the fair Black & Scholes volatility is present in the right hand part of the equation (this is solved through an iterative algorithm).
- The value of the fair Black & Scholes volatility depends on the option (through the gamma).
- The value of the Black & Scholes volatility is an average of realized volatility.
- The averaging is taken under the real probability.
- The calculation is only possible if the term in the denominator permits it. It must keep a constant sign.

As a conclusion, in the case of a gamma map with a constant sign (where it is possible to normalize in t and S), *the fair volatility square in a Black & Scholes Model is an average of the realized volatility square with a kernel issued from the gamma map.* At this stage, we show several examples of gamma maps. This gives intuition into the weighting kernel that transforms the surface of realized volatility – local volatility, in one single volatility number to be plugged into a Black & Scholes formula.

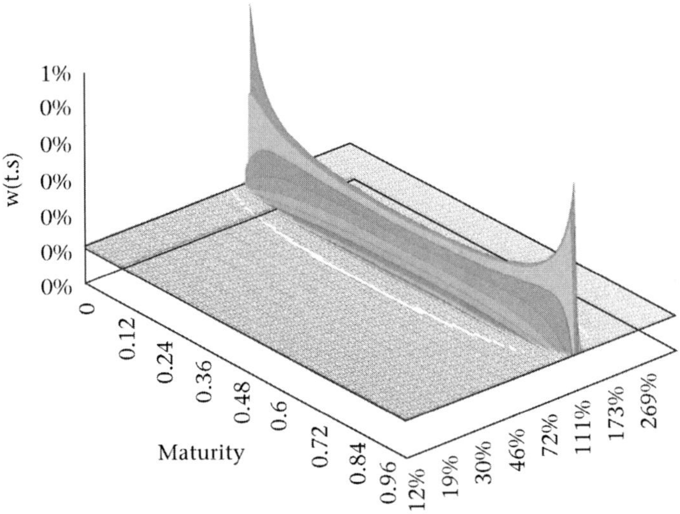

Figure 31 Gamma map European call

In Figure 31, we calculate the kernel for a call option. The sensitivity is concentrated on a path that goes from the initial spot and finishes at the strike level. This is known as the most likely path and will be formally defined in the local volatility section. The gamma map combines the process information through the starting point and the gamma for the product through to the strike of the option.

In Figure 32, we introduce a dividend at half of the maturity of the call option. We again observe that the gamma map is concentrated around the initial spot at the beginning of time and around the strike at maturity. This is similar to the case with no dividends. What is new is the discontinuity at the dividend date. The gamma map shows a discontinuity when crossing the dividend date. In other words, although the equivalent Black & Scholes volatility relies on the gamma map, the presence of a dividend changes the region where the local volatility is used. Via this example, we see that the gamma map combines the information about the product (strike at maturity) and information about the process (starts at the spot and jumps at the dividend date).

In Figure 33, we introduce 3 dividends. As previously, the gamma map starts at the spot (process information) and finishes at the strike (product information). The difference is the number of dividends. Their number is three and at each dividend date the gamma map jumps as well by an amount equal to the dividend amount. In

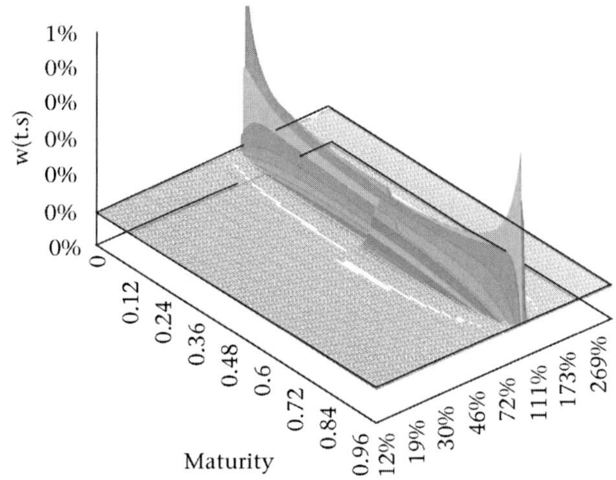

Figure 32 Gamma map European call with 1 dividend

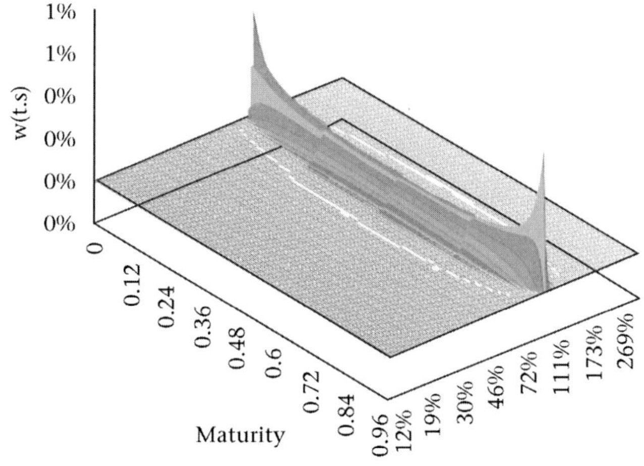

Figure 33 Gamma map European call with 3 dividends

other words, the gamma map weighs the most likely path between the initial spot to the final strike following the process that is jumping at each dividend date. This gamma map shows us the local volatility points which have an impact on the price of the product under study. These points are concentrated around the spot where the process starts and follow the different jumps due to the dividends. Moreover, they finish around the strike where the gamma of the product is maximal.

In Figure 34, we calculate the kernel for an American option in the absence of dividends. The result is exactly the same as for a European option. This is no surprise

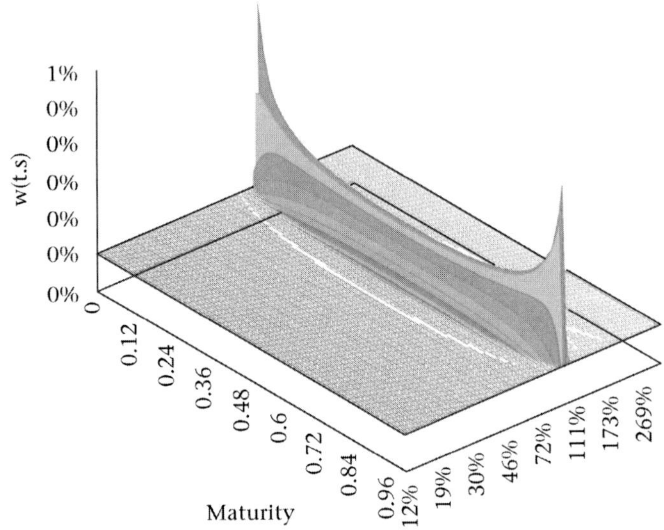

Figure 34 Gamma map American call

as the American call, in the absence of dividends, is nothing other than a European option.

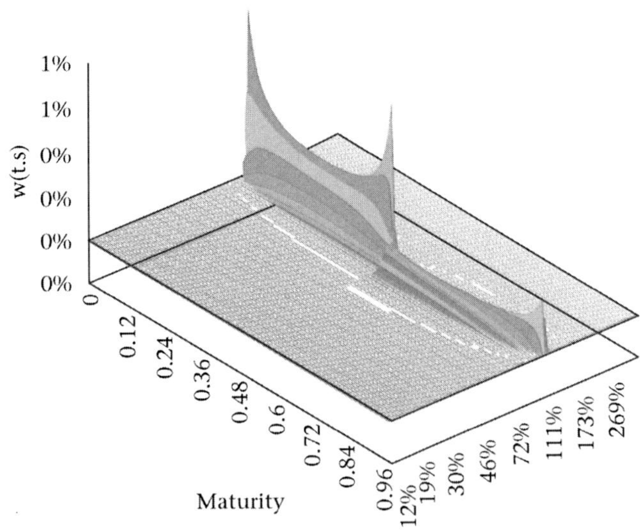

Figure 35 Gamma map American call with 1 dividend

In Figure 35, we introduce dividends and compute the kernel for the American call. This time the kernel is different from the European version. As usual, the kernel starts at the spot, finishes at the strike and drops at the dividend time. What is new is that the mass before the dividend time is greater. This quantifies the high probability that the American can be exercised before the dividend time. It is telling us that the information taken from an American call option with one dividend can differ widely from its European counterpart.

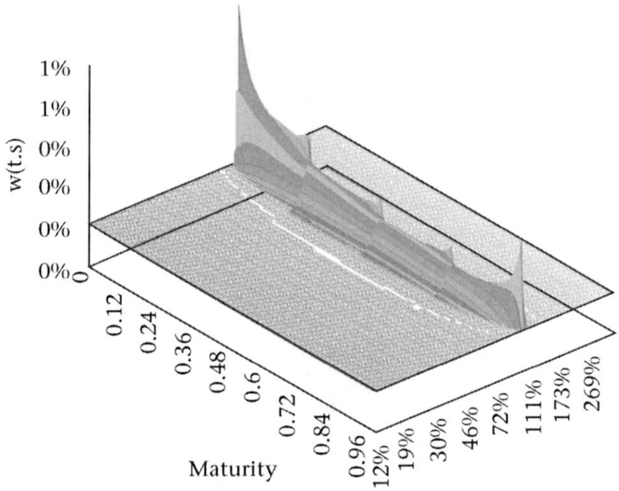

Figure 36 Gamma map American call with 3 dividends

In Figure 36, we introduce three dividends and observe the same phenomenon as for the European. As the amount of dividend is three times smaller, the probability of early exercise is lower and the kernel of the American call option with three dividends is closer to the European call option with three dividends. The gamma map difference between American call and its European counterpart decreases with the size of the discontinuity even if the total amount of paid dividends is the same. In the theoretical limit where everyday a small amount of dividend is paid, the gamma map for the American call becomes very similar to the gamma map of the European equivalent.

In Figure 37, we calculate the kernel of a barrier up and out. We observe this time that it can take positive and negative values. All previous options had only positive values. This change of sign is important to note as it conditions the possibility as to whether the Black & Scholes model can be used in practice. Indeed, the kernel definition can only be correct if the division is possible. In the case of an up & out Barrier option, this division can cause harm and is not defined properly. This is also a serious obstacle that stops practitioners from using the Black & Scholes model for pricing and hedging barrier options.

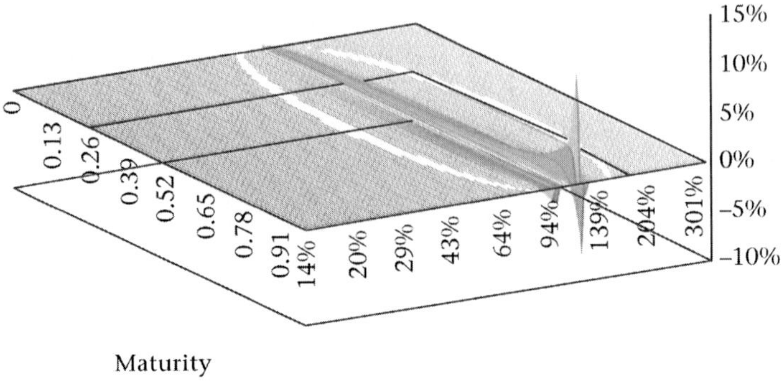

Figure 37 Gamma map barrier option call up & out with no dividends

With these items, we can now answer the question of the validity of the Black & Scholes model. The answer depends on the constant sign property for the gamma map. We have the following list of answers:

Table 8 Is Black & Scholes an appropriate model?

Product	Is Black & Scholes appropriate?
European Call	Yes
European Binary	No
American Binary	Yes
Up & Out Barrier	No
Asian Option	Yes
American Option	Yes

Via this analysis, we have established a sufficient criterion for a product to be priced with a Black & Scholes model. In addition, where possible, that is when the gamma map keeps a constant sign, we have a formula that gives the equivalent Black & Scholes volatility. It is obtained as an average of local volatility weighted by a kernel (normalization of the gamma map). This kernel combines information on the process (starting point, dividends) and information about the product (strike at maturity).

Two remaining questions need answering:

- What do we do to take into account a price definition to the second order?
- What do we do when the Black & Scholes model is not appropriate?

To answer the second question, we shall proceed with an incremental approach by studying different models in the next chapter.

At this stage, we show how to reduce the effect of the second order that is the variance of the Profit and Loss.

In the case where the average PnL is controlled, we have the following result:

$$Var\,(P\&L) = \frac{1}{2}\sigma_B^4 \Delta t \int_0^T E\left(\Gamma_B^2 S^4\right)\, dt \tag{3.16}$$

We see that minimizing the PnL variance entails controlling the gamma. This is realized through a set of techniques known as *gamma smoothing*.

The smoothing technique operates as follows:

When selling an option, the trader creates a new option, known as the replacement contract, which dominates the true one and is more expensive in price. This new contract has also lower convexity – gamma – which insures lower PnL variance.

Table 9 Gamma smoothing technique

True contract	$\phi\,(S_T)$
Replacement contract	$\psi \geq \phi$
Smoothing condition	$\Gamma_\psi \leq \Gamma_\phi$

A classical application of this gamma smoothing technique is the European Binary example.

Table 10 European binary smoothing (by a call spread)

True contract: digital	$1_{\{S_T \geq K\}}$
Replcament contract: call spread	$\frac{(S_T-(K-\Delta K))^+ - (S_T-K)^+}{\Delta K}$
Smoothing condition:	$\Gamma_\psi \leq \Gamma_\phi$

Obviously, the smoothing comes at a cost. The name of the game is to realize cheap smoothing. It is important to note that sometimes perfect smoothing is not possible at inception of the trade. Instead, the trader can dynamically implement the smoothing when the cost is lower. At this stage, we can give an order of magnitude for hedging digitals with a call spread smoothing. Imagine the digital pays 100 mln Euros if active. Also we assume that the spread is equal to 5%. This means that within the distance of 5% the trader needs to generate 100 mln Euros. This corresponds to 20 mln Euros for every 1%. To be able to create such value for 1%, the trader needs to hold 2 Billion Euros worth of the underlying. That is a lot of delta exposure and can have an impact on the market. If the spread is just 1%, the delta holding gets five times bigger up to 10 Billion Euros. This is very high exposure. Traders helped by financial engineers and quants can either spread the option or change it a bit to minimize this exposure. Typically, they can add an asianing over a couple of days to make the delta smoother.

Exercise 3

Let an asset $S_0 = 100$. We assume that interest rates, repo and dividends are zero. We want to price three options: a call at the money, an Asian option and a call lookback max. We consider four-year maturity contracts, recall the payoffs for each of these options and give proxy values and make the numerical applications.

B Study of classical Smile models

In this section, we shall study a set of classical models. The knowledge we obtain from this study is of a mathematical type. More precisely, it concerns the stochastic nature of the models. It is based on clear mathematical assumptions. We like to describe them as the *derivatives algorithms*. Under this set of mathematical results, we dispose of a smile framework and control of its dynamic. Thanks to this framework, we introduce model risk and pricing in the presence of smile and its dynamic.

We shall insist on the validity domain for each model: when we can use the model and more importantly when we cannot.

All the presentation at this stage focuses on the martingale process without taking into account financing costs or dividends. This allows us to focus on the smile problem in its simplest expression. This is in line with our incremental approach.

Black & Scholes model

We shall start with the simplest kind of models: the Black & Scholes model.

The volatility surface generated by this model is a simple flat surface.

However, even if this seems easy one needs to pay attention to some tricky details which play an important role in practice. Indeed, if the volatility is equal to 20%, the Black & Scholes formula depends on variance and is thus dependent on the time measurement.

In practice, we have two classical approaches to measure the time:

- *Calendar time*: the measure is based on the ratio of the number of calendar days over a constant typically worth 365.25 (this constant is the average calendar days in one year computed for the next 10 years),

- *Business time*: in this case, time is measured as the ratio of the number of business days over a constant typically 252 (this constant is the average business days in one year computed for the next 10 years).

In the *market logic* we could ignore this subject and treat it as a convention. In practice, we could just change the volatility number to obtain the right price. This approach will have a disagreeable consequence when it comes to explaining the profit and loss evolution, one of the essential features of a financial model.

In Figure 38, we adjust the volatility in the two time conventions and obtain exactly the same price. We graph the theta for the same option under these two different volatility conventions. Clearly the business convention is smoother and does not create undue weekly seasonality in the theta.

The Black & Scholes model has one degree of freedom and is able to match one vanilla price. In Figure 39, we show the calibration set for the Black & Scholes model. This property can be sufficient in some cases but is rather limiting in most.

Given a smile implied volatility surface it is possible to use this model to price vanilla options (European or American). It is also possible to use such a model to price an Asian option as presented in a previous section. There is however a big drawback when using this model to fit a given volatility surface since one needs to

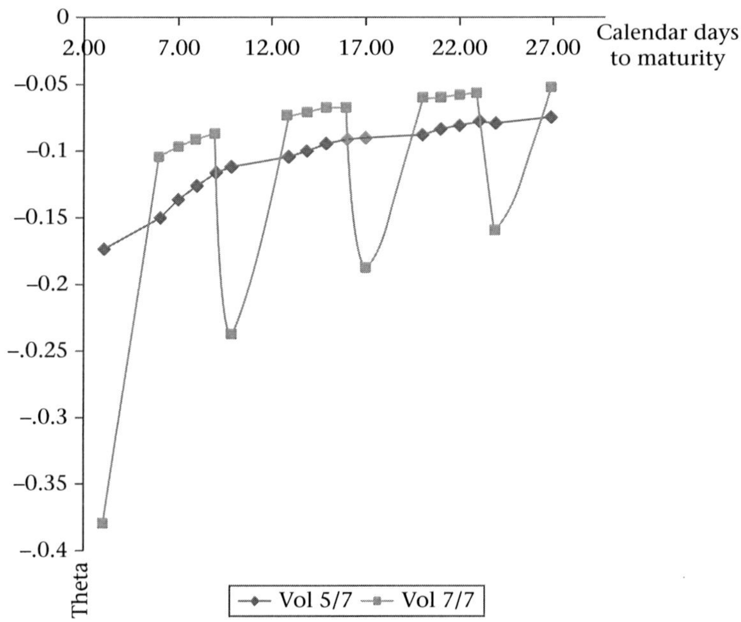

Figure 38 Choice of the time convention and its impact on the theta calculation

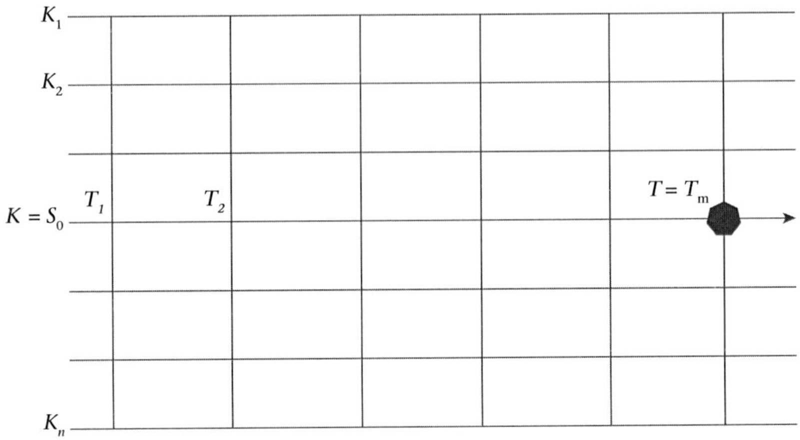

Figure 39 Black & Scholes calibration set

use as many versions of the Black & Scholes models as the number of options to be matched. This limitation is important and one loses consistency between all the different options.

As our objective is to understand the smile effect and its dynamic, we shall make the assumption of a calendar time convention.

Term structure Black & Scholes

Under this model, the dynamic is a bit richer than the pure Black & Scholes model. It enables a whole term structure of vanilla prices to be fitted.

$$\frac{dS_t}{S_t} = \sigma(t)dW_t$$

This model generates a non-flat smile. It is represented by a stationary term structure in time. The calibration set is shown in Figure 40.

More precisely, this smile can be calculated exactly. It is given by a 'Pythagoras-style':

$$\Sigma^2(T) = \frac{1}{T}\int_0^T \sigma^2(t)\,dt \tag{3.17}$$

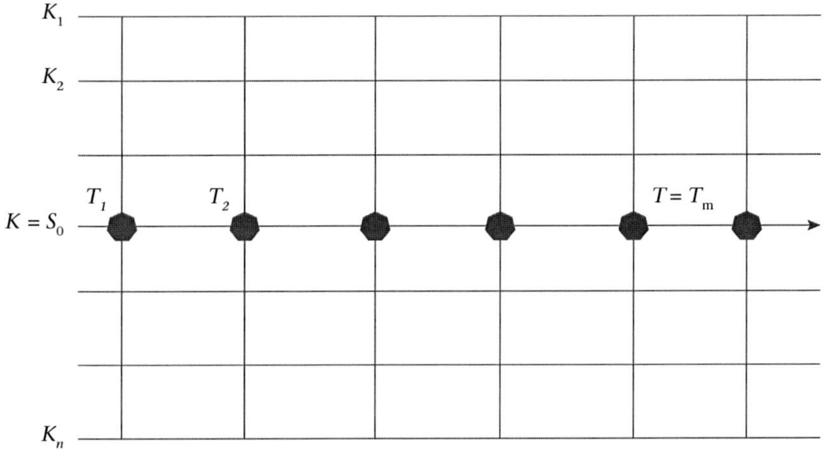

Figure 40 Term structure Black & Scholes calibration set

This means that the implied variance is the arithmetic average of the local variance. We remind that the implied volatility $\{T \rightarrow \Sigma(T)\}$ is the parameter to use in the Black & Scholes formula as in equation Table 1.

The inverse problem which consists of finding the model parameters $\{t \rightarrow \sigma(t)\}$ from the market implied parameters $\{T \rightarrow \Sigma(T)\}$ is also simple to achieve in this model:

$$\sigma^2(T) = \Sigma^2(T) + 2\Sigma(T)\frac{d\Sigma(T)}{dT}T \tag{3.18}$$

This model can be used in case of path-dependency without a change in the sign of the gamma map. As in the basic Black & Scholes, marginal distributions from this process are all log normal. However, there is a change in volatility in the early distributions and a slight change in the auto-correlation between two different maturities.

This model is used also to analyze a product with multiple fixings and also multiple cash flows for a given trajectory.

Sensitivity calculation in this model:

$$vegaT = \frac{\partial \pi}{\partial \Sigma(T)} \tag{3.19}$$

This calculation called vega T represents the sensitivity with respect to each vanilla option for every maturity T.

This type of analysis gives crucial information regarding the duration of the product. The notion of duration replaces the notion of the facial maturity for a path-dependent option. It represents the estimated maturity where most of the risk is located. Traders and practitioners alike use this information to hedge their book and follow their trend in synthetic fashion.

More precisely, the exact term structure volatility contribution is given by the following equation:

$$\Delta PnL = \cdots + \int_0^T \frac{\partial \pi}{\partial \Sigma(t)} d\Sigma(t) + \cdots$$

A typical duration is calculated as the vega weighted maturity as follows:

$$\tau = \frac{\int_0^T \frac{\partial \pi}{\partial \Sigma(t)} t dt}{\int_0^T \frac{\partial \pi}{\partial \Sigma(t)} dt} \tag{3.20}$$

Traders will construct a synthetic PnL evolution equation simply by looking at the duration as a maturity:

$$\Delta PnL = \cdots + \left(\int_0^T \frac{\partial \pi}{\partial \Sigma(t)} dt \right) d\Sigma(\tau) + \cdots$$

In words, traders will allocate the total vega (parallel shift) of the product on a single maturity, the duration.

A good example for such an analysis is the Asian option.

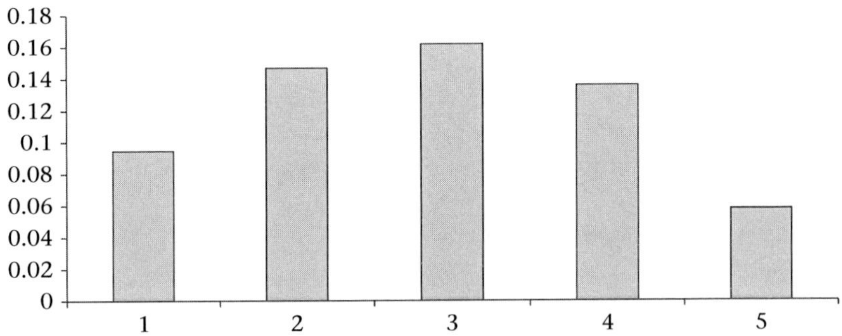

Figure 41 Vega (T) for a five-year Asian option (five fixings)

In Figure 41, we show the vega term structure for a five-year option with yearly fixing. We calculate a duration which is close to two and half years. This is almost true for all Asian options. It deviates from the mid with higher volatility.

Now, given a Smile surface, the choice of the term structure to be fitted is based on common sense and practice. But it is important to include the situation when the product matures while having just one fixing left. In this case, the choice of the strike is well defined.

At this stage we show an example where term structure volatility modeling is essential. Indeed, this is the case of commodity future modeling. Assume you want to model an energy commodity. It is composed per several futures. Nearby future is the one to mature and is typically more volatile than their longer term futures. The local volatility for a given future $F_T(t)$ is modeled in backward time:

$$\frac{dF_T(t)}{F_T(t)} = \sigma_T(t)\, dW_t \tag{3.21}$$

Where

$$\sigma_T(t) = \sigma \exp\left(-\alpha (T-t)\right) \tag{3.22}$$

This can also be achieved using a classical Orstein Uhlebeck. The Orstein-Uhlenbeck process is an extension of the Brownian motion. Its dynamic is given by $dX_t = -\lambda X_t dt + dW_t$.

$$\frac{dF_T(t)}{F_T(t)} = \sigma\, dZ_t \tag{3.23}$$

Where

$$dZ_t = -2\alpha Z_t dt + dW_t \tag{3.24}$$

Monte Carlo simulation

In this model we can simulate the transition between two dates $T_1 < T_2$

- Compute the forward volatility between these $\sigma_{1\to 2} = \sqrt{\frac{\Sigma^2(T_2)-\Sigma^2(T_1)}{T_2-T_1}}$,
- Generate a standard normal variable $\varepsilon \propto N(0,1)$,
- Use the Euler recursion, $\ln S(T_2) = \ln S(T_1) - \frac{1}{2}\sigma_{1\to 2}^2 (T_2 - T_1) + \varepsilon \sigma_{1\to 2}\sqrt{T_2 - T_1}$

Terminal smile model

In this model, we generalize the Black & Scholes by introducing a whole curve of parameters. The difference with the previous model is that this curve is no longer temporal but rather spot-dependent.

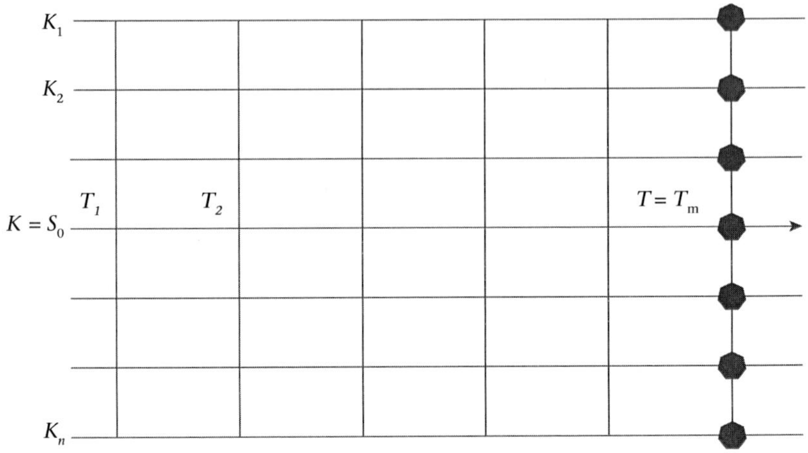

Figure 42 Terminal smile calibration set

More precisely, we introduce a local volatility function of spot $s \to \sigma(s)$ for the following spot dynamic:

$$\frac{dS_t}{S_t} = \sigma(S_t)dW_t \tag{3.25}$$

We do not have analytical results for the pricing of vanilla options except for a short-term maturity. However, we can obtain very good proxy formulae which are exact to the basis point.

In Figure 42, we show the terminal smile calibration set.

The first formulation is due to BBF (Berestycki, Busca, & Florent, 2001). It takes the following form:

$$\Sigma(T,K) \cong \frac{\ln\left(\frac{S_0}{K}\right)}{\int_K^{S_0} \frac{1}{s\sigma(s)} ds} \tag{3.26}$$

The Equation (3.26) is exact[1] for short-term maturity options. The proof is based on Ito stochastic calculus. It is important to note that here the implied volatility is a harmonic average of the local volatility.

---

1 This equation is just an average. Another approximation due to Pat Hagan (Hagan, Kumar, Lesniewski, & Woodward, 2002) gives: $\Sigma(K,T) \cong \sigma\left(\sqrt{S_0 K}\right)$

The previous formula loses its precision when the maturity increases. It is possible to increase its accuracy if we expand to the first order in time.

$$\Sigma_0(K) = \frac{\ln\left(\frac{S_0}{K}\right)}{\int_K^{S_0} \frac{1}{s\sigma(s)} ds} \tag{3.27}$$

$$\Sigma_1(K) = -\frac{\Sigma_0(K)}{\left(\int_K^{S_0} \frac{1}{s\sigma(s)} ds\right)^2} \ln\left(\frac{\Sigma_0(K)}{\sqrt{\sigma(S_0)\sigma(K)}}\right) \tag{3.28}$$

With these two ingredients, we obtain the following formula, which is considerably more precise – up to ten years in practice.

$$\Sigma(T,K) \cong \Sigma_0(K) + \Sigma_1(K)T \tag{3.29}$$

We obtain a quasi-stationary smile (weak dependency on time).

This model is interesting when we need to control the terminal distribution. It can also be applied it to some weakly path-dependent options such as variance swaps. One last use of this model is to interpolate a smile slice in a non-arbitrageable way.

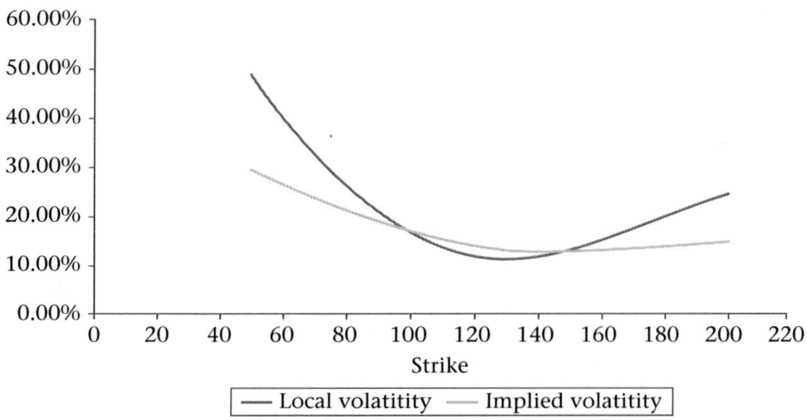

Figure 43 Equity-like smile: local volatility versus implied volatility

In Figure 43, we observe an equity-like smile. It is characterized by a downward slope at the 100 strike.

In Figure 44, we observe an FX-like smile. It is characterized by zero slope at the 100 strike and a symmetry.

In Figure 45, we observe a commodity-like smile. It is characterized by an upward slope at the 100 strike.

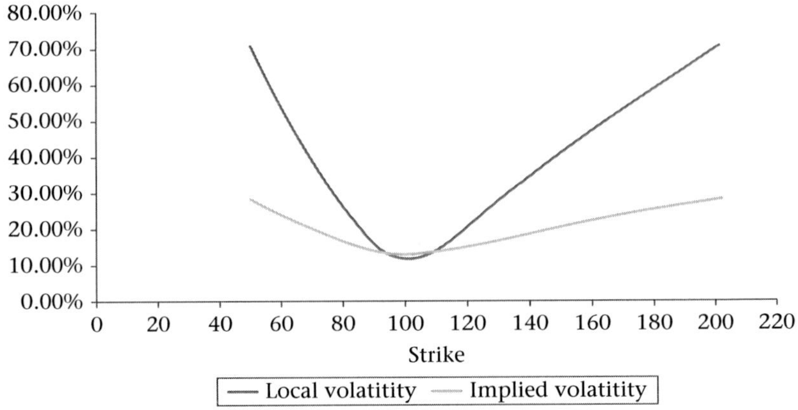

Figure 44 FX-like smile: local volatility versus implied volatility

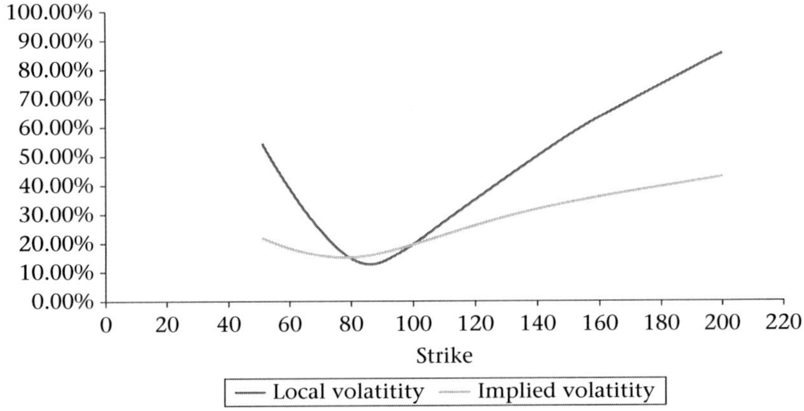

Figure 45 Commodity (Gold)-like smile: local volatility versus implied volatility

Replication approach (an almost model-free approach)

In the case of a terminal European payoff, where this terminal smile model should be used, we can price taking into account the smile quite efficiently, using the Peter Carr and others' formula.

$$\pi_{LV}(f) = \pi_{BS}(f) + \int_0^{F_0} \frac{\partial^2 f}{\partial K^2}\left(\mathrm{Put}_{\mathrm{LV}}(\mathrm{K,T}) - \mathrm{Put}_{\mathrm{BS}}(\mathrm{K,T})\right) dK$$
$$+ \int_{F_0}^{\infty} \frac{\partial^2 f}{\partial K^2}\left(\mathrm{Call}_{\mathrm{LV}}(\mathrm{K,T}) - \mathrm{Call}_{\mathrm{BS}}(\mathrm{K,T})\right) dK$$

Where, F_0 is the forward corresponding to the payoffs maturity.

This states that the price taking the terminal smile model is the price using an inferior model (Black & Scholes) adjusted by the cost of hedge due to the presence of the smile. This approach gives for a smooth payoff f the exact amount $\frac{\partial^2 f}{\partial K^2}$ of the call or the put of strike K to be put in place in order to hedge the smile exposure exactly. This is the super vega KT calculation and it is a special case where this is given analytically.

This approach seems to be model-free. In fact, this is not entirely the case. This is because one needs to price vanilla options for all strikes from zero to infinity. As indicated in the introduction, we can have many models which fit the observed market points and obtain many different extrapolations. This was performed using the mixing weight. A classical contract to illustrate this is the variance swap contract $\frac{1}{T}\int_0^T \sigma_t^2\,dt$. In the absence of jumps, dividends, financing costs and for any diffusion model we can replicate it thanks to a terminal contract $-2\log\left(\frac{S_T}{S_0}\right)$ and delta hedging strategy $\int_0^T \frac{1}{S_t}\,dS_t$. This is shown as an exercise below. For this type of contract, we can extract useful information on how to extrapolate the smile for the left wing where we have most of the dependence.

Monte Carlo simulation (direct approach)

In this model, we can simulate the transition between two dates $T_1 < T_2$ by introducing a set of intermediary dates $t_0 = T_1 < t_1 < \cdots < t_m = T_2$.

- Generate m independent random normal distributions $N(0,1)$,
- Use Euler recursion

$$\ln S(t_1) = \ln S(t_0) - \frac{1}{2}\sigma^2 (S(t_0))(t_1 - t_0) + \varepsilon_1 \sigma (S(t_0))\sqrt{t_1 - t_0},$$

$$\ln S(t_2) = \ln S(t_1) - \frac{1}{2}\sigma^2 (S(t_1))(t_2 - t_1) + \varepsilon_2 \sigma (S(t_1))\sqrt{t_2 - t_1},$$

$$\ln S(t_m) = \ln S(t_{m-1}) - \frac{1}{2}\sigma^2 (S(t_{m-1}))(t_m - t_{m-1}) + \varepsilon_m \sigma (S(t_{m-1}))\sqrt{t_m - t_{m-1}}.$$

Monte Carlo simulation (fast method)

Can we improve the previous scheme to have big step Monte Carlo?

Can we use just one random number?

The answer to this last question is yes. This is explained in details in (A, G, & G, Quantum local volatility, 2012). It is based on operator methods and matrix exponential and we can achieve the same efficiency.

More precisely, for a stationary local volatility $\frac{dX_t}{X_t} = \sigma(\ln X_t)\,dW_t$, we can define the transition probability density function $p(t,T,x,y)\,dy = P(X_T \in [y, y+dy] \,|X_t = x)$.

For a fixed y and t<T, f(t,x) = f(t,T,x,y) satisfies the Kolmogorov Backward equation:

$$\frac{\partial f(t,x)}{\partial t} + Lf(t,x) = 0$$

$$f(T,x) = \delta_{x=y}$$

We define the infinitesimal generator of the diffusion process:

$$Lf(t,x) := \frac{1}{2}\sigma^2(\ln x)\frac{\partial^2 f(t,x)}{\partial x^2}$$

Approximation by a discrete generator on a grid: $x_1 < \cdots < x_N$.

Using finite differences on the x grid, but we do not discretize the time t:

$$A = \begin{pmatrix} d_1 & u_1 & & & & & \\ l_2 & d_2 & u_2 & & & & \\ & \ddots & \ddots & \ddots & & & \\ & & l_i & d_i & u_i & & \\ & & & \ddots & \ddots & \ddots & \\ & & & & l_{N-1} & d_{N-1} & u_{N-1} \\ & & & & & l_N & d_N \end{pmatrix}$$

$$\begin{cases} l_i & = & \frac{1}{2}\frac{\sigma^2(x_i)}{\Delta x^2} \\ u_i & = & -\frac{\sigma^2(x_i)}{\Delta x^2} \\ d_i & = & \frac{1}{2}\frac{\sigma^2(x_i)}{\Delta x^2} \end{cases}.$$

The coefficient of the first and the last row are chosen so that the Markov Chain is reflected on the boundary of the state domain.

The transition probability matrix: $p_d(t,T)\,dy := \left[P\left(t,T,x_i,x_j\right)\right], 1 \leq i,j \leq N$ is the solution of the matrix equation:

$$\frac{\partial p_d}{\partial t} + Ap = 0$$

$$p_d = 1_{\{x_i = x_j\}}$$

Using Operator Theory, the solution can be expressed as a matrix exponential:

$$p_d = e^{A(T-t)}$$

There are many ways to compute the matrix exponential.

We opt for one technique which is efficient and not very time consuming:

dt: = 1 hour
p: = I + A dt
for i = 1..n
p: = p * p
end for

The computation therefore involves n: = log2((T−t)/dt).

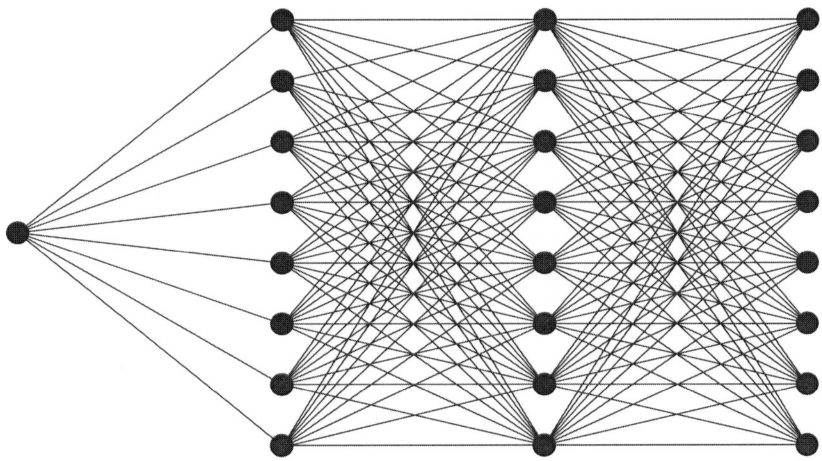

Figure 46 Markov chain calculation representation

In Figure 46, we see the connection from the first point at inception to the next slice. There is a probability of reaching each point and the sum of probabilities sum to one. When we average the probabilities times at the spot at the first slice we obtain the forward for the first time slice. The generator also helps in such a way that options priced by averaging probabilities times the payoff at time one, return the market option prices. For the second slice, there are as many paths coming to a certain point as points in the first slice. When averaging on all possible paths and weighting them by one we obtain a total of one. When we put spot values for the second slice we obtain the forward for the second maturity. We can also put the vanilla option payoffs for the second slice and fit the market options for the second maturity.

With this Markov chain approximation, we can make a big step Monte Carlo just like the Black & Scholes model but in the presence of the smile.

We can also use this chain in a backward approach mimicking the PDE approach with big backward steps.

Classic example

There is a classic example for which the integration is exact but also the Ito integration: The *shifted lognormal.*

The process is given by:

$$dS_t = \sigma\left(bS_0 + (1-b)\,S_t\right) dW_t$$

Local volatility in this case is equal to $\sigma\frac{(bS_0+(1-b)S_t)}{S_t}$. When the parameter $dS_t = \sigma\left(bS_0 + (1-b)\,S_t\right) dW_t$ is zero, we have a lognormal process. When the parameter is set to $b = 1$, we have a Bachelier model (normal model). So both the previous cases are analytically tractable. When b is any value, we consider the process $X_t = \left(bS_0 + (1-b)\,S_t\right)$ which satisfies $dX_t = \sigma\,(1-b)\,X_t dW_t$ implying a log normal process. Therefore,

$S_t = \frac{\frac{e^{(1-b)\sigma W_t - \frac{1}{2}(1-b)^2\sigma^2 t}}{S_0} - bS_0}{1-b}$. We call this process a shifted log normal process and we note interestingly that it converges to a normal process when b goes to 1.

This particular local volatility can be fed to the harmonic average formula and obtain an analytical approximation of the implied volatilities from this model.

$$\Sigma_b(K,T) \cong \sigma\,(1-b)\frac{\ln\left(\frac{K}{S_0}\right)}{\ln\left(\frac{bS_0+(1-b)K}{S_0}\right)}$$

Separable local volatility

A natural way to combine the two models and to keep analytical tractability is to consider separable local volatility:

$$\frac{dS_t}{S_t} = u(t)\,\sigma(S_t)\,dW_t \tag{3.30}$$

In Figure 47, we show the calibration set for a separable local volatility model. We can define a simple approximation by combining the term structure effect and the stationary smile effect. We imply the volatility within this model as follows (this is a very good proxy which is true for short maturities):

$$\Sigma(T,K) \cong \sqrt{\frac{1}{T}\int_0^T u^2(t)\,dt\,\frac{\ln\left(\frac{S_0}{K}\right)}{\int_K^{S_0}\frac{1}{s\sigma(s)}ds}} \tag{3.31}$$

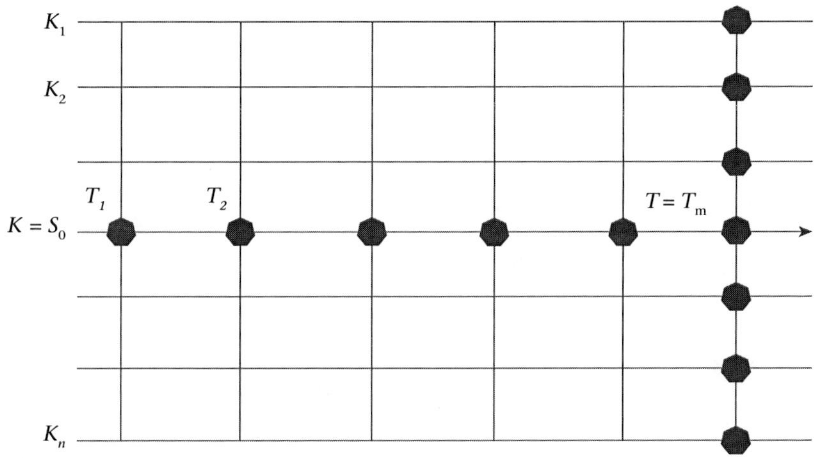

Figure 47 Separable local volatility calibration set

This model controls both a term structure and a terminal smile.

Callable options can be successfully priced with this model. Indeed, we need to have the terminal option right and we need to have, at call date, the whole intermediary smile right.

Term structure of parametric slices

One typical example is the following dynamic:

$$dS_t = \sigma_t \left(b_t S_0 + (1 - b_t) S_t \right) dW_t$$

With this model we can fit not only a term structure at the money options but also the at money skews.

What is interesting in this type of model is that there is a powerful technique called the **Markovian projection** which allows mapping with average type parameters when deriving option pricing formulae for a given maturity. (cf. (Piterbarg, 2006).

The model for a given maturity T behaves just like a stationary terminal smile model with average parameters equal to:

$$dS_t^T = <\sigma>_T (<b>_T S_0 + (1- <b>_T) S_t) dW_t$$

They satisfy:

$$< \sigma >_T = \sqrt{\frac{1}{T}\int_0^T \sigma_t^2 dt}$$

$$< b >_T = \frac{\int_0^T b_t \sigma_t^2 \left(\int_0^t \sigma_s^2 ds\right) dt}{\int_0^T \sigma_t^2 \left(\int_0^t \sigma_s^2 ds\right) dt}$$

These formulae tell us that the average model is obtained by averaging parameters using a particular weight.

Now for the maturity T, we are left with a particular shifted log normal which is quite easy to fit.

If we want to fit the 'at the money volatility,' the skew and the curvature, we can use the following term structure of parameters:

$$\sigma_t^2 (S) = \alpha_t^2 \ln^2 \left(\frac{S}{S_0}\right) + 2\rho_t \sigma_t \alpha_t \ln \left(\frac{S}{S_0}\right) + \sigma_t^2$$

The equivalent terminal model using the averaging technique is given by:

$$< \sigma >_T = \sqrt{\frac{1}{T}\int_0^T \sigma_t^2 dt}$$

$$V_t = \int_0^t \sigma_s^2 ds$$

$$< \rho >_T < \sigma >_T < \alpha >_T = \frac{\int_0^T \rho_t \sigma_t \alpha_t V_t dt}{\int_0^T V_t dt}$$

$$< \alpha >_T^2 = \frac{\int_0^T \alpha_t^2 \left(V_t V_T + 2V_t^2\right) dt}{\int_0^T \left(V_t V_T + 2V_t^2\right) dt}$$

Dupire/Derman & Kani local volatility model

Here the local volatility surface is fully non-parametric (cf. Dupire, Pricing with a Smile, 1994). This model allows a full fitting of an arbitrage-free implied volatility surface.

$$\frac{dS_t}{S_t} = \sigma(t, S_t) dW_t \tag{3.32}$$

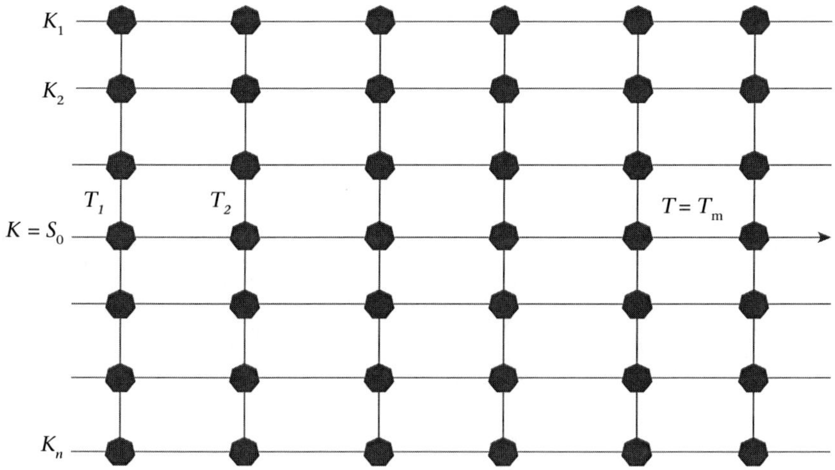

Figure 48 Dupire local volatility calibration set

In Figure 48, we show the calibration set for a general Dupire local volatility. Given a local volatility model, the computation of the implied volatility is only approximate. There exist several methods of approximation, one of which is the most likely path or the gamma map method. We concentrate on the most likely path as it gives intuition as to how the implied volatility is built from local volatility.

The most likely path can be computed using a fixed-point algorithm. It is, indeed, very fast. To maintain the intuition on this calculation we present the Monte Carlo simulation approach. We simulate many paths and keep only the one that finishes around the strike. We obtain a stream of trajectories that start at the initial spot and finish at the strike. We average on each date all these paths and obtain the *most likely path.* We can also extract the variance around this path. We obtain the following implied volatility estimation from this calculation:
In Figure 49, we show in bold the most likely path out of all the simulated paths. Thanks to this most likely path and the width around it we have the following approximation formula (see Reghaï, The Hybrid Most Likely Path, April 2006):

$$\sum{}^2(K,T) \cong \frac{1}{T}\int_0^T E_{K,T}(\sigma^2(t,S_t))dt \tag{3.33}$$

We estimate the integrand using the variance around the most likely path and second order Taylor expansion as follows:

$$E_{K,T}\sigma^2(t,S_t) \cong \sigma^2\left(t, E_{K,T}(S_t)\right) + \frac{1}{2} Var_{K,T}(S_t)\, \partial_{SS}\sigma^2\left(t, E_{K,T}(S_t)\right) \tag{3.34}$$

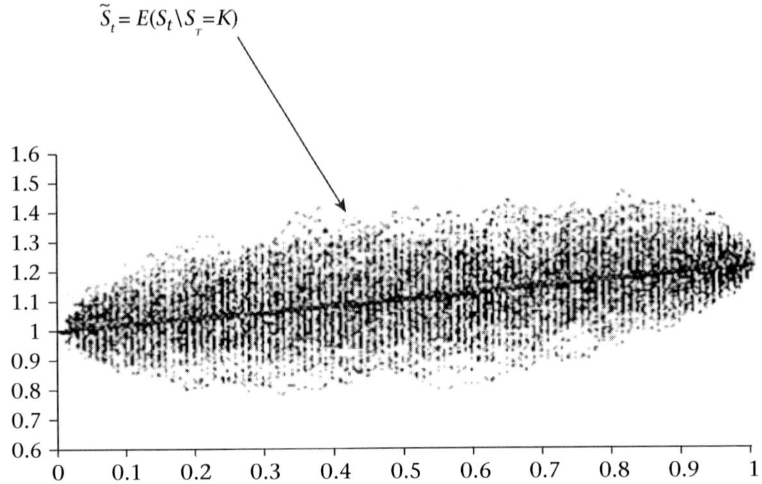

Figure 49 The most likely path

The construction of the local volatility from the implied volatility is a simpler problem theoretically but constitutes a difficult numerical problem. Indeed, the seminal Dupire formula (cf. Dupire, Pricing with a Smile, 1994) allows the local volatility from market prices to be calculated:

$$\sigma^2(T,K) = \frac{\frac{\partial C}{\partial T}}{\frac{1}{2}K^2\frac{\partial^2 C}{\partial K^2}} \tag{3.35}$$

This formula can be expressed solely using implied volatilities (cf. Gatheral, The volatilty surface, a Practitioner's guide, 2006):

$$\sigma^2(t,S) = \frac{\Sigma^2(t,S) + 2t\Sigma(t,S)\left(\frac{\partial\Sigma}{\partial T}|t,S\right)}{1 + 2d_1 S\sqrt{t}\left(\frac{\partial\Sigma}{\partial K}|t,S\right) + d_1 d_2 S^2 t\left(\frac{\partial\Sigma}{\partial K}|t,S\right)^2 + S^2 t\Sigma(t,S)\left(\frac{\partial^2\Sigma}{\partial K^2}|t,S\right)} \tag{3.36}$$

$$d_1 = \frac{\ln\left(\frac{S_0}{S}\right) + \frac{1}{2}\Sigma^2(t,S)\,t}{\Sigma(t,S)\sqrt{t}}, \quad d_2 = d_1 - \Sigma(t,S)\sqrt{t}.$$

We recognize on the numerator the classical term appearing in Equation (3.18). This formula is very practical but is based on the following assumptions:

- It supposes that implied volatility can be computed for every strike and maturity.
- It supposes that there are no dividends, which is not very realistic in equity markets.

In production systems, local volatility calculation remains a difficult numerical problem considering risk, stress test and VaR scenarios.

Instead, we recommend performing the calculation by *optimization* and particularly using a combination of the forward pde (which includes any type of dividend model – even non-linear dividend model) and a fixed-point algorithm to calculate the local volatility (see Reghaï, Boya, & Vong, Quantum local volatility, 2012).[2]

Description of the optimization algorithm by fixed point approach:

- Initialize the local volatility surface:

$$\{\sigma^0(t,S)\}_{t,S} = \{\Sigma_{Target}(T,K)\}_{T,K} \tag{3.37}$$

- Calculate using the 'forward pde' all vanilla prices and imply their volatilities, this is described by the operation.

$$\sigma_{\text{local}} \to \Sigma_{\text{model}} = \Phi\left(\sigma_{\text{local}}\right).$$

- Update the local volatility surface until convergence.

$$\left\{\sigma^{i+1}\right\} = \left\{\sigma^{i}\right\} * \frac{\left\{\Sigma_{\text{Target}}\right\}}{\Phi\left\{\sigma^{i}\right\}} \tag{3.38}$$

Schematically, the local volatility of the *fixed-point* type is built using the following algorithm[3] shown in Figure 50:

Below in Figure 51, Figure 52 and Figure 53 we give examples of the local volatility calculated using the fixed-point algorithm for the following list of underlying FTSE, NKY and SX5E.

Why is the local volatility model so important in practice? This is the case despite several well-known problems with the local volatility model.

Known problems regarding local volatility:

- Forward skew within local volatility is smaller than it should be,
- Volatility of volatility in a local volatility model is small,
- Numerical problems in implementation

Despite all this, polls within investment banks show that the local volatility model is used in more than 90% of production systems in day-to-day risk management.

---

[2] The title 'Relax & Smile' is a play on words. Indeed, the fixed-point algorithm can be seen as a relaxation problem.

[3] Proof can be found in Reghai, Vong, & Boya (2012).

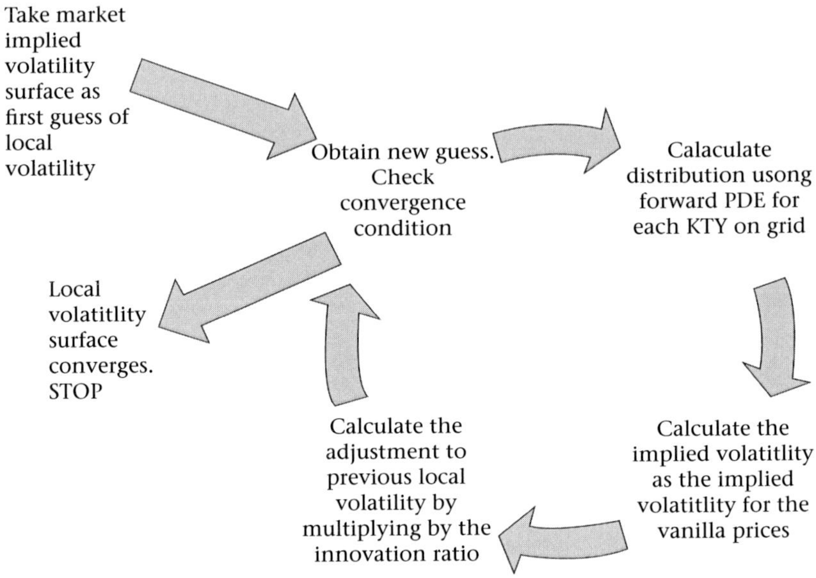

Figure 50 The fixed point algorithm scheme

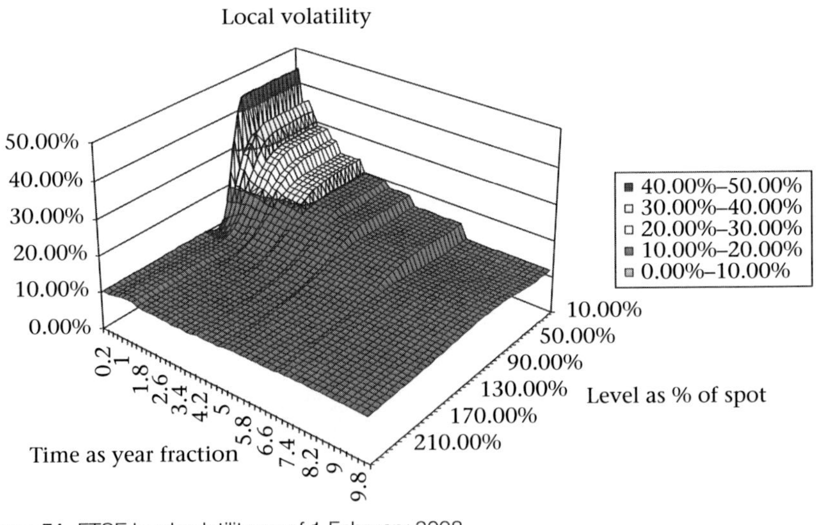

Figure 51 FTSE local volatility as of 1 February 2008

It is important to note at this stage that traders adjust their prices and their greeks if ever the local volatility model is not the adequate pricing model (cliquelets, options on variance swaps).

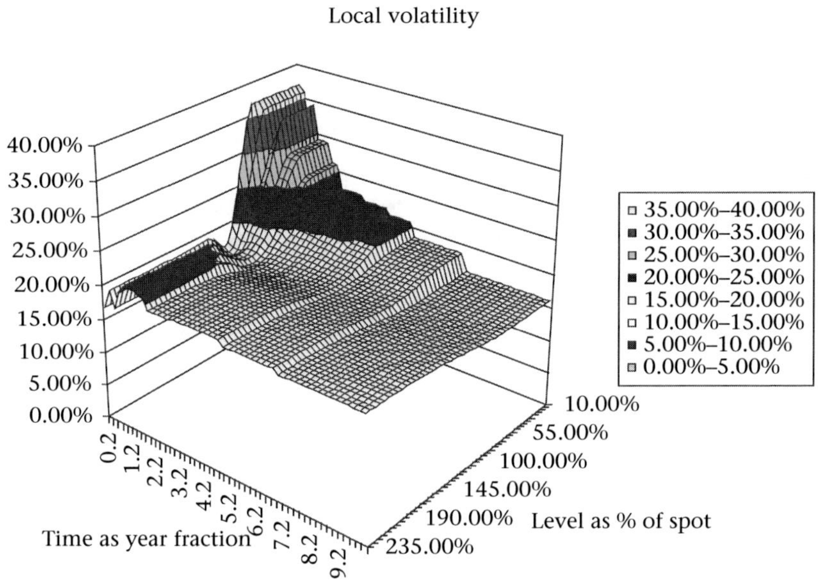

Figure 52 NKY local volatility surface as of 1 February 2008

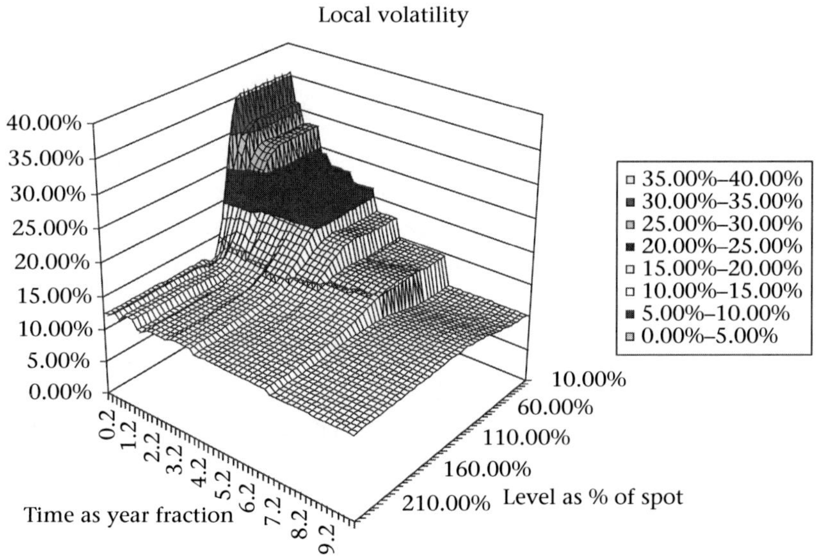

Figure 53 SX5E local volatility surface as of 1 February 2008

The strength of the local volatility model lies in its signature to the product. Only the vega KT map can give precise sensitivities for all vanilla options (K,T).

$$vegaKT = \frac{\partial \pi}{\partial \Sigma (K, T)} \tag{3.39}$$

In other words, the local volatility model allows a more precise projection of the global vega. It provides a powerful means to find the right strikes and maturities whereby to project the total vega. It is also a Profit and Loss explanation for the varied moves in the implied volatility surface. This tool is used every day dozens of times to explain the impact on the book of movements in the volatility surface.

Another useful theoretical aspect of the vega KT hedging (in practice only possible for indices) is that the total immunization of the vega KT ensures total immunization of the gamma map. This is a powerful hedging means that some traders use to prepare for hectic times.

We give the vega KT for some classical products below:

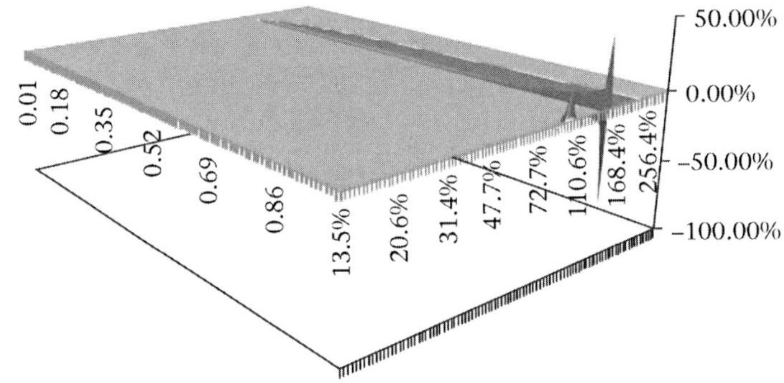

Figure 54 Vega KT of a call up & out

In Figure 54, we recognize at maturity the exposure due to the call at maturity. On the right side, we observe a maximum positive peak followed by a negative minimum. This represents the out deactivating digital. We observe that most of the hedge is concentrated at maturity and this is consistent with the fact that Barrier options are weak path-dependent options. This is also consistent with the gamma map for barrier options in Figure 37.

What is also remarkable is that this vega KT represents the exposure when the product is still alive and one has to unwind the hedging position if the spot hits the barrier. The unwind cost is a key component which enables us to understand the influence of the smile dynamic on derivatives. This example will be examined further.

In Figure 55, we recognize, at maturity, the exposure due to the put. What is new, and contrary to common intuition, is that there is a region with negative vega exposure. This means that adding implied volatility at that point reduces the price of the put down & in. This can be understood as adding more volatility to the process and providing opportunity for the spot to escape from a region where the put was in the money.

In Figure 56, we perform the calculation of the vega KT for an Asian option. We recognize the influence of the different fixings in the construction of the price. As

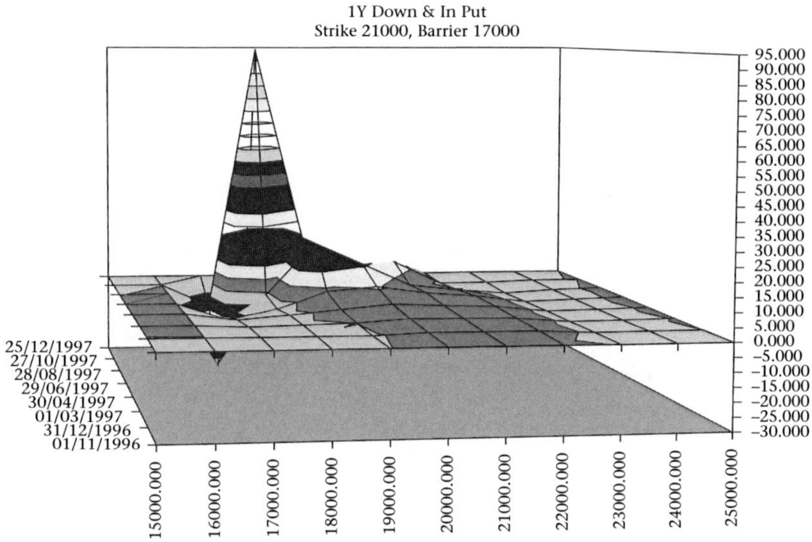

Figure 55 Vega KT for put down & in

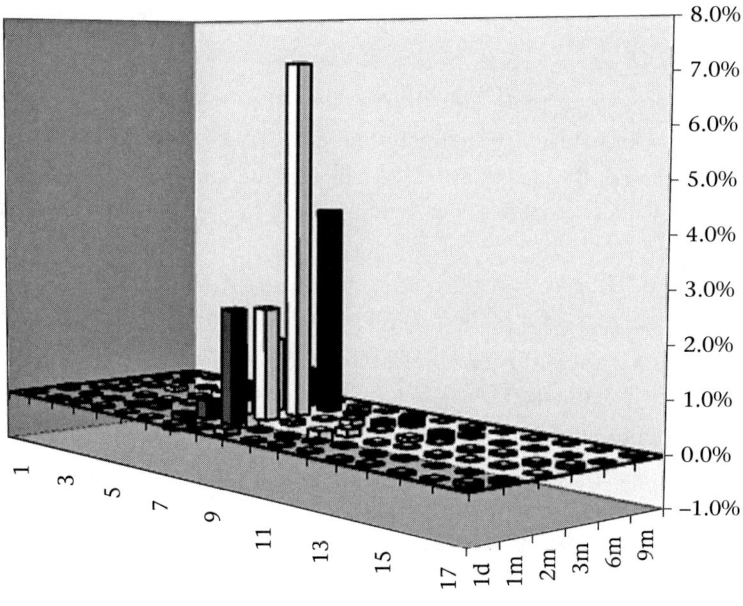

Figure 56 Vega KT for an Asian option

already seen, the Black & Scholes term structure model seems adequate to correctly price an Asian option as all sensitivities are located on the most likely path between the spot today and the strike at maturity. There is no change in sign completely consistent with the gamma of the Asian. What is remarkable is that most of the exposure is located at 2/3 – two thirds – of the final maturity. This is why when traders and practitioners perform a vega hedge of an Asian option, they locate it at 2/3 of the maturity of the deal.

It is possible to obtain *analytical vega (K,T)* for several products expressed as a number of calls times the individual vega of each call.

$$\frac{\partial \pi}{\partial \Sigma(K,T)} = \frac{\partial \pi}{\partial C(K,T)} Vega_{BS}(K,T) \tag{3.40}$$

Exercise 4

1. Consider a market in which one maturity is treated. Calculate the implied volatility derived from a model in which the process is as follows.

$$\frac{dS_t}{S_t} = \sigma \frac{S_t + \lambda}{S_t} dW_t$$

2. Let $\frac{dS_t}{S_t} = \sigma \left(\frac{\sqrt{S_t} - \lambda}{\sqrt{S_t}} \right) dW_t$ a shifted square log normal process. Calculate $d\left(\sqrt{S_t} - \lambda\right)$. Deduce S_t as a function of $S_0, \lambda, W_t, \sigma$.
3. Build a process $\frac{dS_t}{S_t} = \sigma(S_t)\, dW_t$ which gives the same implied volatilities in the short term (maturities goes to zero) as the following stochastic volatility

$$\frac{dS_t}{S_t} = \sigma_t dW_t; d\sigma_t = \alpha \sigma_t \left(\rho dW_t + \sqrt{1-\rho^2} dW_t^{\perp} \right)$$

4. Prove that for any diffusion model the price of the variance swap is equal to minus two log contract. Using Peter Carr's approach, calculate the smile cost of hedge. Hint: apply Ito on the function $\log\left(\frac{S_T}{S_0}\right)$.

Stochastic volatility model

Local volatility models generate stochastic paths for the volatility. However, the volatility of these paths is small compared with models where the volatility is stochastic in itself.

We introduce a Brownian which drives volatility on its own.

$$\begin{cases} dS_t = S_t \sigma_t dW_t \\ d\sigma_t = \alpha \sigma_t d\tilde{W}_t \\ < d\tilde{W}_t, dW_t >= \rho dt \end{cases} \tag{3.41}$$
$$S_0, \sigma_0$$

This model is a simple version of Pat Hagan (cf.Hagan, Kumar, Lesniewski, & Woodward, 2002). It is famous because it is possible to obtain a closed form formula of implied volatility that is very good quality.

It is given by the following equation:

$$\Sigma_{BS}(T,K) = \Sigma(T,S_0) f\left(\frac{\ln\left(\frac{S_0}{K}\right)}{\Sigma(T,S_0)}\right) \tag{3.42}$$

$$f(x) = \frac{\alpha x}{\ln\left(\frac{\sqrt{\alpha^2 x^2 - 2\alpha x \rho + 1} - \rho + \alpha x}{1-\rho}\right)} \tag{3.43}$$

This formula is mainly used in the fixed income market to describe the implied volatility for swaptions. This is called the volatility cube. Thanks to this representation, constant maturity swaps (CMS) developed greatly and became very liquid.

To have a clear understanding of this formula we play with each parameter. More precisely, we consider the following input parameters σ_0, ρ and α in the previous formula. We will perturb them slightly and observe how the smile evolves.

We observe that the parameters induce curve movements that are independent. The first parameter σ_0 steers the global **level** of the volatility curve. The second parameter ρ steers the **slope** of the volatility curve. Finally, the parameter α controls the **curvature** of the volatility curve.

By perturbing the first parameter and re-pricing the contract we can compute the **vega**. By perturbing the second parameter we get the **vega-skew**. For the last parameter we get the **vega-curvature**.

At this stage, we can make a very important remark. If we consider a local volatility model with the following quadratic log-money-ness:

$$\sigma_0^2(S) = \alpha^2 \ln^2\left(\frac{S}{S_0}\right) + 2\rho\sigma_0\alpha \ln\left(\frac{S}{S_0}\right) + \sigma_0^2 \tag{3.44}$$

At small maturities, this model generates exactly the same smile as the stochastic volatility model. This is proved when plugging the local volatility $\sigma_0(S)$ in the harmonic average of BBF. The obtained formula gives exactly the smile of a stochastic volatility process.

This formula can be extended to take the time effect. In this case, the equivalent local volatility which is consistent with a Pat Hagan model is given by:

$$\sigma(t,S) = \sigma_0(S) + t\sigma_1(S) \tag{3.45}$$

Table 11 Stochastic volatility parameters and their impact on the shape of the smile

Parameter	**Slice movement**
σ_0 : The level of the volatility slice at the money. This controls the global level of volatility.	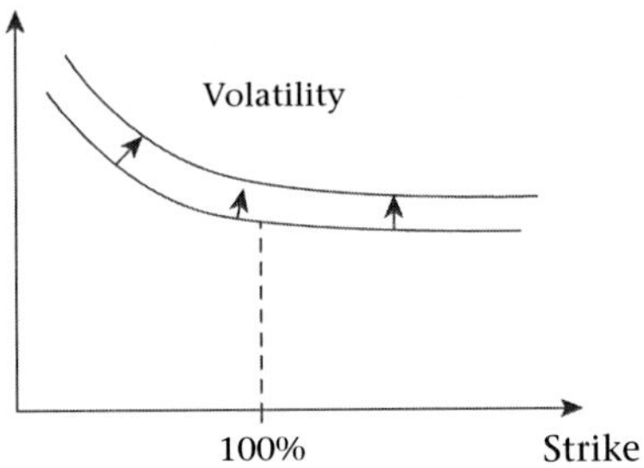
ρ : Correlation of the volatility and the spot. This controls the skew/slope of the smile.	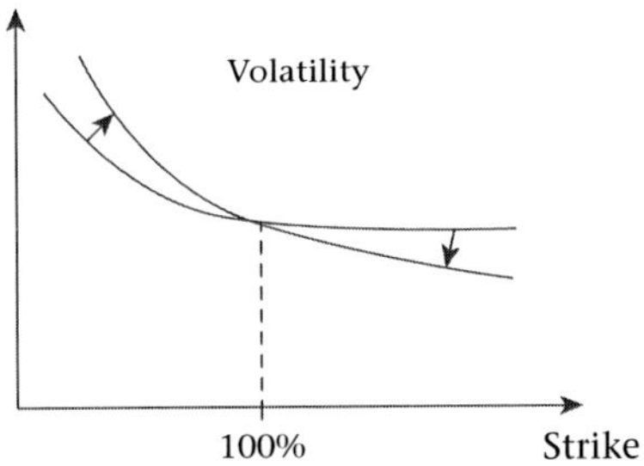
α : The volatility of the volatility. This parameter controls the kurtosis/curvature of the smile.	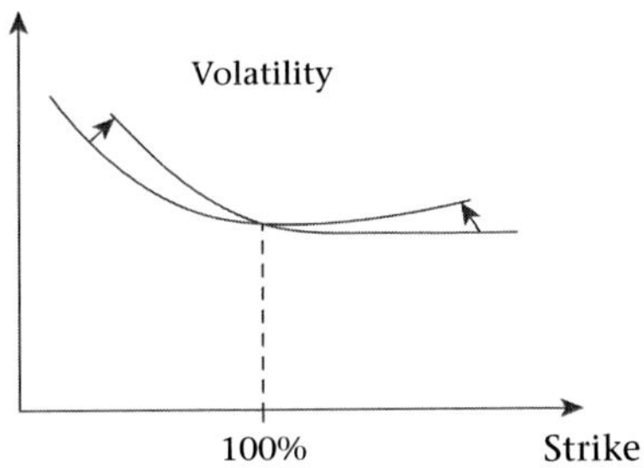

with:

$$\frac{\sigma_1(S)}{\sigma_0(S)} = 2\left(\frac{\rho\alpha\sigma_0}{4} + \left(\frac{2-3\rho^2}{24}\right)\alpha^2\right)$$
$$+\frac{S}{\ln\left(\frac{S}{S_0}\right)}\left(\frac{d\Sigma_0(T,S)}{dK}\sigma_0(S) - \frac{1}{2}\frac{d\sigma_0}{dS}(S)\Sigma_0(T,S)\right) \tag{3.46}$$

Thanks to this construction, we have two models, one is a local volatility model and the other is stochastic volatility model both of which entirely agree on vanilla prices.

Table 12 Stochastic volatility model and its local volatility counterpart

Model	Process	Implied volatility
Local volatility	$\sigma(t,S)=\sigma_0(S)+t\sigma_1(S)$	$\Sigma_{BS}(T,K)=\Sigma(T,S_0)f\left(\frac{\ln\left(\frac{S_0}{K}\right)}{\Sigma(T,S_0)}\right)$
	$\frac{dS_t}{S_t}=\sigma(t,S_t)dW_t$	$\Sigma(T,S_0)=\sigma_0$
Stochastic volatility	$\begin{cases} dS_t=S_t\sigma_t dW_t \\ d\sigma_t=\alpha\sigma_t d\tilde{W}_t \\ <d\tilde{W}_t,dW_t>=\rho dt \end{cases}$	Idem
	S_0,σ_0	

Amongst all stochastic volatility models σ_{SV} we can extract a unique local volatility $\sigma_{LV}(t,S_t)$ model which matches vanilla options exactly. This is possible thanks to the generalized Dupire formula or the Gyongy theorem popularized by Piterbarg (see Piterbarg, 2006).

Indeed, they must satisfy the following relationship.

$$\sigma_{LV}^2(t,S_t)=E\left[\sigma_{SV}^2\,|S_t=S\right] \tag{3.47}$$

What is remarkable here is that we have built an analytical construct that fits this relationship in a special case.

This construction gives us a powerful tool to evaluate the *smile model risk*. In fact, although the previous models agree on the smile photography (vanilla prices), they differ in the way they make this smile evolve, on the one hand, and in the amount of volatility of volatility they inject, on the other.

Therefore, our model risk methodology will start by pricing the same product under the two dynamics. The difference between the two prices gives the smile dynamic impact.

In the case of no impact, such as, but not limited to, vanilla options, the products are fully replicable with European options with static strategies.

In the case of a significant impact, this gives an indication on the path dependency of the payoff on the dynamic of the smile.

To have a normalized measure of the model risk, we introduce the following index:

$$\phi=\frac{\max(LV,SV)-\min(LV,SV)}{\max(LV,SV)+\min(LV,SV)}=\frac{|SV-LV|}{SV+LV} \tag{3.48}$$

We can call this index, a toxicity index and more precisely the *smile dynamic toxicity index.*

When this index is *zero*, it tells us that the payoff is simply replicable by vanilla European options. In other words, this product depends only on marginal distributions.

When the index approaches *one*, we have a very toxic product. Indeed, not only does it tell us that the cheapest model sees no value in the product, but also that the other models (the most expensive model) sees a lot of value. Typically, the cheapest model is the local volatility model and the most expensive the stochastic volatility. This is not always the case.

The toxicity measure is not a deal breaker. By which we mean that that a high toxicity index indicates a high dependency on the dynamic of the smile and gives a warning as to the usage of a local volatility model. It is telling the quant and the trader that the cost of hedge of the product might depend on the shift in the smile.

This toxicity index is a normalized way to classify products and measure their dependence on the smile dynamic. For example, we have seen, through analyzing the gamma map of the Asian option, that the Asian is not very far removed from a European option. We have also seen, through analyzing the vega KT of the barrier option, that the barrier is mainly projected on terminal options. But can we capture a more precise distance between the Asian or the barrier, and the vanilla (zero toxicity)? The toxicity index is such a measure. Once applied to a portfolio of options, it gives a ranking of the different instruments included in the portfolio, hence giving real insight into hedging priorities for the trader and the risk manager.

In the following table, we have calculated the toxicity index for different equity options in a typical equity market.

Table 13 Toxicity index for several products

Product	Toxicity index
Call (T = 1y, k = 100%)	0.0%
Barrier (T = 1y, K = 100%, B = 120%)	7.92%
Asian (T = 1y, K = 100%)	0.71%
Variance Swap (T = 1y)	0.21%
Option on Variance Swap (T = 1y, K = 100% of the level of the Variance Swap)	33.51%

As expected the vanilla option shows zero toxicity regarding the smile dynamic. You can hedge it statically with a European option. A variance swap is a product that depends on the whole set of vanilla for a given maturity. This dependence also means that we are sensitive as to how models extrapolate the smile. The two models, local volatility and stochastic volatility, agree for both very short-term options and near the money options. The small toxicity of 0.21% constitutes a light warning of the variance swap on the smile dynamic. We can now answer the question as to which of the Barrier or Asian is further away from the static vanilla world. Asian options are closer to the static hedging world, with a toxicity of 0.71%, whereas the Barrier option is further away. That said, we saw, from the vega KT, that the Barrier is slightly dependent on the smile dynamic.

We finish our remarks with the case of an option on the variance swap. We know that this option is intuitively an option on the volatility. A toxicity index of 33.51% means that there is a great difference between the local volatility price and the stochastic volatility price. Indeed, the stochastic volatility injects more volatility of volatility than the local volatility model. *We can conjecture that of all stochastic volatility models that match a given smile, local volatility is the one which fits the market with the least volatility of volatility.* In the following lines, we show this for short-term options in the case of a positive curvature.

When we expand the Pat Hagan formula (see Hagan, Kumar, Lesniewski, & Woodward, 2002) to the second order we have an estimate of the volatility of the volatility.

If we note $x = \ln\left(\frac{K}{F}\right)$ the log-money-ness and we compute $A = \frac{\partial \Sigma}{\partial x}(x=0)$ and $B = \frac{\partial^2 \Sigma}{\partial x^2}(x=0)$ then we have the following short term estimators:

$$\alpha_{SV} = \sqrt{3\Sigma_{ATM} B + 6A^2} \tag{3.49}$$

The volatility from the local volatility:

$$\alpha_{LV} = 2\,|A| \tag{3.50}$$

Under these assumptions:

$$\alpha_{LV} \leq \alpha_{SV}.$$

C Models, advanced characteristics and statistical features

We have studied various models in the previous section. We have presented ways, exact or approximate, to transform model parameters into implied volatility parameters. In other words, the previous section exposed means to move from local parameters to implied ones.

This information is very important but not sufficient to fully grasp how a model prices general derivatives.

Another key component for understanding a model is to identify what type of smile dynamic it generates when key factors move that is the spot move.

We have seen that some products under the same smile photography (local volatility matching stochastic volatility) give different prices generating non-zero toxicity indices.

Interestingly, if vanilla prices show zero toxicity their delta is fully impacted by the smile dynamic.

We have the general model independent formula for the delta of a vanilla option which states:

$$\Delta(K,T) = \Delta_{BS}(K,T) + Vega_{BS}(K,T)\frac{\partial \Sigma(T,K)}{\partial S_0} \tag{3.51}$$

We observe terms classified as *photography* $(\Delta_{BS}(K,T), Vega_{BS}(K,T))$. These are fully identified once the model has given the implied volatility for the option KT studied.

We also see one term put in the category *dynamic* $\left(\frac{\partial \Sigma(T,K)}{\partial S_0}\right)$. Here, we need to know how the implied volatility of a given strike K and maturity T moves whenever the spot moves.

This is very *special.* It is a formula which combines *stochastic* calculus via photography and *statistics* via the study of the historical times series composed of the spot and volatility.

We shall now question the models on the induced dynamic and do some statistics to figure out if there is a model which close enough to the observed dynamic.

First of all, *the Black & Scholes model* gives a *sticky strike* dynamic. This is a lazy dynamic. Each option with a strike K and a maturity T will remain at the same level of volatility even if the spot moves.

More precisely, if the spot moves from S_0 to S_1:

$$\Sigma_{BS}(S_1,T,K) = \Sigma_{BS}(S_0,T,K) \tag{3.52}$$

For the stochastic volatility model, the dynamic is known to be a sticky delta dynamic.

$$\Sigma_{SV}(S_1,T,K_1) = \Sigma_{SV}(S_0,T,K_0) \tag{3.53}$$

If the homogeneity relationship is satisfied: $\frac{S_1}{K_1} = \frac{S_0}{K_0}$.

This formula calls for some comments. When we are looking at the implied volatility for the strike K_1 after a movement of the spot at S_1, we can look at the volatility surface before the spot moves at a strike $K_0 = K_1\frac{S_0}{S_1}$. This is true for moving spot while everything else, especially the initial volatility, is left constant. *If we move the volatility accordingly to fit the smile, then all models give the same dynamic imposed by the calibration.* We focus on the dynamic of the smile when just the spot moves. This helps distinguish the models.

In the case of the local volatility model, we do not have exact results as we did before. However, we have good approximation results obtained through a perturbation approach.

$$\Sigma_{LV}(S_1,T,K_1) = \Sigma_{LV}(S_0,T,K_0) \tag{3.54}$$

If the homogeneity relationship is satisfied: $\sqrt{S_1K_1} = \sqrt{S_0K_0}$.

Once again, to estimate the implied volatility for the strike K_1 after a movement of the spot to S_1, we can look at the volatility surface, before the spot moves, at a strike $K_0 = K_1\frac{S_1}{S_0}$.

Each relationship describing the volatility dynamic to the spot is only linked to some homogeneity relationship, representing some sort of invariant after the spot moves.

Table 14 Volatility dynamic for different models

Model type	Volatility dynamic	Invariant quantity
Black & Scholes	$\Sigma_{BS}(S_1,T,K) = \Sigma_{BS}(S_0,T,K)$	K
Local volatility	$\Sigma_{LV}(S_1,T,K) = \Sigma_{LV}(S_0,T,K\frac{S_1}{S_0})$	$\sqrt{SK}$
Stochastic volatility	$\Sigma_{SV}(S_1,T,K) = \Sigma_{SV}(S_0,T,K\frac{S_0}{S_1})$	$\frac{S}{K}$

In particular, we can look at the dynamic induced for options at the money.

In a pure Black & Scholes model with a single volatility:

$$\Sigma_{BS}\,(S_1,T,K=S_1) = \sigma_0$$

In practice, traders use many versions of the Black & Scholes model to trade their implied volatility surface.

$$\Sigma_{BS}\,(S_1,T,K=S_1) = \Sigma_{BS}\,(S_0,T,S_1)$$

In a multi-version Black & Scholes world, the 'at the money' volatility after a move of the spot is the volatility from the previous smile for the same absolute value of the strike.

$$\Sigma_{LV}\,(S_1,T,K=S_1) = \Sigma_{LV}\left(S_0,T,\frac{S_1^2}{S_0}\right)$$

In a local volatility world, the 'at the money' volatility after a move of the spot S_1 is the volatility from the previous smile equal to $\frac{S_1^2}{S_0}$.

$$\Sigma_{SV}(S_1, T, K = S_1) = \Sigma_{SV}(S_0, T, S_0)$$

In a stochastic volatility model, the new at the money is equal to the old at the money.

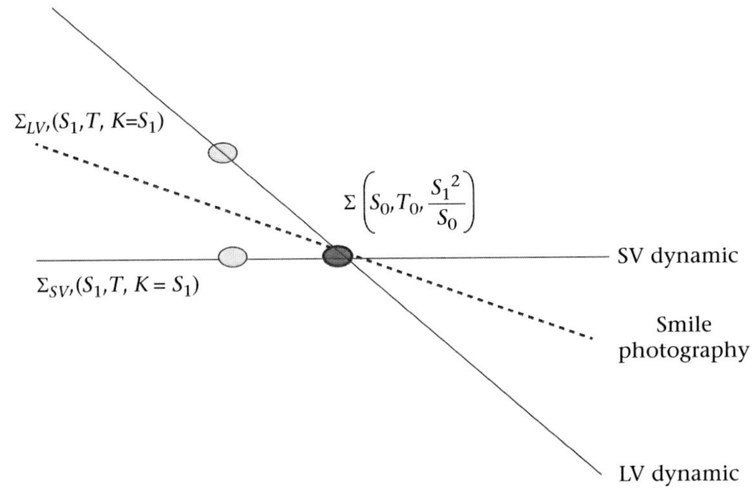

Figure 57 Dynamic of the at the money volatility

In Figure 57, we see that in a stochastic volatility model, if the spot moves and all parameters remain unchanged, the at the money volatility remains at the same level. We also see that in a local volatility model the At the money follows the smile slope twice as fast.

These properties are the result of the dynamic definition.

We need, however, to look at historical data to figure out what is happening in the real world. In this study, we shall at best identify some invariant (quasi-Newtonian approach) and at worst be Keplerian, finding a reasonable description of the data without really understanding the mechanisms.

In Figure 58, and in a qualitative way, we observe that volatility decreases as the spot increases. This is not a property of the smile photography but a statistical observation on the smile dynamic.

In Figure 59, we compare the smile dynamics from the models (local volatility and stochastic volatility) with the historical data. In particular, we have scaled the graphs relative to the historical data (here at 100%). This confrontation with historical data shows that both models, local volatility and stochastic volatility, do not correspond

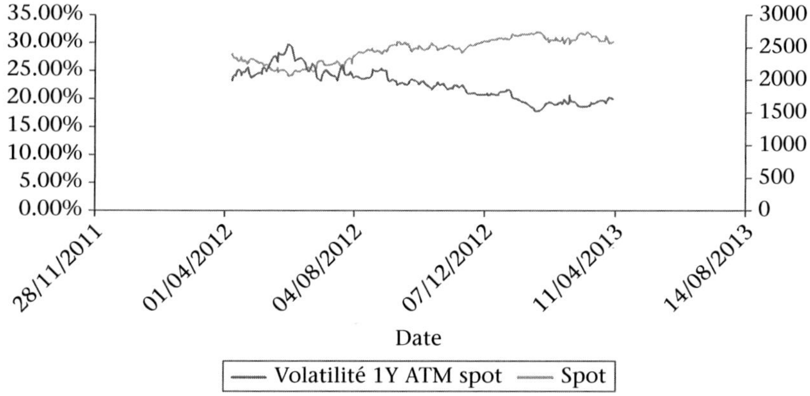

Figure 58 SX5E spot and volatility times series

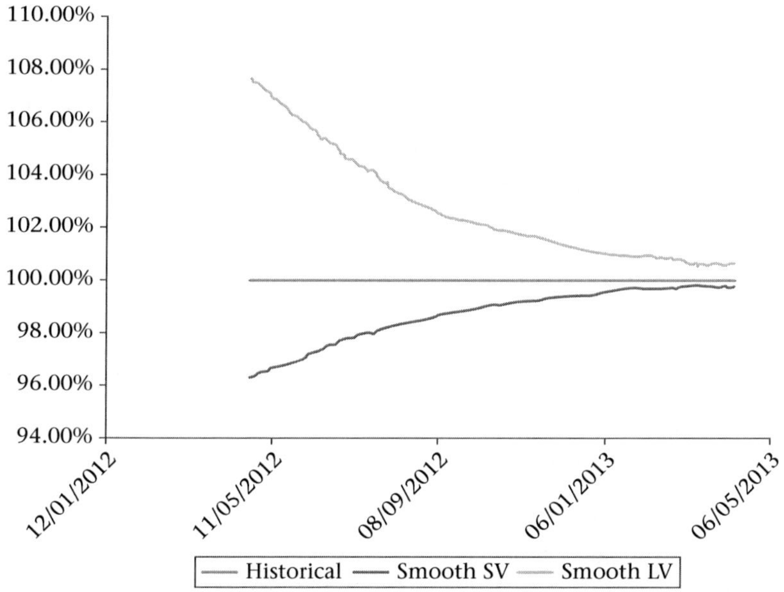

Figure 59 Volatility evolutions (historical versus the model ones)

to the historical realization. Reality or historical data are within the bounds of two synthetic models.

Another useful comparison can be made on the volatility of the volatility. We compare the historical volatility of volatility with that implied by the local volatility and stochastic volatility models.

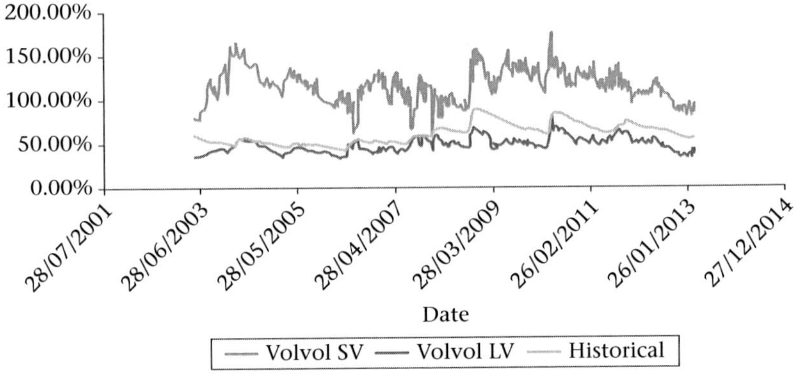

Figure 60 Volatility of volatility under theoretical models and historical observations

In Figure 60, we compare the volatility of volatility calculated in the real world and that issued from the two models the local volatility and the stochastic volatility. We conclude that reality is different from the two models.

However, reality lies in between the two models. We can therefore imagine that we can build a more general process combining the properties of both the local volatility and the stochastic volatility model that approaches the observed data.

This is possible through an extension of the two models, to not only fit the smile photography but also be as close as possible to the real world.

We introduce the local stochastic volatility model (LSV model) with a mixing weight combining the local volatility and the stochastic volatility.

$$\begin{cases} dS_t = S_t \sigma_t f(t, S_t)\, dW_t \\ d\sigma_t = \underbrace{\gamma}_{\gamma \in [0,1]} \alpha \sigma_t d\tilde{W}_t \\ < d\tilde{W}_t, dW_t >= \sqrt{\gamma} \rho dt \end{cases} \quad (3.55)$$
$$S_0, \sigma_0$$

This model has enough parameters to match the smile exactly. It possesses an extra parameter, the *mixing weight*, which offers a degree of freedom in order to match the dynamic of the smile or the volatility of the volatility from historical data.

Another point of view for the *mixing weight* is that it mitigates the stochastic volatility effect stemming from the volatility of the volatility.

Under these new assumptions, the implied volatility in this model combines the local volatility implied volatility with the implied volatility issued from the stochastic volatility.

$$\Sigma_{LSV}(S_1, T, K) = \Sigma_{SV}^{\gamma^2} \left(S_0, T, K\frac{S_0}{S_1} \right) \Sigma_{LV}^{1-\gamma^2} \left(S_0, T, K\frac{S_1}{S_0} \right) \quad (3.56)$$

We are able to use this formula on a daily basis and optimize on the level of the mixing weight in order to match the historical properties of the smile.

We perform this analysis from August 24, 2012 to February 26, 2013. We compute for each day the optimal mixing weight for the maturities 1y, 2y, 3y, 4y and 5y. In Figure 61, we present the results of this historical estimation.

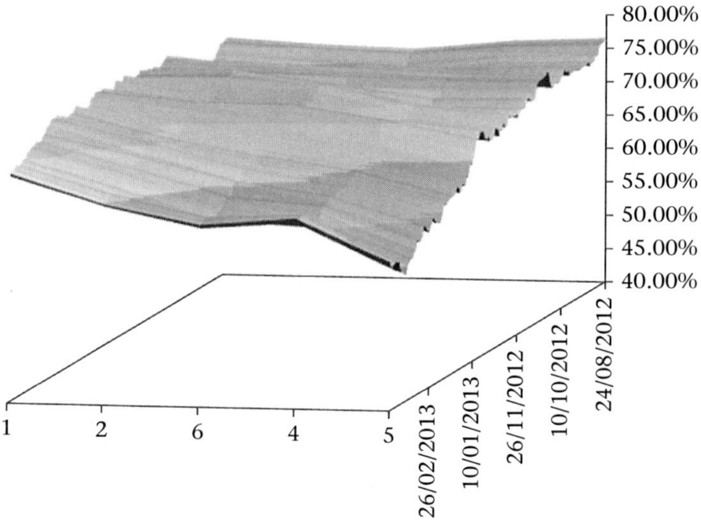

Figure 61 SX5E Estimation of the mixing weight per maturity over time

In Figure 61, we remark that in the past the mixing weight was a bit higher with almost no term structure. More recently, we observe a more pronounced term structure for the mixing weight. It is higher in the short term and lower in the long term.

The current values as of September 2013 for the mixing weights for 1y options for the different asset classes (equity indices, foreign exchange rates and gold) are given in the following table.

Table 15 Typical mixing weights for different markets

Market	Mixing weight
SX5E Index (1y maturity)	70.0%
As of date September 2013	
EURUSD (1y maturity) Foreign Exchange Rate	65.0%
XAUUSD Gold Index (1y maturity)	80.0%

At this stage, we have introduced four different models: Black & Scholes, Local volatility and stochastic volatility and local stochastic volatility.

In fact, they are special versions of the same general class of models: the general stochastic volatility model. There are other stochastic volatility models which are of great interest in practice such as the Heston Model, Bergomi Model, Nandi Model to mention a few.

Let us now see how these special versions can be seen.

Black & Scholes volatility is a special stochastic volatility model with zero volatility of volatility.

In a stochastic volatility model (cf. Hagan, Kumar, Lesniewski, & Woodward, 2002) the volatility of volatility is given by α and the correlation between the spot and the volatility equal to ρ.

In a local volatility model, the correlation is extreme $sign\left(\frac{d\sigma}{dS}(t,S)\right)$ (either $+1$ or -1). The volatility of volatility is given by $\left|\frac{d\sigma}{d\ln S}(t,S)\right|$ and so is spot dependent.

In a local stochastic volatility model, the volatility of the volatility is given by the formula:

$$\sqrt{\sigma^2\left(\frac{d\sigma}{d\ln S}\right)^2+\gamma^2\alpha^2+2\gamma\sigma\alpha\frac{d\sigma}{d\ln S}}$$

We can also present the different partial differential equations (PDE) for pricing.

For the Black & Scholes model, the pricing PDE is the following:

$$\frac{\partial u}{\partial t}+\frac{1}{2}\sigma_0^2 S^2\frac{\partial^2 u}{\partial S^2}=0 \tag{3.57}$$

For the local volatility model:

$$\frac{\partial u}{\partial t}+\frac{1}{2}\sigma^2(t,S)\,S^2\frac{\partial^2 u}{\partial S^2}=0 \tag{3.58}$$

For the stochastic volatility model, the PDE is given by:

$$\frac{\partial u}{\partial t}+\frac{1}{2}\sigma^2 S^2\frac{\partial^2 u}{\partial S^2}+\rho\alpha\sigma^2 S\frac{\partial^2 u}{\partial\sigma\partial S}+\frac{1}{2}\alpha^2\sigma^2\frac{\partial^2 u}{\partial\sigma^2}=0 \tag{3.59}$$

Finally, for the local stochastic volatility model the PDE is given by:

$$\frac{\partial u}{\partial t}+\frac{1}{2}\sigma^2 f^2 S^2\frac{\partial^2 u}{\partial S^2}+\gamma^2\left(\rho\alpha\sigma^2 f^2 S\frac{\partial^2 u}{\partial\sigma\partial S}+\frac{1}{2}\alpha^2\sigma^2\frac{\partial^2 u}{\partial\sigma^2}\right)=0 \tag{3.60}$$

We apply our incremental approach to solve the local and stochastic volatility PDEs.

Local volatility model

We express the local volatility model price as a function of the Black & Scholes model.

The first approach uses a perturbation approach:

$$\pi_{LV} \cong \pi_{BS} + \frac{1}{2}\int_0^{\infty}\int_0^{T} \phi_{BS}(t,S)\,\Gamma_{BS}(t,S)\,S^2\left(\sigma^2(t,S) - \sigma_0^2\right) dSdt$$

We see that the gamma map plays an important role in the price adjustment.

A second formula is possible using a first-order expansion of the local volatility model.

$$\pi_{LV} \cong \pi_{BS} + \int_0^{\infty}\int_0^{T} \frac{\partial \pi_{BS}}{\partial \sigma(t,S)}\left(\sigma(t,S) - \sigma_0\right) dSdt$$

A final formula uses a first order expansion of the implied volatility:

$$\pi_{LV} \cong \pi_{BS} + \frac{1}{2}\int_0^{\infty}\int_0^{T} \frac{\partial \pi_{BS}}{\partial \Sigma(t,K)}\left(\Sigma(t,K) - \sigma_0\right) dKdt$$

Stochastic volatility model

As previously, we express the price under the stochastic volatility as an adjustment of the Black & Scholes price:

$$\begin{aligned}\pi_{SV} \cong \pi_{BS} &+ \int_0^{T}\int_0^{\infty}\int_0^{\infty} \rho\alpha\sigma^2 S\phi(t,S,\sigma_0)\frac{\partial^2 \pi_{BS}}{\partial S\partial\sigma} dS\, d\sigma\, dt \\ &+ \frac{1}{2}\int_0^{T}\int_0^{\infty}\int_0^{\infty} \alpha^2\sigma^2\phi(t,S,\sigma_0)\frac{\partial^2 \pi_{BS}}{\partial \sigma^2} dS\, d\sigma\, dt\end{aligned}$$

For European products, we have a simple version of the previous formulae:

$$\pi_{SV} \cong \pi_{BS} + \frac{1}{2}\rho\alpha\sigma_0^2 S_0 T\frac{\partial^2 \pi_{BS}}{\partial\sigma_0\partial S_0} + \frac{1}{6}\alpha^2\sigma_0^2 T\frac{\partial^2 \pi_{BS}}{\partial\sigma_0^2}$$

Thanks to a perturbation approach, it is possible to approximate the LSV price as a combination of the local volatility and stochastic volatility prices[4]:

$$\pi_{LSV} \cong \gamma^2 \pi_{SV} + \left(1-\gamma^2\right)\pi_{LV} \tag{3.61}$$

Let us now summarize all the model observations $\frac{dS_t}{S_t} = \sigma_0 dI$ around pricing and induced dynamic:

Table 16 Different models and summary of pricing formulae

Model	Dynamic	Pricing
Black & Scholes	$\frac{dS_t}{S_t} = \sigma_0 dW_t$	π_{BS}
Local volatility	$\frac{dS_t}{S_t} = \sigma(t,S_t) dW_t$	$\pi_{LV} \cong \pi_{BS} + \frac{1}{2} E \int_0^T \Gamma_{BS}(t,S)\, S^2 \left(\sigma^2(t,S) - \sigma_0^2\right) dt$
Stochastic volatility	$\begin{cases} dS_t = S_t \sigma_t dW_t \\ d\sigma_t = \alpha \sigma_t d\tilde{W}_t \\ < d\tilde{W}_t, dW_t >= \rho dt \end{cases}$ S_0, σ_0	$\pi_{SV} \cong \pi_{BS} + E\int_0^T \rho\alpha\sigma^2 S \frac{\partial^2 \pi_{BS}}{\partial S \partial \sigma} dt + \frac{1}{2} E \int_0^T \alpha^2 \sigma^2 \frac{\partial^2 \pi_{BS}}{\partial \sigma^2} dt$
LSV	$\begin{cases} dS_t = S_t \sigma_t f(t,S_t)\, dW_t \\ d\sigma_t = \underbrace{\gamma}_{\gamma \in [-1,1]} \alpha \sigma_t d\tilde{W}_t \\ < d\tilde{W}_t, dW_t >= \sqrt{\gamma} \rho dt \end{cases}$ S_0, σ_0	$\pi_{LSV} \cong \gamma^2 \pi_{SV} + \left(1-\gamma^2\right)\pi_{LV}$

All previous models belong to the same large class of stochastic volatility models. We can distinguish them via their different highlighted characteristics:

1. *To Smile or not to Smile*: Black & Scholes is the only model with no smile. The three others fit the same smile and cannot be distinguished.
2. *Smile dynamic*: the three models local volatility, stochastic volatility and the LSV models differ in their implied dynamic,
3. *Volatility of volatility*: this is an important way to distinguish all models. If we note α_{BS} the volatility of volatility of the Black & Scholes model, α_{LV} that for the local volatility model, α_{LSV} that for the local stochastic volatility model and α_{SV} that for the stochastic volatility model, we have:

$$\alpha_{BS} = 0 \le \alpha_{LV} \le \alpha_{LSV} \le \alpha_{SV} \tag{3.62}$$

4 Proof can be found in Reghaï, Klaeyle, & Boukhaffa, LSV with a mixing weight (2012).

We know that none of the three models Black & Scholes, local volatility or stochastic volatility fits the photography and dynamic of the smile. We know that the LSV model resembles a mixture of local volatility and stochastic volatility. We also know that there is a configuration of the LSV (defined by a specific choice of the mixing weight) that fits both the photography of the smile and its dynamic. Based on all this information, we can now answer the question of fair valuation.

4 What is the Fair Value in the Presence of the Smile?

A What is the value corresponding to the cost of hedge?

Until now, we have studied a few products using simple models. To build the fair value, we need to fully understand the way to hedge. We shall describe the fair value from the point of view of an investment bank, that is from the sell side. In particular, the hedging portfolio immunizes the book against spot and volatility movements.

$$\begin{aligned} C_{t+1} - C_t =& d\, S_t \Delta t + (C_t - \Delta_t S_t)\, r \Delta t + \Delta_t (S_{t+1} - S_t) \\ &+ \iint\limits_{\mathrm{K,T}} \frac{\partial \pi}{\partial \Sigma(K,T)_t} \left(\Sigma(K,T)_{t+1} - \Sigma(K,T)_t \right) dK dT \end{aligned} \tag{4.1}$$

To simplify the PnL equation, we make the following assumptions:

- Ignore dividends (first term in the right-hand side).
- Ignore financing (second term in the right-hand side).
- Focus on convexity through one option hedging (with At the money option).
- Mono underlying option.
- Discrete hedging and no impact of discontinuities.

$$\begin{aligned} \Delta PnL =& \frac{1}{2} \frac{\partial^2 \pi}{\partial S^2} S^2 \left(\left(\frac{\Delta S}{S} \right)^2 - \sigma_{\mathrm{Model}}^2 \Delta t \right) \\ &+ \frac{1}{2} \frac{\partial^2 \pi}{\partial \sigma^2} \sigma^2 \left(\left(\frac{\Delta \sigma}{\sigma} \right)^2 - \alpha_{\mathrm{Model}}^2 \Delta t \right) \\ &+ \frac{\partial^2 \pi}{\partial \sigma \partial S} \sigma S \left(\frac{\Delta S}{S} \frac{\Delta \sigma}{\sigma} - \rho_{\mathrm{Model}} \sigma_{\mathrm{Model}} \alpha_{\mathrm{Model}} \Delta t \right) \end{aligned} \tag{4.2}$$

In this equation, we once again observe the contributions of the three ingredients:

- *Option* through the terms:
  Gamma $\frac{\partial^2 \pi}{\partial S^2}$,
  Vanna $\frac{\partial^2 \pi}{\partial \sigma \partial S}$,
  Volga/Voma $\frac{\partial^2 \pi}{\partial \sigma^2}$,
- *Market*, through the terms:
  Realized Volatility $\left(\frac{\Delta S}{S}\right)^2$,
  Realized Covariance $\frac{\Delta S \Delta \sigma}{\sigma S}$,
  Realized volatility of volatility $\left(\frac{\Delta \sigma}{\sigma}\right)^2$,
- *Model*, through the terms:

$$\sigma^2_{\text{Model}}, \ \alpha^2_{\text{Model}}, \ \rho_{\text{Model}} \ \alpha_{\text{Model}} \ \sigma_{\text{Model}}$$

As previously, we shall apply the same incremental methodology to build our understanding, starting with a simple model that is Black & Scholes.

We apply our methodology to a barrier option.

We shall apply our approach to barrier options at the same time. Each has a different barrier level.

We shall examine the different sources of risk for these two options in an incremental way.

We perform the following risk scenarios:

- The Delta spot ladder (identifies the gamma map),
- The Vega volatility ladder (identifies the vomma, or the gamma with respect to the volatility),
- The Vega spot ladder (identifies the vanna).

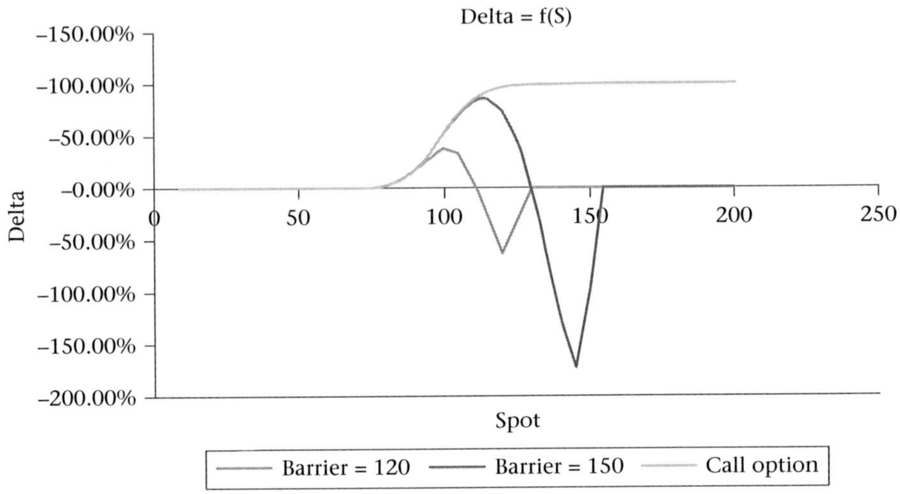

Figure 62 Delta spot ladder for two barrier options

The Delta spot ladder for two barrier options

In Figure 62, a study of the delta as function of spot is performed. It is essential to detect the rapid variation of the delta when the spot moves. This helps the risk manager for two usual issues:

- *Gap risk identification*: you can indeed find regions of the spot where the delta moves rapidly. In particular, we have a negative delta when crossing the barrier. This means that when the option ends, the trader needs to unwind his/her delta hedging position. He needs to buy back the spot with higher price. The Gap risk is in this case detrimental to the trader, unlike the American binary option case.
- *Gamma map*: With this scenario, we can color regions of the spot. When the graph is increasing for increasing spot we then have positive gamma. When the delta is decreasing for increasing spot then the gamma is negative. Changing sign gamma limits the use of the Black & Scholes model. In this case, there is an impact from the local volatility on the pricing.

If there is a presence of Gap risk one needs to consider smoothing the payoff. If there is a change of sign for the Gamma, then one knows that the simplest model, the Black & Scholes is not enough. We need to use a model that takes the smile into account.

The vega volatility ladder

In Figure 63, we observe that the barrier option will have different behaviors depending on the experienced volatility. We observe that there are zones of positive vomma (vega increases with volatility) and there are other zones of negative vomma (vega decreases with volatility).

Let us remember the PnL equation and zoom in particularly on the vomma term:

$$\Delta PnL = \cdots + \frac{1}{2}\frac{\partial^2 \pi}{\partial \sigma^2}\Delta\sigma^2 + \cdots \tag{4.3}$$

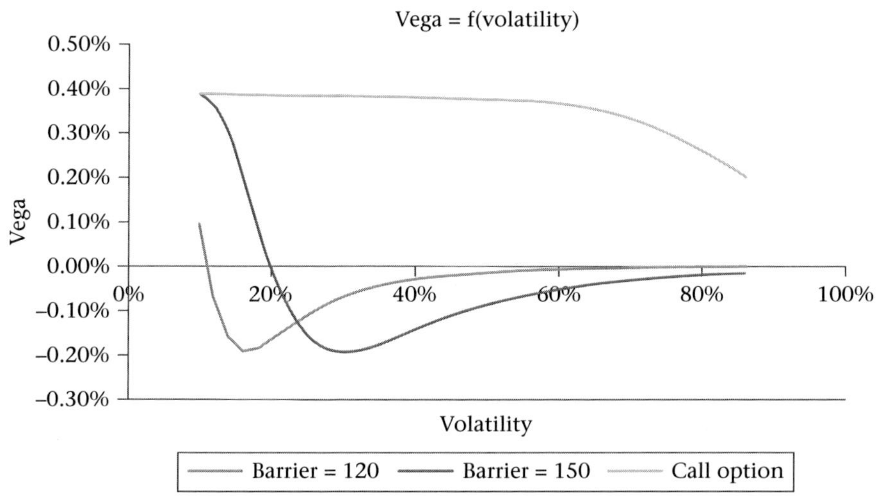

Figure 63 Vega volatility ladder for the barrier option

In a volatility regime equivalent to Equity and Commodity, between 15% and 35%, we typically observe a positive vomma.

When a trader in such a market shorts a barrier option and vega hedges, his/her position becomes vomma negative. This creates a loss in the PnL equation. The trader needs to increase the price compared to the Black & Scholes price to take into account this extra hedge cost.

One has to be careful of market changes which vibrate at different volatilities and also regime change in a given market.

The vega spot ladder

In Figure 64, we study the vega as a function of the spot. This captures the vanna effect on the PnL evolution. Unlike the vomma, the sign of the vanna is not

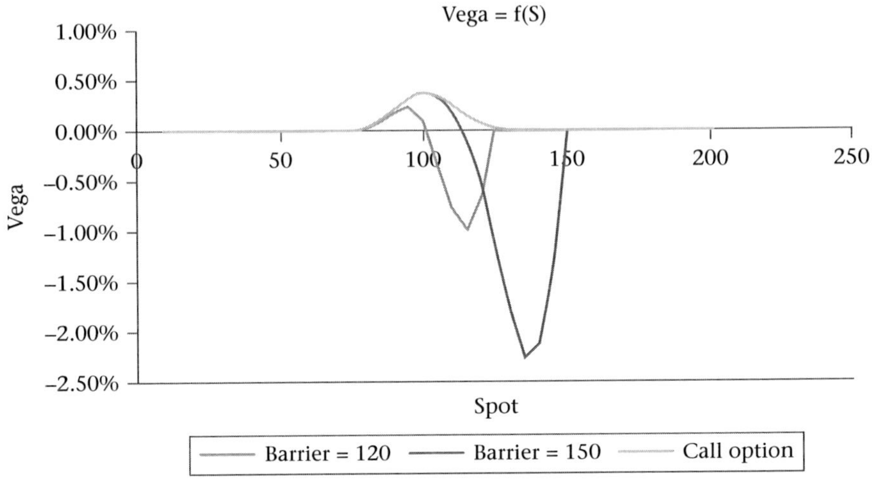

Figure 64 Vega spot ladder of two different barrier options

enough to understand the effect on the product. We need to know the sign of the co-movements of the spot and the volatility.

In Equation (4.4) we zoom in on the on the vanna term in the PnL evolution equation:

$$\Delta PnL = \cdots + \frac{1}{2}\frac{\partial^2 \pi}{\partial \sigma \partial S}\Delta\sigma\Delta S + \cdots \tag{4.4}$$

If the co-movements of the spot and the volatility are negatively correlated and the vanna position is positive then the trader loses money.

To compensate for this loss, the trader needs to increase the price relatively to the Black & Scholes price.

Once again, we observe that with a simple Black & Scholes model we can investigate if this is enough for pricing the product or if we need to have a more elaborate model. For the stochastic volatility model, we have to look at vomma (volatility convexity) and vanna (cross convexity spot and volatility). The effects on the price depend on the regime of volatility and the regime of co-movements for the spot and volatility.

At the inception of the transaction, the trader implements vanilla hedging. The exact composition of the hedging portfolio is a result of the vega KT. Then, either at maturity or when the barrier is hit, the trader unwinds his/her hedging position. Movements of the spot imply movements in the volatility. If the underlying assumptions of the model generate different assumptions than reality, the trader will not be well hedged. This will generate a profit or a loss. On the contrary, if the underlying assumptions of the model fit the realized dynamic, the trader will generate just enough value in his/her portfolio to replicate the option value.

Let us now provide some numerical applications and we shall give results on the same barrier option under different markets.

Here are the results for the equity and the foreign exchange markets:

Table 17 Barrier option pricing in two different markets

	Equity markets $\sigma_0 = 30\%$, $\alpha = 50\%$, $\rho = -60\%$	Foreign exchange rate $\sigma_0 = 10\%$, $\alpha = 100\%$, $\rho = 0\%$
Black & Scholes	0.43%	0.63%
Local volatility	0.62%	0.54%
Stochastic volatility	0.68%	0.74%
Toxicity index	3.1%	12%
Local stochastic volatility	0.63%	0.62%

We discover what practitioners in the different business lines use in practice. In the Equity world, the local volatility model is generally enough to obtain the right pricing for barrier options. In the Foreign Exchange business, we may have the illusion that market prices are built thanks to a simple Black & Scholes model. Indeed, the Black & Scholes price is close to the fair pricing which is the result of the LSV model with 65% mixing weight. However, one should not forget that the right pricing is a small part of the life of the derivative. A model is designed to build the hedging strategy from the beginning of the option until it matures. Only with the right modeling can the trader price correctly and also implement a hedging strategy that takes him/her from the fair value to the payoff for every realized path.

Conclusion

We have presented a set of useful results to play with models and question them in different situations. We have also presented an incremental methodology to explore product toxicity. This starts by studying products under a simple model first and looking at the gamma map. This helps identify rapid changes (gap risk) or sign changes (smile exposure). Then extensions to price with smile are proposed. The simplest of all smile models can suffice if the toxicity index is at zero. If this is not the case, a statistical study of a certain type of smile dynamic combined the volatility of volatility, allows the right mixture between local volatility and stochastic volatility to be built. This mixture fits the initial smile (photography) and captures some quasi-Newtonian property of its dynamic. This fine-tuning helps obtain the fair value and right hedging strategy. In Figure 65, we summarize the incremental methodology presented in this chapter.

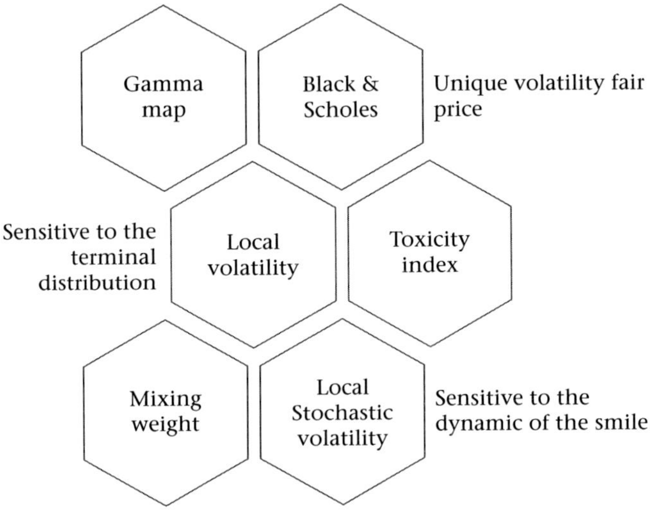

Figure 65 Incremental model identification in the presence of the smile

This approach can be generalized to take into account other effects such as correlation, interest rate exposure, forward skew exposure, dividend risk. In the next chapter, we follow the same lines and expose an incremental modeling approach for the dividend, interest rate and forward skew risk.

5 Mono Underlying Risk Exploration

We have seen how to analyze the smile risk. We have learnt how to decompose this risk in a photography risk (fitting the initial smile) and a dynamic risk (capturing elements of its dynamic). Not all products need full exposure to the smile and its dynamic. This question is answered via a progressive approach in which we start by exploring the gamma map. We also compute the smile toxicity index to know if a model extension is necessary. In the most complex case, where the gamma map shows changes of exposure and the presence of an important smile toxicity index, we need to figure out the right mixing weight, the right blending factor issued from a statistical study of the volatility dynamic in the market. We developed a large set of models and approaches for which we have full access, analytically or semi-analytically, to their properties.

This set of models can then be used to fit each situation according to the need and the analysis of the three main building blocks the option, the market and the model.

It is now time to cover other areas of model risk in the case of the mono asset pricing.

In this chapter, we shall present different versions of the toxicity risk indicators covering many axis of risk. More precisely, we are interested in the following axis:

- Dividend modeling.
  In equity models, dividends play an important role. Typically, investments banks sell options (call options) and thereafter they become long dividends. The cost of hedging depends dramatically on the assumptions of the dividends. We model the expected dividends and the variability of this amount subject to the main driver that is the equity spot. To be able to explain the PnL evolution, we need to model the realized dividend for a given equity path accurately.
- Interest rate modeling.
  Most contracts happen to be packaged in equity notes. Typically, there is a swap option next to the equity option that cancels when the option matures. It becomes clear that even for non-hybrid options (no clear dependence on the interest rate underlying) the unwind value of the swap can change and depends

on the correlation between the equity and interest rate. To explain the trader's PnL, we have to accurately model the level of the swap for a given equity path.

- Forward skew modeling.
  Cliquets are contacts where the payoff depends on the forward performance. Fitting the smile in such a situation does not help in the pricing and hedging such instruments. Model-wise, we need one that generates fat tails in its increments. At the same time, when a cliquet has fixed, it becomes a vanilla option. Therefore, the model needs to fit vanilla options. The difficulty of building such models is to be able to explain the PnL variation due to the static hedge with vanillas and the dynamic hedge that captures the fat-tail nature of the returns.

Dividends

Models: discrete dividends

The natural model extension of the previous models in the equity world is to add a *discontinuity* to the diffusion to represent the jump due to the dividend. This is shown in Figure 66, where we have two possible trajectories of a stock with and without dividends. The modeling of the amount of the drop differentiates the models. This modeling can possibly rely on the existing spot factor. In general, this is enough except when we tackle options on dividends. In that case, we look at the proper dividend convexity. For this situation, we need a proper dividend factor. There is a parallel with what has previously been done with the smile. We saw, for example, that options on variance swaps could not be priced just with a local volatility model and that an extra factor was needed to price and hedge them.

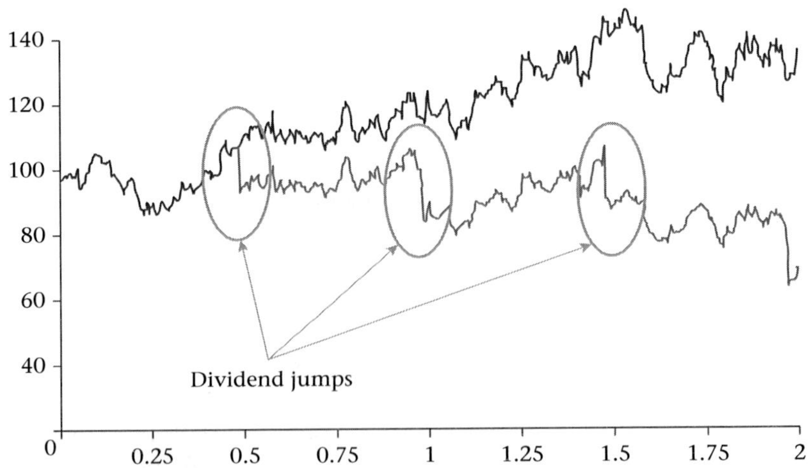

Figure 66 Black & Scholes Spot Path with and without dividends

We shall concentrate on one-factor models only. Within this class of model, we have different possible assumptions.

We assume that analysts have come with a modeling of the expected dividends to be paid in the future. We need in/out modeling to be able to shift this amount in the future depending on the equity path. If we zoom in on the contribution of the dividends to the PnL equation we have:

$$\Delta PnL = \cdots + \Delta_t D_r + \cdots \tag{5.1}$$

Where Δ_t is the delta at time t and D_r is the realized dividend amount. At the same time, the model price has implicitly made the assumption that the dividend model is equal to D_m. So, the total cost due to the difference between the realized dividends D_r and the modeled ones D_m generates an impact in the pricing that is equal to:

$$\Delta\pi = \sum_{i \in div} E_{T_i}^{P}\left(\Delta_{T_i}\left(D_r(T_i) - D_m(T_i)\right)\right) \tag{5.2}$$

Here again, we observe the influence of the real world on the hedging performance. We also identify some kind of wrong risk assessment. Indeed, we can become long dividend in a given model with an amount that is too high compared to the reality.

To obtain the fair valuation we need to obtain the right modeling of the dividends. For stocks, we only have a few points and statistics have little meaning, unless we perform a collaborative statistical modeling.

For this reason, we make a statistical study on the large universe of stocks of the Eurotop600.

This will give us the right blend between the different dividend models that best fits reality.

The process of the spot in the presence of discrete dividends is given by:

$$\frac{dS_t}{S_t} = rdt + \sigma(t, S_t)\, dW_t$$
$$S_{t_d}^{+} = S_{t_d}^{-} - D\left(S_{t_d}^{-}\right) \tag{5.3}$$

In this class of one-factor models, we may have many types of assumptions to model function$D(S)$. All of them will have to generate the same expected amount of dividends $E\left(D\left(S_{t_d}^{-}\right)\right)$.

Models: cash amount dividend model

In this model, the amount of the dividend is constant for all trajectories. The amount of dividend as a function of the spot is shown in Figure 67. The model can generate negative spots after the drop of the dividend. The terminal distribution generated with this model in no more log normal and we lose a closed form formula for simple options. The calibration of the local volatility is also a difficult problem and there is no equivalent for the Dupire formula.

$$D(S) = D \tag{5.4}$$

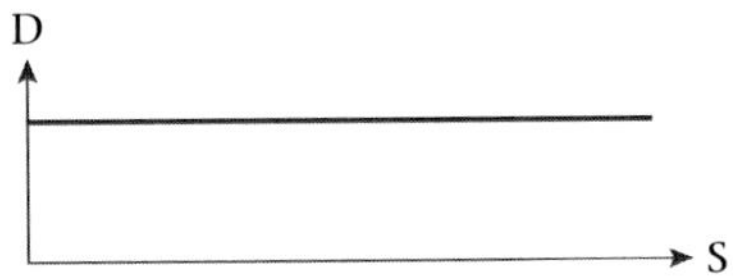

Figure 67 Cash amount dividend modeling

Buehler designed an affine transformation that allows the negativity problem to be solved and makes it is easy to solve for local volatility.

Models: proportional dividend model

In this case, we extend the Black & Scholes model with a drop in the dividend with an amount proportional to the spot before the jump. The amount of dividend as a function of spot is shown in Figure 68. This has some interesting properties. The spot never goes negative. We also notice that the marginal distribution of the spot is always log normal in the case of constant volatility. This gives us closed form formulae for vanilla options. The calibration of the local volatility is also possible thanks to easy adaptation of the Dupire formula.

$$D(S) = yS \tag{5.5}$$

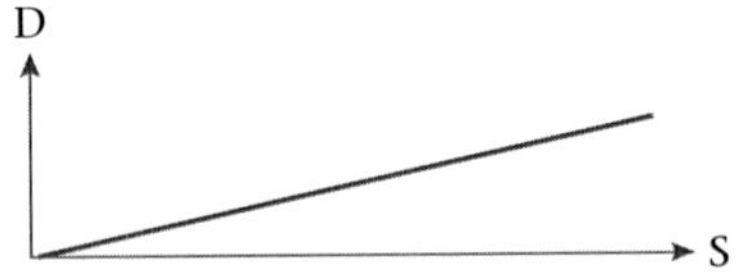

Figure 68 Proportional dividend modeling

Models: mixed dividend model

In this model, d is the minimum dividend level, which can grow linearly with spot thanks to the yield y. This modeling is a trade-off approach to model partial uncertainty on dividends. The amount of dividend as a function of spot is shown in Figure 69.

We introduce a new parameter to determine dividends split: it is noted γ_ε. This quantity represents the proportion of the proportional dividend out of the total dividend. Cash and proportional parts are determined by the following system of equations (we note $F^-$the forward just before the dividend drop):

$$\begin{cases} y = \gamma_\varepsilon \frac{D}{F^-} \\ d = (1 - \gamma_\varepsilon) D \end{cases} \tag{5.6}$$

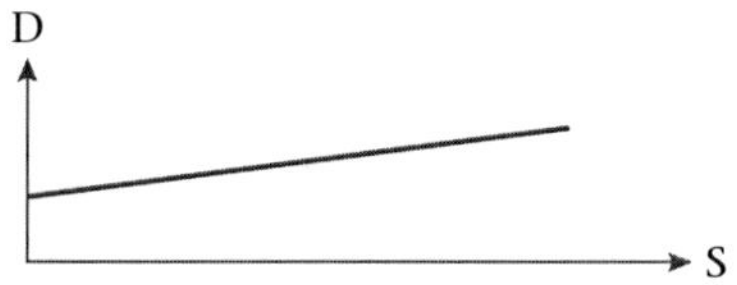

Figure 69 Mixed dividend modeling

This model can be solved as the cash amount dividend by an affine representation of the spot.

Models: dividend toxicity index

When we study a new product, we can design a dividend toxicity index. We compute the price using the proportional dividend model π_{pd} and the one obtained with a cash amount dividend model π_{cad}.

$$\phi_{div} = \frac{\max(\pi_{pd}, \pi_{cad}) - \min(\pi_{pd}, \pi_{cad})}{\max(\pi_{pd}, \pi_{cad}) + \min(\pi_{pd}, \pi_{cad})} = \frac{|\pi_{pd} - \pi_{cad}|}{\pi_{pd} + \pi_{cad}} \tag{5.7}$$

When this quantity is zero, it means that the structure in question does not only depend on the expected amount of dividends. In the case where this quantity differs from zero, the trader knows that the randomness around the representation has an impact on the pricing and hedging.

Typically the trader's position is long dividends. So when the prices π_{pd} and π_{cad} of his or her option differ, this means that the trader is long on the dividends only in a region of values of the spot.

If the trader sells an auto call on the high side, he/she becomes long dividends on the downside. Therefore, in the proportional dividend model assumption, he/she becomes long a smaller amount of dividend as compared with the cash amount dividend model. Therefore, the price π_{pd} is more expensive than π_{cad}. We have a proxy formula which links the prices within the two models:

$$\pi_{pd} - \pi_{cad} \cong \sum_{div} \left.\frac{\partial \pi_{cad}}{\partial D}\right|_{(t_d,S)} E_{t_d}^{Q}\left(D - yS\right) \tag{5.8}$$

We use the dividend sensitivity for every dividend time and at any spot level.

At this stage, we need to collect data and extract some statistical invariants to find the right mix between the two models.

Statistical observations on dividends

Statistical modeling of dividends is a complex matter. Several non-quantitative factors come into play in the determination of the dividend level.

Therefore, modeling dividends as a function of the spot is a real challenge.

In this study, we shall concentrate on the universe of the FTSE. In this universe, there exist futures on dividends that are very liquid. T1/T2/T3/T4/T5 correspond to the dividend futures for the first five years ahead. In Figure 70, we observe that dividend futures move along the future index. They are not as volatile as the future index.

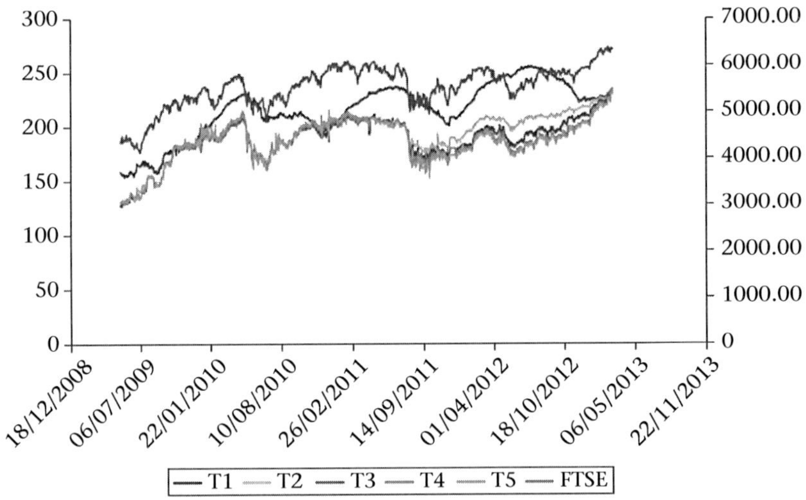

Figure 70 FTSE index and dividend futures evolution

The simplest model of the dividend futures as a function of the spot can be formulated as linear regression. The proportion of the proportional part of the dividend out of the total dividend represents the blend or the dividend mixing weight γ_ε. The estimation of this parameter is quite stable for each dividend future (quasi-Newtonian model). There are periods when it changes a great deal.

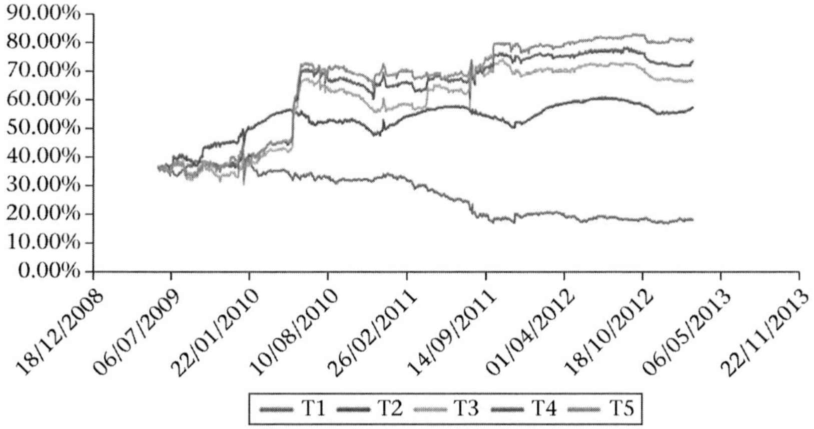

Figure 71 Trend for the dividend mixing weight as a function of time

It is interesting to observe in Figure 71, that there is a regime change in April 2010. The reason for this was that the market was mainly driven by hedgers. They were becoming long dividend on the downside forcing them to sell dividend futures to hedge their positions. The fact that after a transition period, the proportions seem to converge to some equilibrium, suggests that there is a shift in the composition of the players in this market. This is like having a new gravitational constant subject to this regime.

The identification of the right blend allows the right pricing to be built.

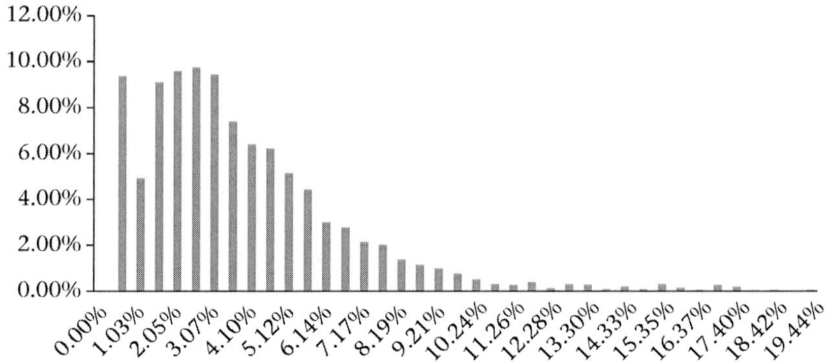

Figure 72 Annual dividend yield distribution for the Euro top 600

To complete the subject of dividends, we need to pay attention to stocks. The dividend can be affected by special events that happen during the life of a company. This generates extra randomness and extreme cases are to be considered. Statistically speaking, we observe in Figure 72, that the dividend yield is capped at 20%.

In some countries the regulation sets a limit, for example as in Italy, at 10%. In the following graph, we see the global distribution for the Euro top 600.

From this distribution it is also possible to compute quartiles:

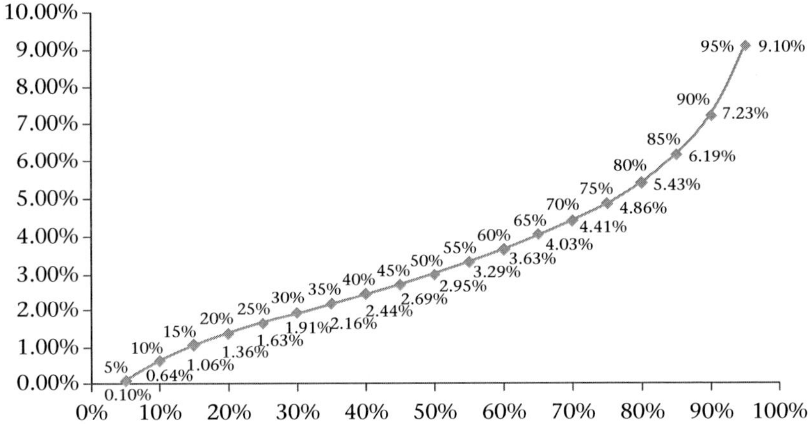

Figure 73 Quartile dividend yield distribution

Indeed, in Figure 73, the third quartile is equal to 4.86%, that is 75% of the observed dividend yields are below 4.86%. No dividend yield has ever exceeded 20%.The median dividend yield is equal to 2.69%.

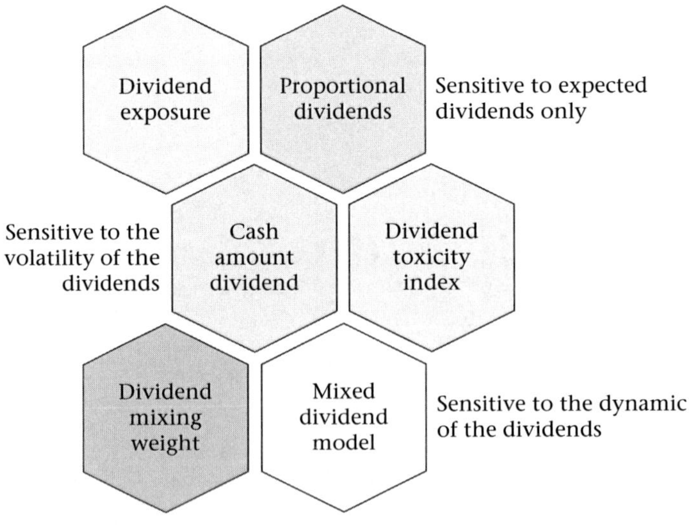

Figure 74 Incremental model identification in the presence of the dividend risk

In Figure 74, we summarize the incremental steps in the discovery of the dividend toxicity and the choice of the model to obtain the fair price.

Interest rate modeling

Models: why do we need stochastic interest rates?

Consider a derivative position with an interest rate swap. In the case where this option terminates before the maturity, the trader needs to unwind the swap hedging position. The hedging mechanism resembles the barrier position hedging. The trader is short a swap as long as the deal has not been called. When it is called, he/she needs to buy back the swap. The question that determines its fair price is to be able to have the right estimate of the unwind cost when the spot is at the level of the barrier.

If we zoom in on the contribution of the interest rates to the PnL equation we have:

$$\Delta PnL = \cdots + \frac{\partial^2 \pi}{\partial S \partial r}\Delta S \Delta r + \frac{1}{2}\frac{\partial^2 \pi}{\partial r^2}\Delta r^2 + \cdots \tag{5.9}$$

Where $\frac{\partial^2 \pi}{\partial S \partial r}$ (cross term) represents the change of the delta when the rates move and $\frac{\partial^2 \pi}{\partial r^2}$ represents the change of the Rho (sensitivity to the rate move) when the rates move (gamma rates).

For products that do not depend explicitly on the rates, gamma rates are usually close to zero. Therefore, only the cross term $\frac{\partial^2 \pi}{\partial S \partial r}$ contributes to the PnL evolution. Its total impact can be estimated as follows:

$$\Delta \pi = E \int_0^{\tau} \int_{-\infty}^{\infty} \int_0^{\infty} \frac{\partial^2 \pi}{\partial S \partial r} dS\, dr\, dt \tag{5.10}$$

τ is the time when the contract effectively ends.

Without models, traders know this type of extra cost when hedging Autocall options and they have developed proxy formulae of the following type:

$$\Delta \pi \cong \frac{\partial^2 \pi}{\partial S_0 \partial r_0} E(\tau)\, \rho_{S,r}\, \sigma_S\, S \sigma_r \tag{5.11}$$

This formula is like a Keplerian result. As usual, it contains information from the product and the market it belongs to. We need to develop a more precise theory to capture the real effect. We propose here a simple hybrid model which is easy to implement. It captures the cost of trading and hedging the stochastic interest rates as an impact between two simple models. The formula used is inspired from the impact formula of the stochastic volatility impact as in Equation (3.62).

Models: simple hybrid model

In this case, the task is to calibrate to both the option vanilla market (calls and puts) and swaption volatility cube. This can be difficult in practice and can be replaced efficiently by a decomposition of effects. Indeed, as the calibration of a log normal process with stochastic interest rates is an easy task because it is analytical, one can do that and calculate the effect of stochasticity of interest rates comparing it to a Black & Scholes model. The final price is obtained by adding the last effect on a local volatility price that matches the whole vanilla surface.

This approach can be summarized as follows:

- The joint dynamic price is obtained using a hybrid equity rate model with the following dynamic:

$$\frac{dB(t,T)}{B(t,T)} = r_t dt - \Gamma(t,T)\, dW_t$$
$$\frac{dS_t}{S_t} = r_t dt + \sigma^S(t)\, d\tilde{W}_t \qquad (5.12)$$

This model is simple to calibrate for two reasons. The rate model assumes normal rates with one factor. Under this assumption, we have analytical formulae for swaptions and the rate model is easily calibrated. The second reason for simplicity is that based on these assumptions the equity stock remains log normal and the rest of the calibration is thus readily achieved.

- The Black & Scholes price is calculated under the following dynamic:

$$\frac{dS_t}{S_t} = r_t dt + \sigma^S(t)\, dW_t \qquad (5.13)$$

- The equity smile price is obtained with a local volatility process for which we switch off the interest rate volatility. The dynamic of process is given by:

$$\frac{dY_t}{Y_t} = \sigma(t, Y_t)\, dW_t \qquad (5.14)$$

and the spot is reconstructed as follows $S_t = F_t Y_t$(F_t represents the forward).

The three building blocks presented above are assembled to mimic the model dynamic which combines local volatility for the equity and interest rates volatility.

The final price can be approximated at first order with all effects as follows:

$$\pi \cong \pi_{LV} + \pi_{IR-BS} - \pi_{BS}$$

The overview of the pricing algorithm is given by:

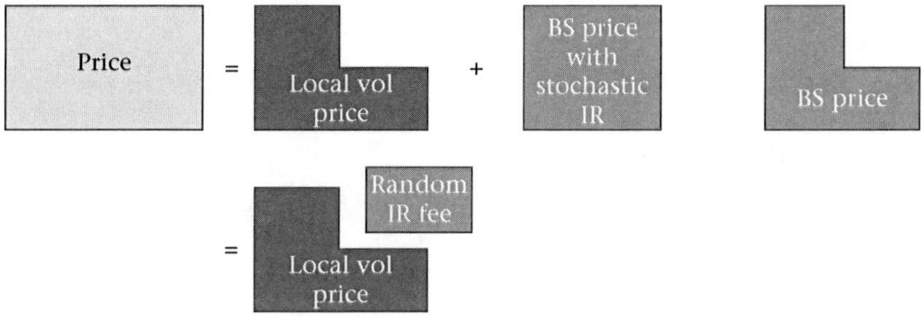

Figure 75 The interest rate model fudge approach

This modeling approach is a practitioner's model in replacement of a more complex model which is given by:

$$\begin{aligned}\frac{dB(t,T)}{B(t,T)} &= r_t dt - \Gamma(t,T)\, dW_t \\ \frac{dS_t}{S_t} &= r_t dt + \sigma^S(t,S_t)\, d\tilde{W}_t\end{aligned} \tag{5.15}$$

This model is more complex and can be calibrated using a forward PDE and in some cases we can use the Markovian projection in parametric smiles as in Reghai (cf. A, The Hybrid Most Likely Path, April 2006), Piterbarg, 2006 (cf. V, 2006) and Chibane, 2013 (cf. M & D, October 2012).

The proposed approach is much simpler and directly gives the interest rate toxicity index:

$$\phi_{IR} = \frac{\max(\pi_{IR-BS}, \pi_{BS}) - \min(\pi_{IR-BS}, \pi_{BS})}{\max(\pi_{IR-BS}, \pi_{BS}) + \min(\pi_{IR-BS}, \pi_{BS})} = \frac{|\pi_{IR-BS} - \pi_{BS}|}{\pi_{IR-BS} + \pi_{BS}} \tag{5.16}$$

Models: statistics and fair pricing

At this stage, we need to know how to estimate the interest rate volatility contribution. In other words, we need to identify the interest rates mixing weight.

For this, we use a regression of the forward implied volatility onto the spot volatility and the bond's volatility. We obtain a statistical model of the interest rate mixing weight $\gamma_r$as the coefficient of regression which satisfies:

$$\Sigma_F^2(0,T) - \Sigma_S^2(0,T) \cong \gamma_r R(T) \tag{5.17}$$

Where $R(t) = \frac{1}{T}\int_0^T \Gamma^2(t,T)\,dt$ and $\Gamma(t,T) = \lambda_r \sigma_r e^{\frac{t}{\lambda_r}}\left(e^{-\frac{T}{\lambda_r}} - e^{-\frac{t}{\lambda_r}}\right)$ are calibrated from the swaption volatility cube.

Estimates of the interest rates mixing weight for SX5E give a value of $\gamma_r = 50\%$.

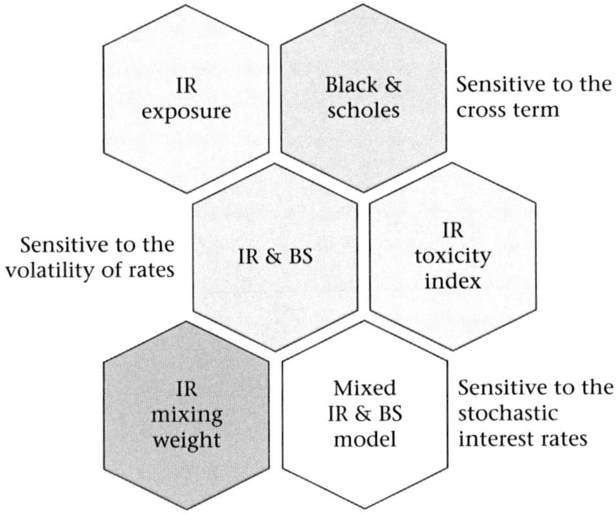

Figure 76 Incremental model identification in the presence of interest rate risk

In Figure 76, we summarize the incremental steps in the discovery of the interest rate toxicity and the choice of model to obtain the fair price.

Forward skew modeling

Forward skew modeling is a key component in financial modeling. It is known from the study of historical data (cf. Mandelbrot, 4 Juin 1962) that returns are not Gaussian. Jumps can occur and make the tail fatter than implied by diffusion. Using the smile models we can achieve non-Gaussian distributions. However, this is obtained in a smooth way and over a long period of time, one month or more. Now imagine that you want to set up a crash put. An option which is a daily cliquelet Put 80% to 90%. If the market goes down by less than 10%, there is no payout. If it goes down more than 20% then you receive one dollar. In between 10% and 20% you get a value between zero and one dollar. Whenever the contract pays something it stops. A stochastic volatility model will be blind and won't be able to generate a value for this payout. This is because over one day diffusion is smooth and cannot generate enough movements of the spot to impact the payoff. We need to model jumps. This is usually done by adding a Poisson process to the Brownian which counts the jumps and a distribution of the jump. For example, we note the Merton approach. Where the jumps are exponentially distributed in time and the jumps are lognormal. This approach has the advantage of having analytical formulae. However, it is not parsimonious (needs many extra parameters) and the obtained underlying's distribution does not fit observed data. An improvement in the data fit is achieved thanks to the Kou model. Again, we have tractable formulae but the distance to the observed data is still large and there are too many parameters.

In the following section, we shall not apply a Poisson process. Instead, we shall opt for a parsimonious approach and privilege the link with one of the most documented statistical invariants from the data. We shall replace the diffusion by a distribution that generates fatter tails with just one extra parameter. This approach captures the so-called **power law** observed in the data. It is a martingale extension of the Brownian with controlled fatter tails.

In this section, we shall present features of the local volatility Dupire Model. We show its limitations when generating the forward skew. We then replace the Brownian generator with an inspired alpha stable process and complete the vanilla market calibration, introducing the alpha local volatility surface, an extension of the Dupire local volatility surface.

We finally price crash puts within this framework and give the corresponding results.

The local volatility model is not enough

Local volatility, as described earlier, is a powerful model that helps practitioners in their day-to-day trading. In earlier sections, we saw that of all stochastic volatility models which match a given vanilla market, local volatility is the one that generates the least volatility of volatility. Local stochastic volatility was a response to this in accordance with the statistics of the volatility. Now, we shall fatten the tails in accordance with what is commonly observed in raw data returns.

The forward skew issued from a local volatility model decays too fast, as shown in the next graphs:

In Figure 77 and Figure 78, we first fit a local volatility model to the vanilla prices issued from SPX and SX5E markets. We then price forward start options. We back out the implied volatility of these options and calculate the differential with at the money option volatility and name it the forward skew. The first points in the two

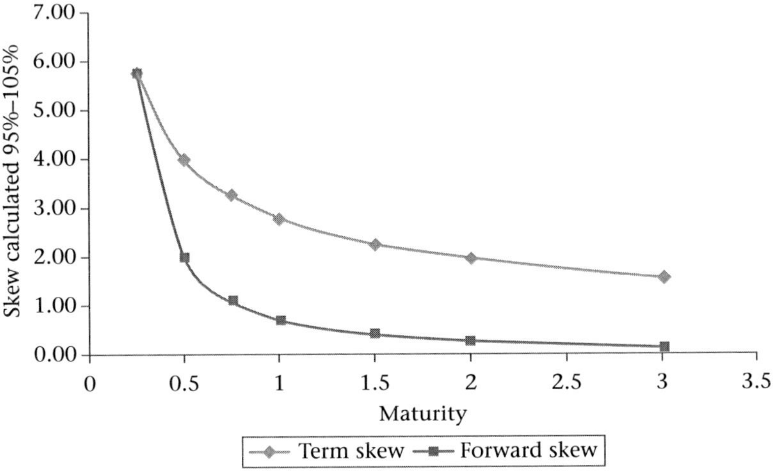

Figure 77 Fast decay of the forward skew SPX

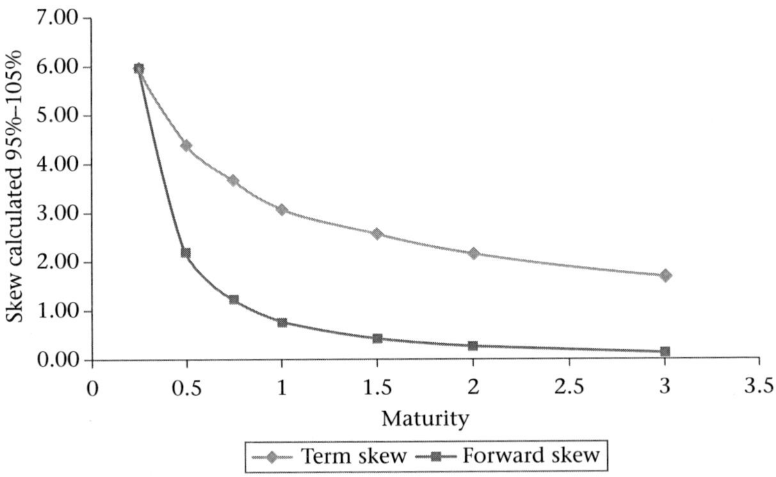

Figure 78 Fast decay of the forward skew SX5E

graphs match naturally because the 3m forward start option has already fixed and is a spot start option.

The aim of this section is to show how to implement local volatility with fat tails (statistical property). This also shows the role of the local volatility as it accommodates for these jumps quite naturally.

Local volatility calibration

There are fundamentally two approaches for the local volatility calibration as described earlier:

1. The direct way with the use of the *Dupire formula*
2. The optimization way with either classical optimization technique or the *fixed point algorithm.*

We concentrate on the fixed point algorithm. In the next section, we present our building block which aims at replacing the Brownian increment and better fitting the observed returns. We rely on a description of a PhD thesis in (Jacques-Levy & Christian, 2006).

Alpha stable process

The alpha stable process is built from increments of the alpha distribution $S_{\alpha,\beta}(\mu,\gamma)$.

The meaning of these parameters is as follows:

μ : drift of the distribution,
$\gamma\sqrt{2}$: standard deviation of the distribution,
β : plays the role of the skew and controls the asymmetry of the distribution,
α : is the kurtosis and controls the fat tails.

Stability of this distribution is seen through the following property:

$$S_{\alpha,\beta_1}(\mu_1,\gamma_1) + S_{\alpha,\beta_2}(\mu_2,\gamma_2) \propto S_{\alpha,\beta}(\mu,\gamma)$$

With

$$\begin{cases} \mu &= \mu_1 + \mu_2 \\ \gamma^\alpha &= \gamma_1^\alpha + \gamma_2^\alpha \\ \beta\gamma^\alpha &= \beta_1\gamma_1^\alpha + \beta_2\gamma_2^\alpha \end{cases}$$

In some cases, we can find the analytical expression of its distribution as in the following case $S_{2,0}(0,\gamma) \propto N\left(0,\gamma\sqrt{2}\right)$. In general, we can only do this with the **characteristic** function:

$$\begin{aligned}\Psi_X(t) &= E\left(e^{itX}\right) \\ &= \exp\left(i\mu t - |\gamma t|^\alpha\left(1 - i\beta sgn(t)\Phi\right)\right)\end{aligned} \tag{5.18}$$

Where $\Phi = \tan\left(\frac{\pi\alpha}{2}\right)$ for allαexcept for $\alpha = 1$in which case $\Phi = -\frac{2}{\pi}\log|t|$.

We can simulate this distribution using the Chambers Mallows Stuck technique to generate a random variable $X \propto S_{\alpha,\beta}(0,1)$ as follows:

- Generate a uniform random variable Von $\left]-\frac{\pi}{2},\frac{\pi}{2}\right[$,
- Generate an exponential variable $W$with parameter 1,
- Fabricate the random variable X as follows:

$$X = \Delta_{\alpha,\beta}\frac{\sin\left(\alpha\left(V+\Omega_{\alpha,\beta}\right)\right)}{(\cos V)^{\frac{1}{\alpha}}}\left\{\frac{\cos\left(V-\alpha\left(V+\Omega_{\alpha,\beta}\right)\right)}{W}\right\}^{\frac{1-\alpha}{\alpha}}$$

Where

$$\Omega_{\alpha,\beta} = \frac{\arctan\left(\beta\tan\left(\frac{\pi\alpha}{2}\right)\right)}{1-|1-\alpha|},$$

$$\Delta_{\alpha,\beta} = \left\{\cos\left(\arctan\left(\beta\tan\left(\frac{\pi\alpha}{2}\right)\right)\right)\right\}^{-\frac{1}{\alpha}}.$$

More details can be found in (Vehel & Walter, 2001).

We shall add an asymmetric truncation to the asymmetric alpha stable process.

We shall note this random variable $Y = \min\left(l_u, \max\left(l_d, X_{\alpha,\beta}\right)\right)$.

The process $L_\alpha(t)$ is built through the following equation:

$$dL_\alpha(t) = dt^{\frac{1}{\alpha}}Y \tag{5.19}$$

The problem with alpha stable process is the fact that returns are not bounded and therefore may not be useful in practice.

The construction of the alpha-stock process is achieved as follows:

$$\frac{dS_t}{S_t} = \sigma_\alpha\, dL_\alpha(t) \tag{5.20}$$

The choice of this process prompts comments:

- This Levy process comes with a parsimonious representation.
- The asymmetric distribution brings the short term skew and makes it persist.
- The (asymmetric) truncation is here to produce reasonable values.
- Hedging is still possible when annihilating the dependency with respect to the process increments.

We simulate paths generated by this process. With a certain probability some increments are extremely high.

In Figure 79, we show a typical simulated path issued from the alpha process. What is remarkable with this modeling is that we generate large movements within the same martingale process.

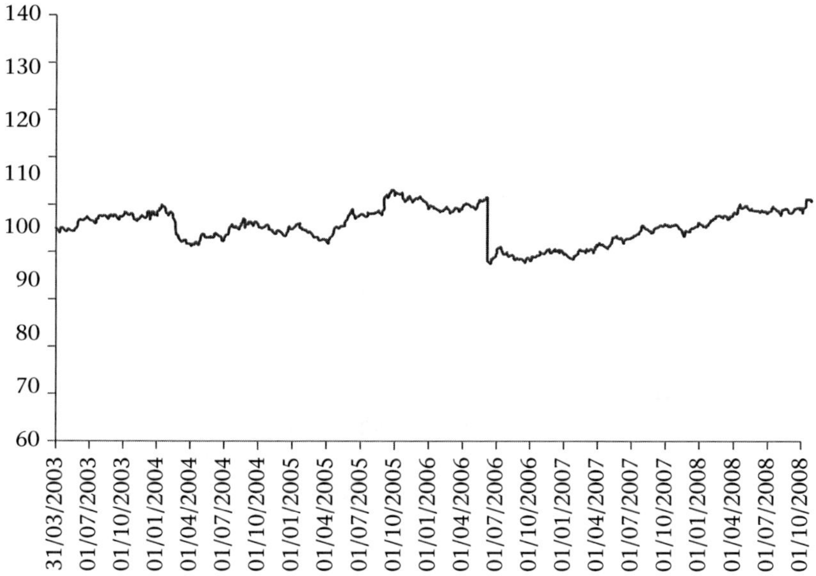

Figure 79 A possible path issued from the alpha spot path

Truncated alpha stable invariants

Although we are not dealing with physics, with its well-established laws of nature, in financial markets different invariants prevail and need to be taken into account.

Statistical invariants: Studying daily returns one can estimate the fat tails properties, as previously done by Benoit Mandelbrot and al. Recent returns for 2008, and especially the second half of the year, have presented a series of highly skewed returns. Using the asymptotic result of the following type **power law:**

$$\begin{aligned} P(X < x) &\propto C(1-\beta)\,x^{-\alpha} \\ P(X > x) &\propto C(1+\beta)\,x^{-\alpha} \end{aligned} \tag{5.21}$$

This method is not a very good one to estimate as it is sensitive to the set of returns selected for the estimation. There is another method that is more efficient. It is based on the norm of the characteristic function. The Koutrouvélis technique works very well – more details in (Jacques-Levy & Christian, 2006).

One can establish good estimates for the following indices:

Table 18 Power law estimates and impact of the 2008 crisis

Index	Alpha estimates before 2008 crisis	Alpha estimates after 2008 crisis
SPX	1.66	1.39
SX5E	1.79	1.58
CAC40	1.83	1.61

Persistent skew: the historical behavior of the skew shows that it persists independently of the level of the spot or volatility.

The two previous observations are obtained from historical data studies. The next invariant is read directly for the volatility surface. It is just photography of the smile.

Smile invariants: the implied skew structure behaves as a function of $\frac{1}{\sqrt{T}}$. This timescale invariance is observed in smile surfaces for all asset classes.

The pricing with the truncated alpha stable process generates a term structure of skew of the right shape with only a few parameters.

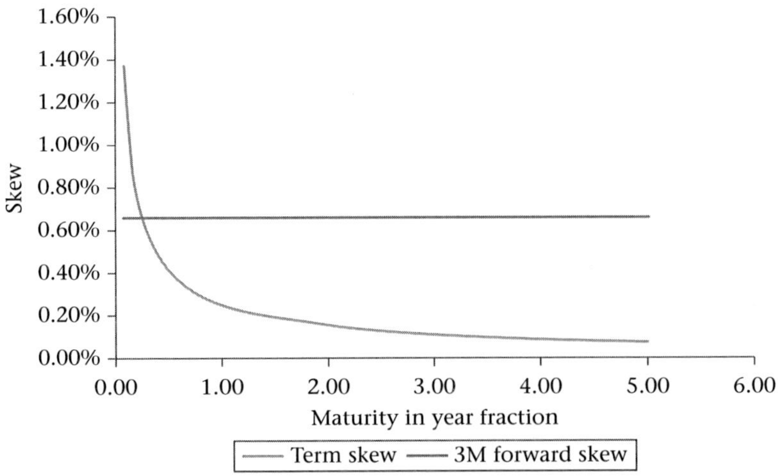

Figure 80 Implied 3m forward skew in the alpha stable model

In Figure 80, we observe that using this process we can use statistical invariants and generate a persistent skew and a term skew of the observed shape. All these features are obtained with very few parameters.

It is interesting to study the skew as a function of the volatility level. Indeed, in Figure 81, we observe that the skew varies slowly as a function of the volatility level. This is interesting as we have almost achieved independent control variables (volatility and skew).

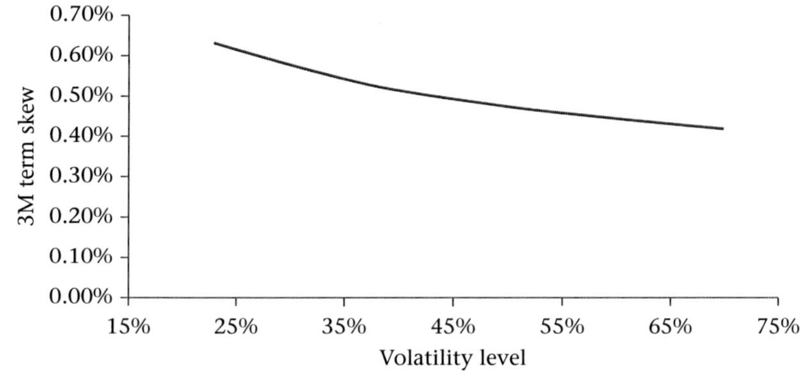

Figure 81 3m Forward skew as a function of the volatility level

Local volatility truncated alpha stable process

To improve the fit we shall introduce the local volatility alpha stable process as follows:

$$\frac{dS_t}{S_t} = \sigma(t, S_t)\, dL_\alpha(t) \tag{5.22}$$

This process fits all vanilla options and has a persistent forward skew. To calibrate this process we shall use the fixed-point algorithm technique. It can be done on a Monte Carlo with some natural control variate given by the model:

$$\frac{dS_t}{S_t} = \sigma_D(t, S_t)\, dW(t) \tag{5.23}$$

It can also be done using a forward PDE approach.

In Figure 82, we observe that the calibrated local volatility within the alpha process is less steep on the downside compared to the original Dupire local volatility. This is intuitive as the alpha process generates skew on itself and local volatility in this case acts like an adjustment.

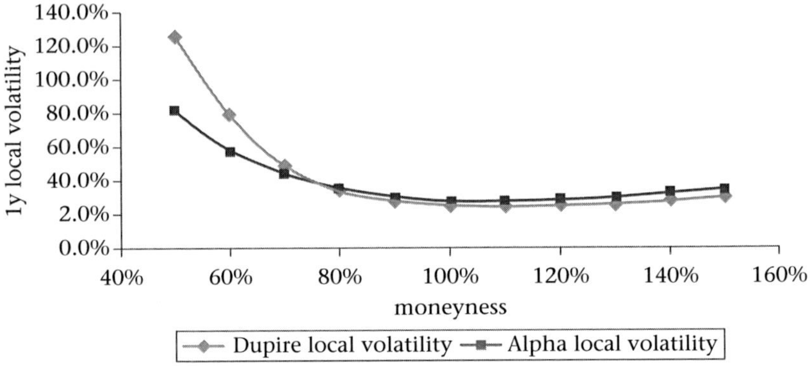

Figure 82 Dupire local volatility versus alpha local volatility

We can now define a forward skew toxicity index.

Table 19 Comparison of prices of a 1y crash put option on SX5E under two different models

1y Crash put price under local volatility model	0
1y Crash put price under alpha local volatility model	0.13%

In the previous table, we observe that the price of the crash put option under the local volatility model is nil. However, for the alpha local volatility model, we start seeing some value.

As before, we can define a toxicity index to measure the importance of a particular risk axis. The fat tail toxicity index is defined by the following quantity:

$$\phi_{FS} = \frac{\max(\pi_{lv}, \pi_\alpha) - \min(\pi_{lv}, \pi_\alpha)}{\max(\pi_{lv}, \pi_\alpha) + \min(\pi_{lv}, \pi_\alpha)} = \frac{|\pi_{lv} - \pi_\alpha|}{\pi_{lv} + \pi_\alpha} \quad (5.24)$$

In the case of the crash put (a client pays a running premium to obtain protection against a large daily movement, 10% or more down) we obtain the maximum score at 100%. This means that we just cannot ignore fat tails for such products.

The proportion to take into account is dependent, however, on a statistical estimation and some learning from the market. Short dated frequency cliquelets provide this type of information. Otherwise, the statistical alpha estimation is enough to correctly price the fat tail effect. It is important to note that for some other products however, not as toxic as the crash put, we need to take this risk into account. Typically, a constant proportion portfolio insurance (CPPI) structure, which is a trading strategy which allows an investor to maintain exposure to the upside potential of a risky asset while providing a capital guarantee against downside risk, also shows fat tail risk. For a daily CPPI, the toxicity index can reach as much as 65% which is non-negligible. So it must be computed and at least provisioned.

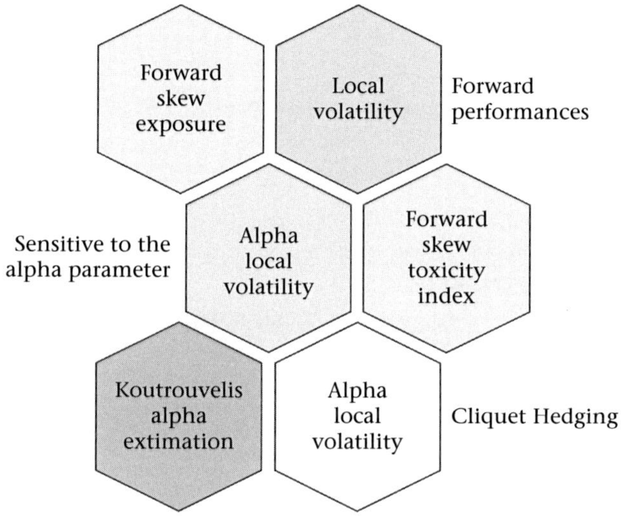

Figure 83 Incremental model identification in the presence of Forward skew

In Figure 83, we summarize the incremental steps in the discovery of the forward skew toxicity and the choice of model to obtain the fair price.

Exercise 5

Let an asset $S_0 = 100$. We assume zero interest rates and zero repo. We consider the following cliquelet $\frac{S_{T_2}}{S_{T_1}}$ payoff paid at time $T_2 > T_1$. We assume a dividend D_{12} paid during the period $]T_1, T_2]$.
Calculate the dividend toxicity index under Black & Scholes? Calculate a proxy for small dividend yield and volatility.

6 A General Pricing Formula

When we collect all the axis of risk for a general mono underlying product, we need to take into account all the previous effects according to their contribution to the price and hitherto the cost of hedge.

It is possible to derive a first order general formula that takes into account all these effects:

$$\pi_{\text{Fair Price}} - \pi_{lv} = \gamma^2 (\pi_{sv} - \pi_{\text{lv}}) + \gamma_\varepsilon \left(\pi_{\text{cad}} - \pi_{\text{pd}}\right) + \gamma_r (\pi_{\text{IR-BS}} - \pi_{\text{BS}}) + \gamma_\alpha (\pi_\alpha - \pi_{\text{lv}}) \tag{6.1}$$

As of the end of 2013, the mixing weights are given by $\gamma = 70\%, \gamma_\varepsilon(1y) = 20\%$, $\gamma_r = 50\%, \gamma_\alpha = 70\%$. These parameters are the quasi-invariants of our pricing theory.

In this global approach to pricing and risk management, we can define the relative toxicity of each axis by considering the following quantities:

$$\begin{aligned}
\Phi_{SV} &= \frac{\gamma^2 |\pi_{\text{sv}} - \pi_{\text{lv}}|}{\gamma^2 |\pi_{\text{sv}} - \pi_{\text{lv}}| + \gamma_\varepsilon \left|\pi_{\text{cad}} - \pi_{\text{pd}}\right| + \gamma_r |\pi_{\text{IR-BS}} - \pi_{\text{BS}}| + \gamma_\alpha |\pi_\alpha - \pi_{\text{lv}}|} \\
\Phi_\varepsilon &= \frac{\gamma_\varepsilon \left|\pi_{\text{cad}} - \pi_{\text{pd}}\right|}{\gamma^2 |\pi_{\text{sv}} - \pi_{\text{lv}}| + \gamma_\varepsilon \left|\pi_{\text{cad}} - \pi_{\text{pd}}\right| + \gamma_r |\pi_{\text{IR-BS}} - \pi_{\text{BS}}| + \gamma_\alpha |\pi_\alpha - \pi_{\text{lv}}|} \\
\Phi_r &= \frac{\gamma_r |\pi_{\text{IR-BS}} - \pi_{\text{BS}}|}{\gamma^2 |\pi_{\text{sv}} - \pi_{\text{lv}}| + \gamma_\varepsilon \left|\pi_{\text{cad}} - \pi_{\text{pd}}\right| + \gamma_r |\pi_{\text{IR-BS}} - \pi_{\text{BS}}| + \gamma_\alpha |\pi_\alpha - \pi_{\text{lv}}|} \\
\Phi_\alpha &= \frac{\gamma_\alpha |\pi_\alpha - \pi_{\text{lv}}|}{\gamma^2 |\pi_{\text{sv}} - \pi_{\text{lv}}| + \gamma_\varepsilon \left|\pi_{\text{cad}} - \pi_{\text{pd}}\right| + \gamma_r |\pi_{\text{IR-BS}} - \pi_{\text{BS}}| + \gamma_\alpha |\pi_\alpha - \pi_{\text{lv}}|}
\end{aligned} \tag{6.2}$$

We have a multi-dimensional scale to measure the relative importance of each risk axis. These are not absolute numbers. However, they offer a way to compare products within the same market or alternatively compare the same products across different asset classes or different market regimes.

7 Multi-Asset Case

Correlation plays a tremendous role when pricing and hedging multi-asset derivative products. It is also a fundamental element in asset allocation.

We present an incremental approach for three products: baskets, worst of and best of. We use three different models: Black & Scholes, local volatility and local volatility local correlation.

A Study of derivatives under the multi-dimensional Black & Scholes

This is the first step in our incremental approach. We use the relatively simple model: Black & Scholes. We shall also consider a homogeneous version of it. This simplification, combined with other approximations, permits the derivation of simple closed-form formulae in the case of the Basket option.

Using the Johnson method, it is also possible to obtain closed-form formulae for Best of and Worst of options. In this simple framework, we can analytically study the internal model greeks and also the sensitivities with regard to the model parameters.

Methodology

Our methodology is to define a very simple dynamic with the ability to enhance the products and dissect them completely.

$$\frac{dS_t^i}{S_t^i} = \sigma_i dW_i(t), < dW_i(t)\, dW_j(t) >= \rho_{i,j} dt \tag{7.1}$$

The basket underlying is given by:

$$\frac{1}{n}\left(\frac{S_T^1}{S_0^1} + \cdots + \frac{S_T^n}{S_0^n}\right) \tag{7.2}$$

We can calculate the volatility for the basket using a two-moment matching formula:

$$\sigma_B^2 \left(\sum_{i=1}^{n} S_0^i \right)^2 = \sum_{i,j} \rho_{ij} \sigma_i \sigma_j S_0^i S_0^j \tag{7.3}$$

In the case of the **homogeneous basket**, where all volatilities are equal and so are the correlations and initial spots, we obtain the following approximation formula:

$$\sigma_B^2 = 2 \frac{\rho \sigma^2}{n^2} \frac{n(n-1)}{2} + \frac{\sigma^2}{n} \tag{7.4}$$

As the number of assets goes to infinity, we obtain the very simple equation for the basket equivalent volatility:

$$\sigma_B = \sqrt{\rho} \sigma \tag{7.5}$$

It tells us that a basket is less volatile, less risky than each individual stock. This is known as the **diversification effect**. So with **diversification** and **hedging** we can obtain the following proxy pricing formula for the at the money option:

$$0.4 \sqrt{\rho} \sigma \sqrt{T} \tag{7.6}$$

This is powerful as we have an effective way to diminish option pricing through the construction of appropriate baskets. It is fair to say that thanks to this simple remark and the computation power mentioned in the introduction, the pace of products and innovation exploded in the early 1990s.

With the previous calculation of the option price, we can build a portfolio which replicates the options payoff. The treasury evolution for the replication portfolio (we ignore financing, dividends, and any value adjustments for simplicity) is as follows:

$$C_{t+1} - C_t = \sum_{i=1}^{n} \Delta_t^i \left(S_{t+1}^i - S_t^i \right) \tag{7.7}$$

This equation explains the quality of the hedging of a given model. It is important to notice that this quantity depends on the following variables $\Delta_t^i = f_i\left(t, S_t^1, \ldots, S_t^n\right)$. So applying our methodology of exploring the greeks within the model becomes a bit complex.

Can we envisage fewer scenarios without losing too much information?

The answer is yes and is based on common sense. Indeed, in the simple case of a homogeneous basket we can have the following statistical representation, which is extremely useful to design scenarios.

Indeed,

$$dW_i(t) = \sqrt{\rho} dB_0(t) + \sqrt{1-\rho} dB_i(t) \tag{7.8}$$

Now, all Brownians $dB_i(t), i = 0, 1, \ldots, n$ are independent.

This representation is not parsimonious because it uses an extra Brownian (n+1 Brownians versus n assets). However, it explicitly shows that $dB_0(t)$ is the common factor that drives all assets. It generates the fully **correlated move**. Besides when taking $dB_i(t), i \neq 0$ we get control on one, unique asset 'i' move. This is the **fully uncorrelated move**.

We can reasonably apply our one dimensional methodology just by extending the type of spot scenarios (fully correlated and fully uncorrelated).

We also notice that most of the payoffs are symmetric and for the uncorrelated case we can move any of the assets alike.

In the general case, we use the Principal Component Analysis (PCA) to design the scenario space.

$$\Delta PnL = \frac{1}{2} \sum_{i,j} \frac{\partial^2 \pi}{\partial S_i \partial S_j} S_i S_j \left(\frac{\Delta S_i \Delta S_j}{S_i S_j} - \rho_{i,j} \sigma_i \sigma_j \Delta t \right) \tag{7.9}$$

We observe that as for the one-dimensional case we have a succession of fair pricing questions around the terms $\frac{\partial^2 \pi}{\partial S_i \partial S_j} S_i S_j \left(\frac{\Delta S_i \Delta S_j}{S_i S_j} - \rho_{i,j} \sigma_i \sigma_j \Delta t \right)$. These terms involve the option through the cross gamma $\frac{\partial^2 \pi}{\partial S_i \partial S_j} S_i S_j$, the market through the term $\frac{\Delta S_i \Delta S_j}{S_i S_j}$ and the model through the term $\rho_{i,j} \sigma_i \sigma_j$. As in the one-dimensional case, a key indicator is the sign of the cross gamma. If the cross gamma has a constant sign, say positive, we can imagine to define the fair pricing correlation $\rho_{i,j} = \frac{E^P \int_0^T \frac{\partial^2 \pi}{\partial S_i \partial S_j} \Delta S_i \Delta S_j}{E^P \int_0^T \sigma_i \sigma_j \frac{\partial^2 \pi}{\partial S_i \partial S_j} S_i S_j dt}$. The problem with this analysis is that it does not ensure that the obtained correlations are valid as a whole (it works in the two dimensional case only). Indeed, the correlation matrix needs to be definite positive. At this stage, fair pricing in the multi-dimensional case is not addressed. Its complexity is clear however. We continue our incremental approach to analyze the product within this simplified model.

More precisely, if we want to understand the PnL evolution, we need to consider the entire diagonal gamma $\frac{\partial^2 \pi}{\partial S_i^2}$ and the cross gamma $\frac{\partial^2 \pi}{\partial S_i \partial S_j}$.

What should we look at to understand the dynamic of the hedging portfolio?

This is a difficult question and we try to answer based on the specifics of multi-dimensional payoffs.

We can reduce this complexity by considering specific analysis. Indeed, when the payoff is a basket option, we have a useful symmetry argument to play. All assets play the same role and looking just at any two assets is enough. Besides, in the full correlated move the PnL evolution equation exhibits a quantity $\frac{1}{2}\left(\sum_{i,j}\frac{\partial^2\pi}{\partial S_i \partial S_j}\right)\Delta S^2$ which can be obtained thanks to a global calculation (more precise and faster to do).

$$\pi\left(S_1+\Delta S,\ldots,S_n+\Delta S\right)-2\pi\left(S_1,\ldots,S_n\right)$$
$$+\pi\left(S_1-\Delta S,\ldots,S_n-\Delta S\right)\cong\frac{1}{2}\left(\sum_{i,j}\frac{\partial^2\pi}{\partial S_i \partial S_j}\right)\Delta S^2$$

This is called the *total gamma.*

To summarize our observations in the case of a basket option: we shall explore the PnL explanation though a list of *scenarios* and look at a list of *observables.*

Scenarios: Fully correlated move, fully uncorrelated move.

Observables: Total gamma, diagonal gamma, any cross gamma.

We perform these analyses to understand the risk dynamic got a basket option. As in the one-dimensional case, we need to be able to assess if the restrictive assumption of constant parameters (volatility and correlation) is enough to value the derivative contract. We also need to propose incremental models.

PCA for PnL explanation

Eigenvalue decomposition for symmetric operators

Consider a real symmetric square matrix M:

$$M^T = M$$
$$M_{ij} \in \Re$$

Then there exists an orthogonal matrix P and a diagonal matrix D such that:

$$P^T P = I \quad \text{P is an orthogonal matrix}$$
$$D_{ij} = \begin{cases}\lambda_i & \text{if } i=j\\ 0 & \text{if } i\neq j\end{cases} \quad \text{D is a diagonal matrix}$$
$$PDP^T = M$$

Note that this is different from the Cholesky decomposition:

$$QQ^T = M$$

where Q can be chosen to be upper diagonal.

Stochastic application

Consider N normal random variables ξ_i with covariance matrix C and mean zero:

$$E[\xi_i \xi_j] = C_{ij}$$

How can we represent these random variables in term of N independent random variables?

Since C is real symmetric then C can be represented as follows:

$$PDP^T = C$$

Consider N normal random variables η_i that are independent. Take a real $N \times N$ matrix R.

Define N random variables V_i such that:

$$V_i = \sum_{j=1}^{N} R_{ij}\eta_j \quad \text{i.e. } V = R\eta$$

Then these random variables are normally distributed and the covariance matrix of these random variables is:

$$E[V_i V_j] = \sum_{l=1}^{N} R_{il}R_{jl} = (RR^T)_{ij}$$

In particular, choose

$$R = P\sqrt{\mathrm{D}}\ P^T.$$

The matrix $\sqrt{D}$ is a diagonal matrix with diagonal elements, the square root of the diagonal elements of D.

Then the covariance matrix of the random variables V_i is:

$$RR^{\mathrm{T}} = P\sqrt{D}P^T P\sqrt{D}\ P^T = PDP^T = C.$$

Hence the N normal random variables V_i have the covariance matrix C and thus have the same distribution as the ξ_i.

Note that the same result holds with$R = P\sqrt{D}$.

In practice:

Simulate N independent normal random variables and then multiply these random variables by $R{=}P\sqrt{\mathrm{D}}\ P^T$ to obtain N correlated random variables.

Note that one can also use the Cholesky decomposition.

The advantage of using the eigenvalue decomposition is to isolate the various modes of deformation.

Consider a string made of N points with 'random' high V_i.

Suppose that theses points are 'rigid' that is to say they do not move independently. Suppose we find by experience that the high of these points has a normal distribution with covariance matrix C. Then we have:

$$\begin{pmatrix} V_1 \\ \\ V_n \end{pmatrix} = \sqrt{\lambda_1}\begin{pmatrix} P_{11} \\ \\ P_{n1} \end{pmatrix}\eta_1 + \cdots + \sqrt{\lambda_n}\begin{pmatrix} P_{1n} \\ \\ P_{nn} \end{pmatrix}\eta_n \tag{7.10}$$

Here the first mode corresponds to the largest eigenvalue and the last mode to the smallest eigenvalue.

Profit and loss explanation

Consider a position that depends on N different asset values. More precisely, the position value can be written as:

$$\pi\left(S_1, \ldots, S_N\right)$$

The market moves from one day to another from the $(S_1, \ldots, S_N)$ to $(S_1 + \Delta S_1, \ldots, S_N + \Delta S_N)$.

The variation of the position value can be explained thanks to the second order Taylor approximation as follows:

$$\Delta\pi\left(S_1, \ldots, S_N\right) = \sum_{i=1}^{N} \frac{\partial \pi}{\partial S_i}\Delta S_i + \frac{1}{2}\sum_{i,j=1}^{N} \frac{\partial^2 \pi}{\partial S_i \partial S_j}\Delta S_i \Delta S_j \tag{7.11}$$

Although it is a simple formula, all the necessary greeks to calculate the expansion are difficult in the present case. To give an idea, with the current position it takes 25h for 2*N+2 scenarios and for the previous formula it is necessary to have N*(N+1)/2 scenarios which would take something around 7 days of computation time. To avoid such a burden, we shall model the joint movements of the spots using a statistical model.

If we assume $E[\Delta S_i \Delta S_j] = C_{ij}$ and using the same notations as previously we can have the following representation:

$$\begin{pmatrix} \frac{\Delta S_1}{S_1} \\ \frac{\Delta S_n}{S_n} \end{pmatrix} = \sqrt{\lambda_1}\begin{pmatrix} P_{11} \\ P_{n1} \end{pmatrix}\Delta\eta_1 + \cdots + \sqrt{\lambda_n}\begin{pmatrix} P_{1n} \\ P_{nn} \end{pmatrix}\Delta\eta_n \tag{7.12}$$

We operate a spectral truncation by keeping only the first r factors:

$$\begin{pmatrix} \frac{\Delta S_1}{S_1} \\ \frac{\Delta S_n}{S_n} \end{pmatrix} = \sqrt{\lambda_1}\begin{pmatrix} P_{11} \\ P_{n1} \end{pmatrix}\Delta\eta_1 + \cdots + \sqrt{\lambda_r}\begin{pmatrix} P_{1r} \\ P_{nr} \end{pmatrix}\Delta\eta_r \tag{7.13}$$

In matrix form, this can be written as follows:

$$\begin{pmatrix} \Delta S_1 \\ \Delta S_n \end{pmatrix} = \begin{pmatrix} \alpha_{i,j} \end{pmatrix}\begin{pmatrix} \Delta\eta_1 \\ \\ \Delta\eta_r \end{pmatrix}$$

With $\alpha_{i,j} = S_i\sqrt{\lambda_j}P_{i,j}$.

Therefore the differential operator can be calculated as follows:

$$\frac{\partial}{\partial S_i} = \sum_{k=1}^{r}\alpha_{i,k}\frac{\partial}{\partial\eta_k}$$

From here, we can use the Hermite States to generate a list of scenarios for each normal variable η_i. If we assume$p$scenarios for each variable we would have a total of p^r scenarios. From these we can estimate the cross gammas with respect to the normal factors $\frac{\partial^2\pi}{\partial\eta_i\partial\eta_j}$. This in turn enables us to estimate the cross gammas using the following formula:

$$\frac{\partial^2\pi}{\partial S_i\partial S_j} = \sum_{k,l=1}^{r}\alpha_{i,k}\alpha_{j,l}\frac{\partial^2\pi}{\partial\eta_k\partial\eta_l} \tag{7.14}$$

If we use symmetric differences, we shall need 2*N calculations for the deltas, one calculation for the price and p^r for the cross gammas.

In practice, $r = 2$, $p = 3$ is enough and we shall need 1+2*N+9 which is of the same order as the previous calculations and would be possible to perform on a daily basis.

The source of the parameters

To feed the multi-asset Black & Scholes model and start an analysis we are confronted by the major need for parameters. Some of these parameters are already present in the mono-asset case, such as dividends, interest rates and volatility. The correlation, on the contrary, is a new parameter and needs to be fed to the pricer to be able to start a first-step analysis. For some baskets of stocks there exists a liquid product that delivers the realized correlation. For most baskets, we can just estimate the realized correlation from historical data. This estimation needs to be performed very carefully to cope with asynchronous data. We typically use the *Hayashi Yoshida* estimator for the correlation as proven in (Bergomi, 2010). This estimator calculates the ratio of the covariance of the returns divided by the product of the realized volatilities. The innovation is that the covariance term is composed of all the returns that have a temporal overlap. Once we have this historical estimation of the correlation parameter, can we use it as it is for the list of products mentioned above baskets, worst of, best of? In other words, is the historical correlation the right number to put in the basket option?

The answer is no. This is because the basket option uses a covariance term. We observed that the price of a basket at the money option uses correlation and volatility. These are two measures of risks and they appear in a multiplicative form in the pricing. Multiplication generates convexity. Roughly speaking, by hedging a basket option with respect to volatility and correlation, there is a contribution in the PnL evolution of the form:

$$\Delta PnL = \cdots + \frac{\partial^2 \pi}{\partial \sigma \partial \rho} \Delta \rho \Delta \sigma + \cdots \tag{7.15}$$

For a basket option, the position of the trader is short the cross-term $\frac{\partial^2 \pi}{\partial \sigma \partial \rho} < 0$. Besides, the co-movements of the volatility and the correlation in the equity market are aligned and we have$\Delta \rho \Delta \sigma > 0$. The result on the PnL evolution for the trader's position is negative. To compensate for such an effect, he/she needs to charge more, that is put a higher mark for basket options than the estimated correlation historically. It is interesting to notice that in the case of a basket composed of equity underlying and an interest rate underlying typical co-movements are negatively aligned $\Delta \rho_{rS} \Delta \sigma > 0$. In this case, the trader puts a lower correlation mark when pricing a basket involving equity and an interest rate instrument than the number he puts in the corresponding correlation swap.

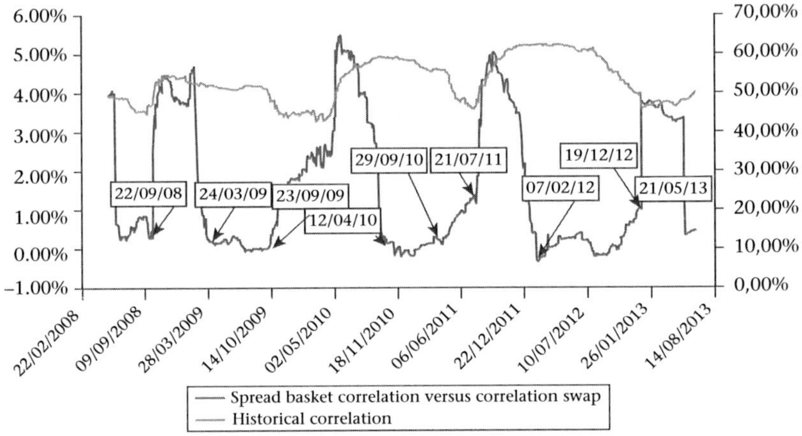

Figure 84 Comparison between the historical correlation and the basket-implied correlation

In Figure 84, we observe that the difference between the basket correlation and the historical correlation is almost always positive. This denotes the extra cost of hedging. At the same time, we observe that for periods of market stress the spread tends to increase. This will be discussed further when building risk-monitoring tools based on correlation.

At this stage, taking all these precautions, estimation of the historical correlation taking into account the non-synchronicity of the markets and the cost of hedge we are ready to use the Black & Scholes model in an exploration of the risks dynamic.

Basket option

This is the simplest option to be considered in a multi-asset framework. We perform the different analyses presented in the section above, crossing the type of scenarios and the type of observables. This is key information that will serve as a benchmark for other options, just as the mono-dimensional vanilla option serves as a benchmark for different options presented in the first part of the book.

We shall undertake our study on three asset basket options, the exact payoff is given by:

$$\left(\frac{1}{3}\left(\frac{S_T^1}{S_0^1}+\frac{S_T^2}{S_0^2}+\frac{S_T^3}{S_0^3}\right)-K\right)^+ \tag{7.16}$$

We can derive analytical formulae that are good approximations of the real price. This is obtained by moment-matching just as for the Asian option in the mono underlying case.

Before producing our observables (the greeks) we shall see how the prices evolve:

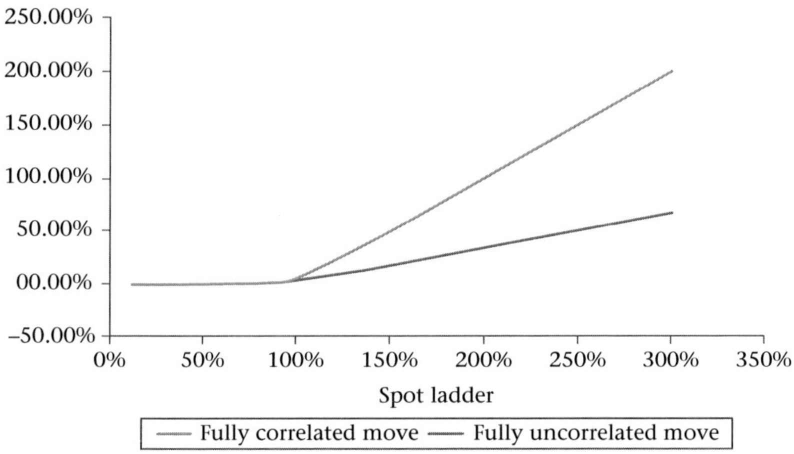

Figure 85 Basket price spot ladder (correlated and uncorrelated move)

In Figure 85, we observe that for the correlated move the price goes up when the spot goes up and at a faster speed than in the case of the uncorrelated move. This is rather intuitive behavior. Indeed, the uncorrelated move is like looking at a fraction of the nominal. Also on the downside, the red line representing the uncorrelated move is slightly above the one from the correlated move. This tells us that the option is not completely out of the money in the uncorrelated move as the rest of the underlying can create some positive payout.

Now let us look at the delta spot ladder:

In Figure 86, we observe that the delta converges to 100%, as expected in the correlated move case. This is intuitive as the basket option behaves exactly as a mono vanilla call option. In the case of the uncorrelated move, the delta converges to 33% as expected in a three-asset basket option when just one asset moves (only a fraction of the nominal is impacted).

We now look at the total gamma (corresponding to a fully correlated move) and compare it with an individual diagonal gamma (corresponding to a fully uncorrelated move).

In Figure 87, we observe that the when gamma is at its maximum, the ratio between the correlated move and the uncorrelated one is around 9. This is equal

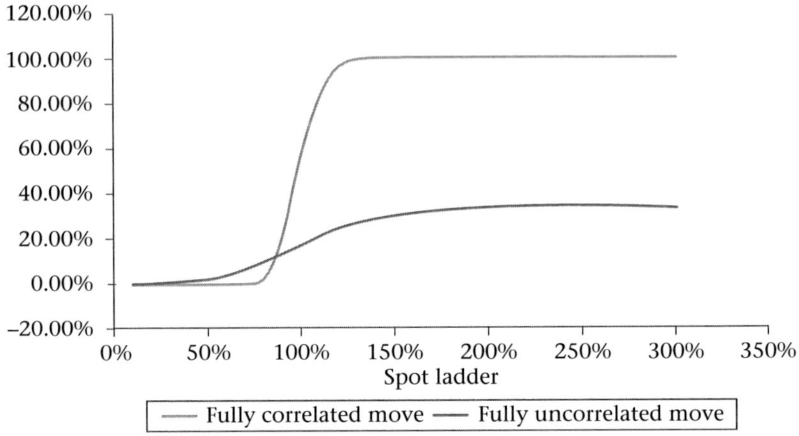

Figure 86 Basket delta spot ladder (correlated and uncorrelated move)

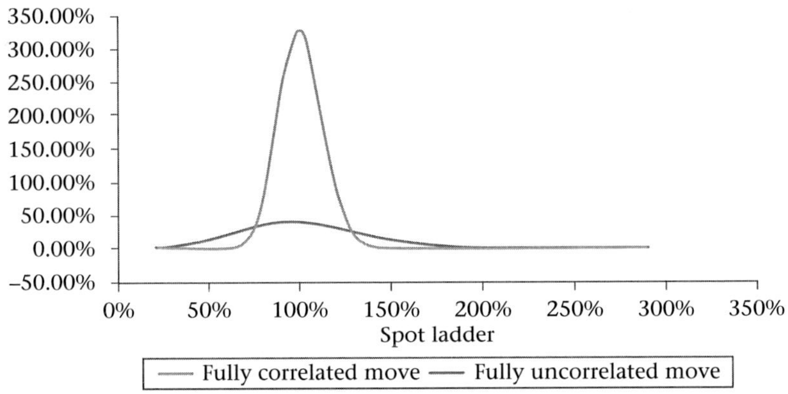

Figure 87 Gamma price spot ladder (correlated and uncorrelated move)

to the number of assets square.

$$\frac{\partial^2 \pi}{\partial S_i \partial S_j} \approx \frac{\partial^2 \pi}{\partial S_i^2} \approx \frac{1}{n^2} \sum_{i,j} \frac{\partial^2 \pi}{\partial S_i \partial S_j} \tag{7.17}$$

Another useful measure to capture the effect of the cross gamma is to calculate the sensitivity with respect to the correlation. This is known as the *cega*.

$$\text{Cega} = \frac{\partial \pi}{\partial \rho} \tag{7.18}$$

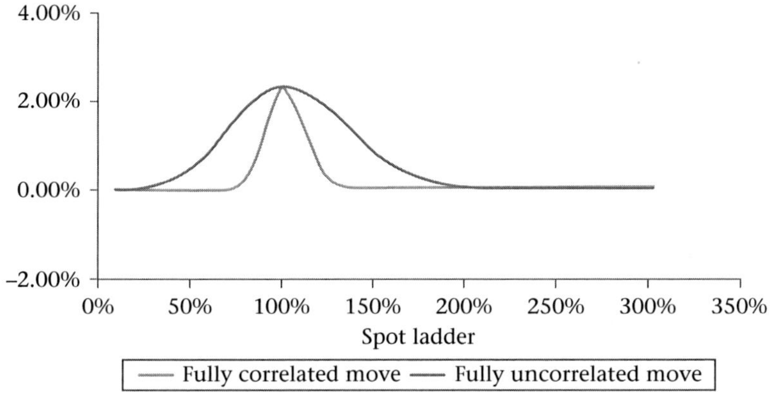

Figure 88 Cega spot ladder (correlated and uncorrelated move)

In Figure 88, we observe that the cega for a basket option is positive for all scenarios. Its shape looks like the vega exposure. In the correlated case, the exposure is concentrated, whereas in the uncorrelated case it is more dispersed. Once again, this represents the benchmark to compare with future payoffs.

In the basket example, we observe how typical the different greeks are and their dynamic for some of the most important scenarios. We shall now proceed to different payoffs.

Worst of option (wo: call)

This option is a classic. The reason for this is very simple. In the previous basket option, we controlled the level of the volatility by diversification. We could create a synthetic asset with lower volatility. The latter has a forward that is just an average of the different forwards of the assets composing the basket. It remains comparable to the forward of each asset. By taking the worst of the different assets, we have a powerful way to diminish the resulting forward. For a call option, this helps decrease the price of the option sometimes significantly.

In this case, we can derive analytical types of prices using either the multi-normal or a statistical technique of recursively identifying the resulting asset after taking the forward.

We shall apply the same type of analysis for the following three assets' worst of option. The payoff is given by:

$$\left(\frac{1}{3}\min\left(\frac{S_T^1}{S_0^1}, \frac{S_T^2}{S_0^2}, \frac{S_T^3}{S_0^3}\right) - K\right)^+ \tag{7.19}$$

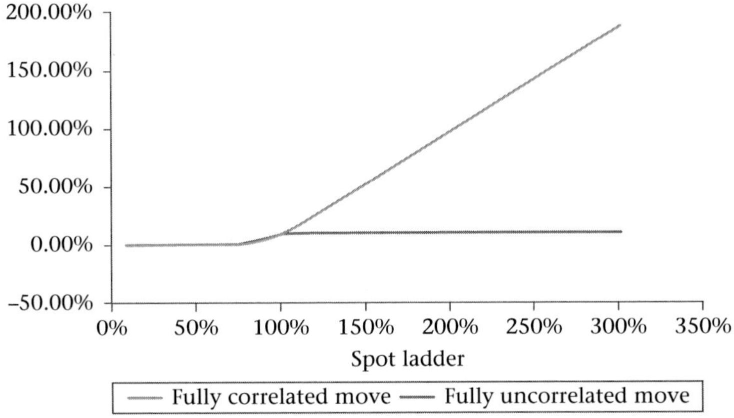

Figure 89 Worst of price spot ladder (correlated and uncorrelated move)

In Figure 89, we recognize in the fully correlated case the price profile of a regular basket option. This is not surprising as all assets move together, the worst of is one of the elements. Now, when we de-correlate the moves, imagine that we just move the first asset $\frac{S_T^1}{S_0^1}$. This asset goes up and we keep the others assets fixed, the worst of option converges to its intrinsic value

$$\left(\frac{1}{3}\min\left(\frac{S_T^2}{S_0^2}, \frac{S_T^3}{S_0^3}\right) - K\right)^+$$

This creates a delta behavior analogue to that for a digital option. It starts at zero for small spots because the worst of option is out of the money. Then it needs to create value similar to a digital. Beyond a certain level of the spot the delta returns to zero.

What is interesting to note is that in the fully correlated move none of these special behaviors appear: the product is just like a mono underlying classic call option.

In Figure 91, we look at the gamma spot ladder. It comes as no surprise that the product in the fully correlated move is just like a simple vanilla option, whereas, in the fully uncorrelated move the digital call behavior of the gamma surfaces again.

In Figure 91, we also notice something remarkable about the risk dynamic. There is a break in symmetry that happens during the life of the contract. Indeed, in the fully correlated case the gamma does not change sign and looks very similar to a benign call option. In the case of uncorrelated move, we observe a change of sign of the gamma. This now looks similar to the gamma spot ladder of a European binary option. We know that this type of gamma map implies the use of a smile model. We can also illustrate this phenomenon in the following scenario. We assume that one asset went up, another did not move and the last moved down. This is a typical

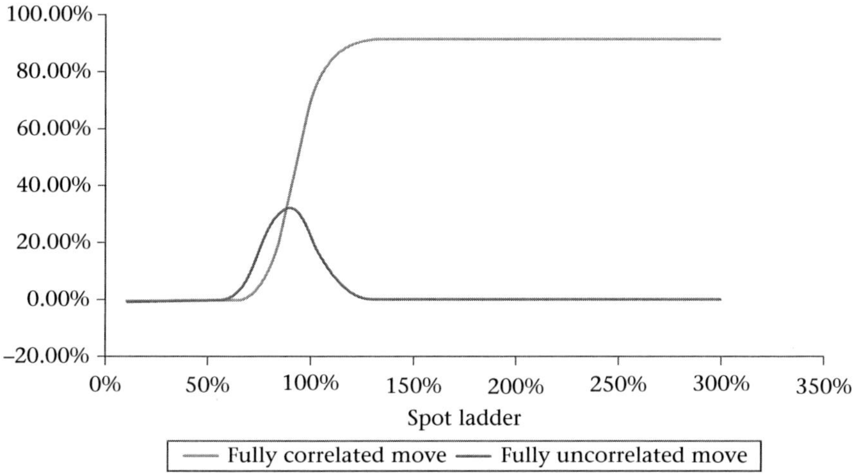

Figure 90 Worst of delta spot ladder

dispersion situation. We look at the cross gammas matrix: for such a situation and compare it with the matrix at inception when everything is symmetric.

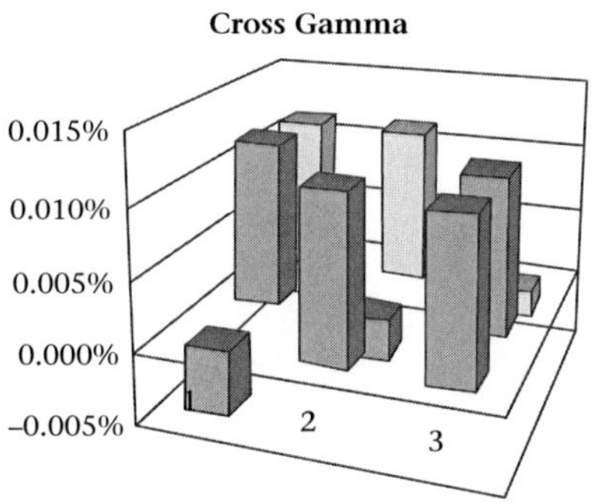

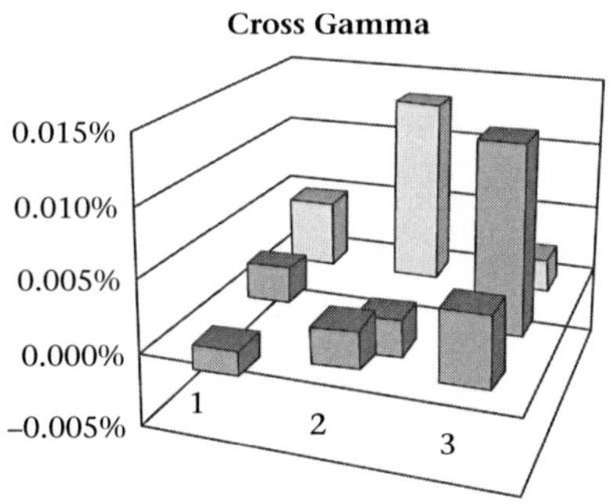

At inception, the off diagonal terms have the same positive weight. This reflects the speed of change from one asset to the other when the asset representing the worst of changes. They are all equivalent. For the diagonal terms the gamma are negative as any individual move implies a loss in value.

After a *dispersion* move, the off diagonal terms lose their symmetry. Asset1>Asset2>Asset3.
The Gamma (3.2) is more important than Gamma (1.3) and Gamma (1.2). The Diagonal terms remain positive for the assets 1 and 2. The asset 3 which is more likely to be the worst of has a simple option written on it and generates positive gamma.

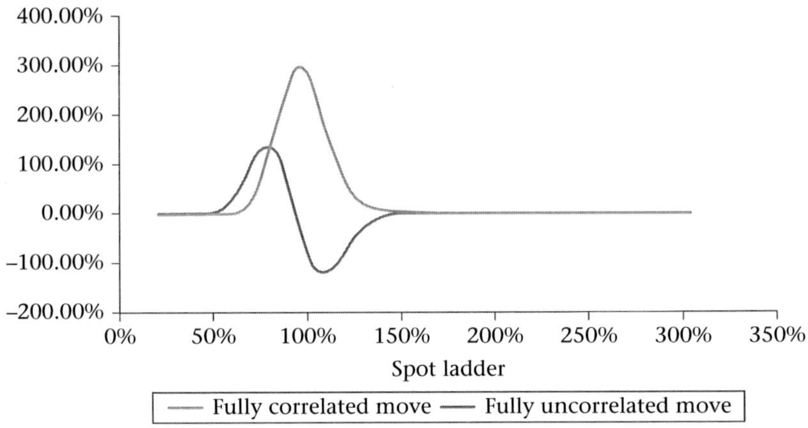

Figure 91 Worst of Gamma spot ladder

The change of sign in the gamma reminds us that the Black & Scholes model is not enough.

Now we complete our analysis with a cega scenario.

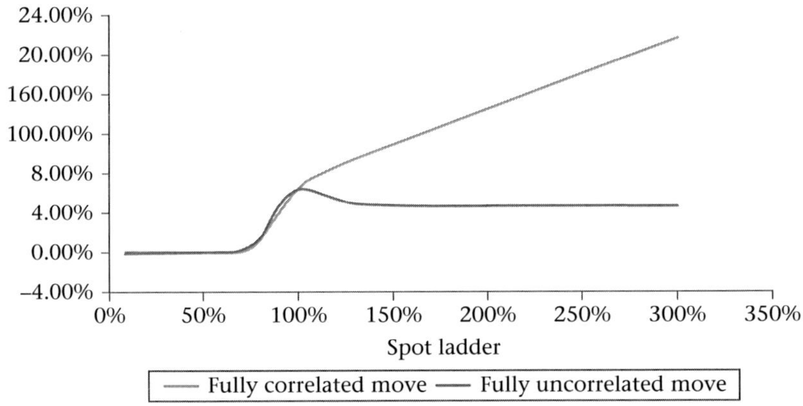

Figure 92 Cega spot ladder worst of

In Figure 92, we observe that the cega remains positive (no change of sign). However, it is not concentrated around the strike of the option as for our basket option benchmark. Instead it shows exposure to different levels of strikes on the high side. The fair level of correlation is somewhat of an average of correlation above the strike.

We can conclude that for worst of call options, the pricing model needs to include the smile for each underlying (to cope with the changing sign of the gamma in the fully uncorrelated move) and needs to use a correlation level which is an average of correlations above the strike.

Best of option (Bo: put)

We shall consider a put on the best of performer. It is a common method to make an option cheaper. The payoff is given by:

$$\left(K - \frac{1}{3}\max\left(\frac{S_T^1}{S_0^1}, \frac{S_T^2}{S_0^2}, \frac{S_T^3}{S_0^3}\right)\right)^+ \tag{7.20}$$

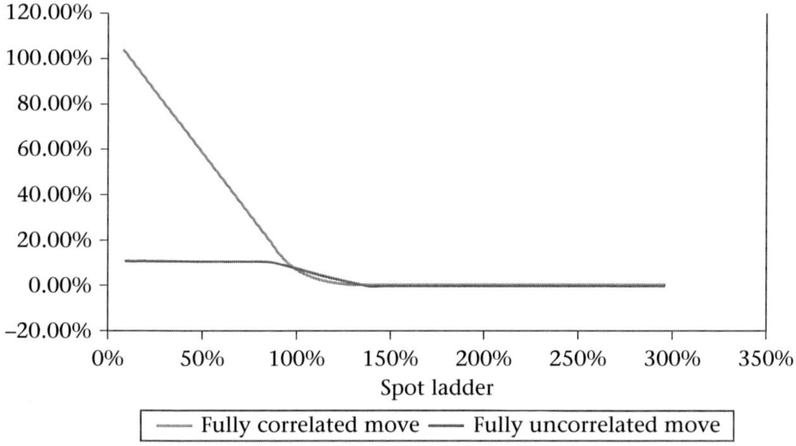

Figure 93 Best of put spot ladder

In Figure 93, we exhibit the price scenario analysis. In the fully correlated case we recognize the price profile of a regular basket put option. This is not surprising, as all assets move together the best of is one of the elements. Now, when we decorrelate the moves, imagine that we move the first asset $\frac{S_T^1}{S_0^1}$ and leave the other assets unchanged. In such a scenario, the best of put option converges to intrinsic value:

$$\left(K - \frac{1}{3}\max\left(\frac{S_T^2}{S_0^2}, \frac{S_T^3}{S_0^3}\right)\right)^+$$

In the uncorrelated move, the generated profile resembles a digital put. We recognize the delta and the gamma issued from such a payoff.

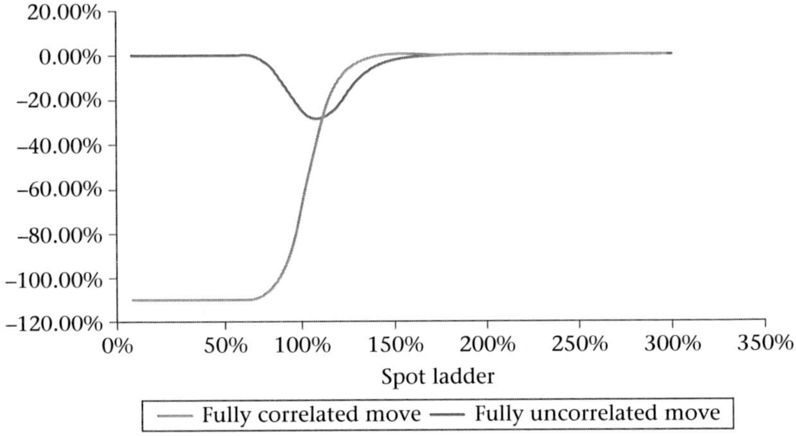

Figure 94 Best of put delta spot ladder

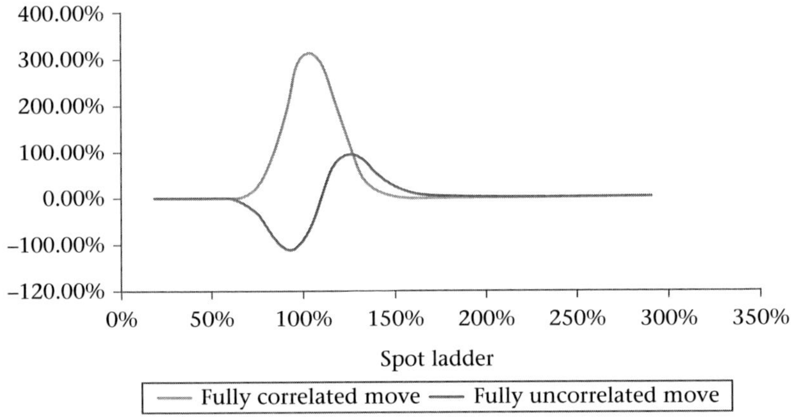

Figure 95 Best of put gamma spot ladder

Here the analogy concerns a digital put.

In Figure 96, we note that the cega remains positive. However, it is not concentrated around the strike of the option like our basket option benchmark is. Instead, it shows exposure to different levels of spots on the downside. The fair level of correlation is somewhat of an average of correlation below the strike.

We can conclude that for pricing best of put options, we need to include the smile for each underlying (to cope with the changing sign of the gamma) and we need to use a correlation level which is an average of correlations below the strike.

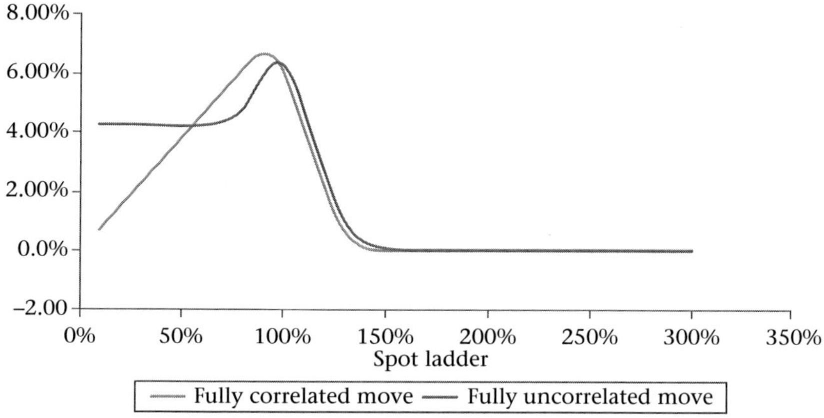

Figure 96 Cega spot ladder

Other options (Best of call and worst of put)

These options are not very common as they make the price too expensive. When we look at their greeks' gamma and cega exposures, we obtain the following graphs.

From these scenarios, we conclude that the Black & Scholes model can be used for both products if the parameters are appropriately adjusted.

If we return to the fair pricing problem, all the considered products can be priced using a local volatility model (to cope with changing diagonal gammas) and a fair level of correlation.

To determine this fair level we assume that the reality is given by a local correlation model and try to infer the fair level of correlation to price these products.

Our process now includes local volatility and local correlation:

$$\begin{cases} \frac{dS_t^1}{S_t^1} = \sigma_1\left(t, S_t^1\right) dW_t^{\rho(\lambda),1} \\ \cdot \quad \cdot \qquad \cdot \\ \frac{dS_t^n}{S_t^n} = \sigma_n\left(t, S_t^n\right) dW_t^{\rho(\lambda),n} \end{cases} \tag{7.21}$$

Where $W^{\rho(\lambda)} = [W^{\rho(\lambda),1}, \ldots, W^{\rho(\lambda),n}]$ is a multi-dimensional Brownian motion with stochastic correlation:

$$\rho(\lambda)_t := \left(1 - \lambda\left(t, S_t^1, \ldots, S_t^n\right)\right)\rho + \lambda\left(t, S_t^1, \ldots, S_t^n\right)\Theta \tag{7.22}$$

Table 20 Worst of put and best of call sensitivity analysis

Worst of Put

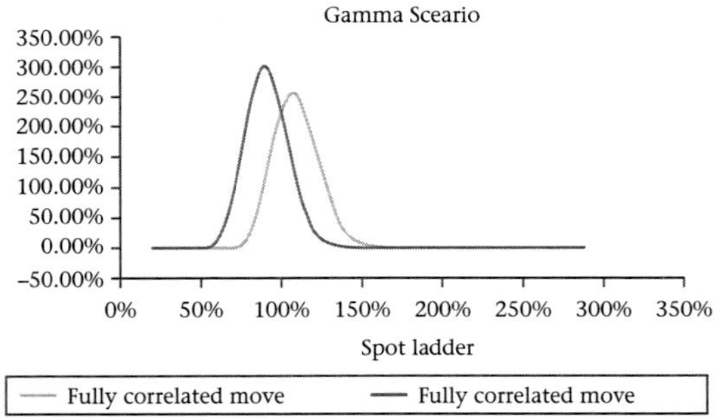

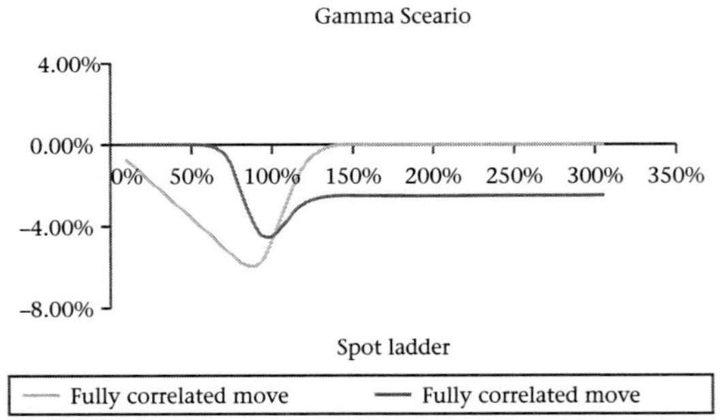

Best of call

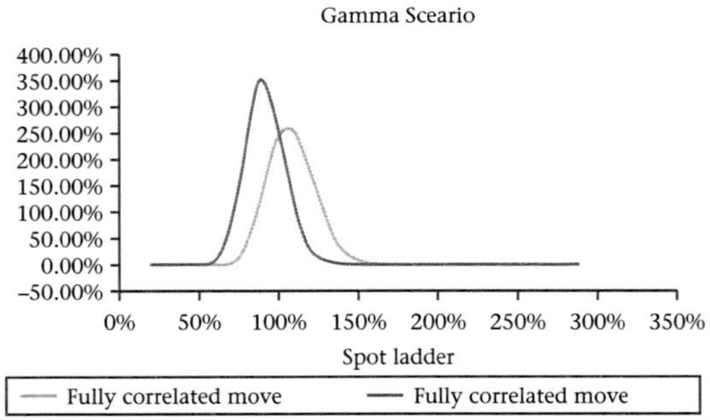

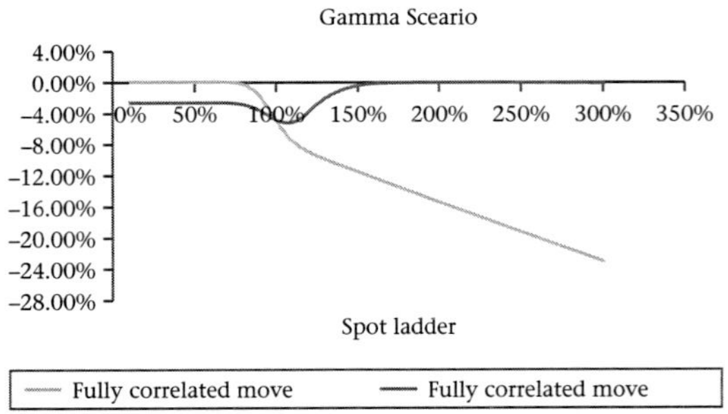

ρ is a valid correlation matrix and $\rho(\lambda)$ remains a valid correlation matrix for any value λ in [0,1].

$$\lambda\left(t, S_t^1, \ldots, S_t^n\right) = \lambda_0 f\left(t, L_t\right) \tag{7.23}$$

With the Lt function is an aggregator function $L_t = h\left(S_t^1, \ldots, S_t^n\right)$ that is constructed depending on the product and the business. Later on, we shall explain different strategies for the aggregator's choice. This setting is also a key feature so as to have a well-posed problem in the calibration or the estimation process.

The local lambda function λ is fine-tuned according to payoff and available information:

1. *Implied approach – mostly appropriate for world indices or baskets of very liquid stocks*

Basket option market quotes on various strikes and maturity provide first-hand information about implied correlation. Therefore, we opt for a model calibration to market observables by building a simplified local lambda function:

$$\lambda\left(t, \sum_{i=1}^{n} w_i \frac{S_t^i}{S_0^i}\right) \tag{7.24}$$

Fitting the basket implied volatility surface.

In Equation (7.23), if we make the lambda depend only on time and the weighted basket, a particular aggregator, we transform an ill-posed calibration problem into a well-posed one. Indeed, there is now a one-to-one correspondence between the model parameters and the surface of implied volatility to be calibrated.

(2) *Direct approach – mostly appropriate for regular stock baskets*

Suppose basket options are not liquid enough to extract relevant information from the market. We can still analyze the statistical distributions of the correlation with respect to the basket components as a whole or in some directions to infer a judicious functional form that mimics historical behavior. For instance, for rainbow options, we suggest:

$$\lambda\left(t, S_t^1, \ldots, S_t^n\right) = \lambda_0 f\left(t, L_t\right) \tag{7.25}$$

With λ_0 in [0,1] and L defined by

$$L_t = \sum_{i=1}^{n} w_{(i)} \ln\left(\frac{S_t^{(i)}}{S_0^{(i)}}\right) \tag{7.26}$$

Where $S_{(i)}$ is the ith best performing asset of the basket.

You can think of λ_0 as a bump so that the function f introduces vibrations depending on current market conditions L_t. Notice that f also depends on the time t so that short-term and long-term correlation dynamics can differently respond to market moves. This is of particular relevance when estimation follows an abnormal market period as from September 08 to March 09. The model embeds a view on future correlation according to market regimes.

In both cases, local correlation adjusts S_i-delta by $\frac{\partial \pi}{\partial \lambda}\frac{\partial \lambda}{\partial S_i}$.

$$\underbrace{\Delta_{i,LVLC}}_{\text{Local Vol Local Correl Delta}} = \underbrace{\Delta_{i,LV}}_{\text{Local Volatility Delta}} + \frac{\partial \pi}{\partial \lambda}\frac{\partial \lambda}{\partial S_i} \tag{7.27}$$

A naïve approach to diffuse a basket of n spots under a local correlation scheme consists in performing successive Cholesky decompositions – with $O(n^3)$ complexity – at each time step of the Euler discretization grid according to current time and spot levels. This is extremely time-consuming: neither a price nor all necessary risk measures can be produced in a reasonable amount of time.

The key ingredient for the numerical implementation, both for the calibration, on the one hand, and the pricing and risk management, on the other, is to use a dimension extension similar to what was introduced in (Burtschell, Gregory, & Laurent, 2005) helping by-pass this limitation.

The natural way to produce correlated paths with a different correlation matrix at each time step is to perform a Cholesky decomposition for every path and every time step. This is a cumbersome calculation. We instead produce these correlated Brownians with their complicated path dependent structure as the result of a linear interpolation between deterministic correlation Brownians and one extra independent Brownian.

In fact, we easily remark that $W^{\rho(\lambda)}$ is the weighted sum of two independent n-dimensional Brownian motions W^{ρ} and W^{Θ}:

$$dW_t^{\rho(\lambda)} = \sqrt{1-\lambda(t,L_t)}\,dW_t^{\rho} + \sqrt{\lambda(t,L_t)}\,dW_t^{\Theta} \tag{7.28}$$

Given that W^{Θ} degenerates into a single Brownian motion, we only need to factorize ρ to build Brownian increments with instantaneous correlation $\rho(\lambda)$.

More generally, assume λ in $[\lambda_{min},1]$ included in $[-1,1]$, then

$$dW_t^{\rho(\lambda)} = \sqrt{1-\frac{\lambda(t,L_t)-\lambda_{\min}}{1-\lambda_{\min}}}\,dW_t^{(1-\lambda_{\min})\rho+\lambda_{\min}\Theta} + \sqrt{\frac{\lambda(t,L_t)-\lambda_{\min}}{1-\lambda_{\min}}}\,dW_t^{\Theta} \tag{7.28}$$

And the matrix to decompose becomes $(1-\lambda_{min})\rho+\lambda_{min}\Theta$.

This algorithm has the same complexity as the classic multi-dimensional local volatility model with a unique Cholesky decomposition to perform before starting the Monte Carlo simulations. Here, the innovation is that an extra independent Brownian motion is simulated to generate Brownian increments under the local correlation framework at each node of the path. [1]

We notice as in the previous examples that the determination of the equivalent level of correlation depends on a whole averaging region of the local correlation.

Model calibration using fixed-point algorithm

Basket options with payoff $\left(\sum_{i=1}^{n} w_i \frac{S_T^i}{S_0^i} - K\right)^+$ are mainly sensitive to global correlation shift so that we search for a local lambda function which depends on stock spots through basket level $B_t = \sum_{i=1}^{n} w_i \frac{S_t^i}{S_0^i}$.

In the presence of a set of basket option quotes for various strikes and maturities, the functional form λ is calibrated with the *fixed-point algorithm.*

Given a local surface λ, we evaluate basket options on various maturity/strike buckets (T,K) in order to imply the Black & Scholes volatility surface (λ) generated by the local correlation model.

The **contracting** mapping[2] is then the application which turns the local lambda surface λ into a basket implied volatility surface (λ):

$$\lambda(*,\bullet) \rightarrow \Phi(\lambda)(*,\bullet) \tag{7.29}$$

We proceed as with the local volatility calibration previously discussed in (A, The Hybrid Most Likely Path, April 2006) (A, Relax and Smile: calibration du modèle de volatilité locale et extensions, Février 2008):

- Start with a relevant initial guess λ_0; rely on asymptotic formula given in papers (Dupire B., 2004; Karoui & Durreleman, 2007);
- Price basket options in the local correlation/volatility framework;
- Imply volatilities to obtain the mapping (λ);

---

[1] We can also diminish pathwise correlation of the different Brownians by simulating n extra independent Brownians (doubling the dimension) and using a similar formula as Equation (7.28).

[2] Asymptotically, when maturity goes to zero, $\Phi(\lambda)^2 = \frac{1}{n^2}\sum_{i,j=1}^{n} \sigma_i\sigma_j\left(\rho_{i,j} + \left(1-\rho_{i,j}\right)\lambda\right)$ which gives the following first derivative $\frac{d\Phi(\lambda)}{d\lambda} = \frac{1}{2}\frac{\sum_{i,j=1}^{n}\sigma_i\sigma_j\left(1-\rho_{i,j}\right)}{\sum_{i,j=1}^{n}\sigma_i\sigma_j\left(\rho_{i,j}+\left(1-\rho_{i,j}\right)\lambda\right)}$. For a 50% average correlation the maximum of this quantity is 0.5.

- Repeat the following iterative scheme until convergence holds

$$\lambda_{i+1}(*,\bullet) = \lambda_i(*,\bullet) + \ln\left(\frac{\Sigma_{\text{Market}}(*,\bullet)}{\Phi(\lambda_i)(*,\bullet)}\right) \tag{7.30}$$

Σ_{Market}, a matrix value function, denotes the Black & Scholes surface implied from quoted basket options in the market. (7.30) is a change of the matrix values point per point.

The interest of this technique is the robustness of the obtained results, as happens for the local volatility calibration in (A, The Hybrid Most Likely Path, April 2006; A, Relax and Smile: calibration du modèle de volatilité locale et extensions, Février 2008). This is a key feature for the greeks' stability. Also, the implementation is merely 20 lines of code easy to maintain in a production environment.

We run the algorithm on an equally weighted basket composed of eight stock market indices. For a given expiry the iterative steps to build a functional form λ so that the local correlation model fit a fictitious market basket skew – in gray – are displayed below in Figure 97. In this example, the initial guess for lambda was a zero surface. This is the worst obtained performance in terms of iterations. It is not an issue because in practice this calculation is done once every 24 hours during the night.

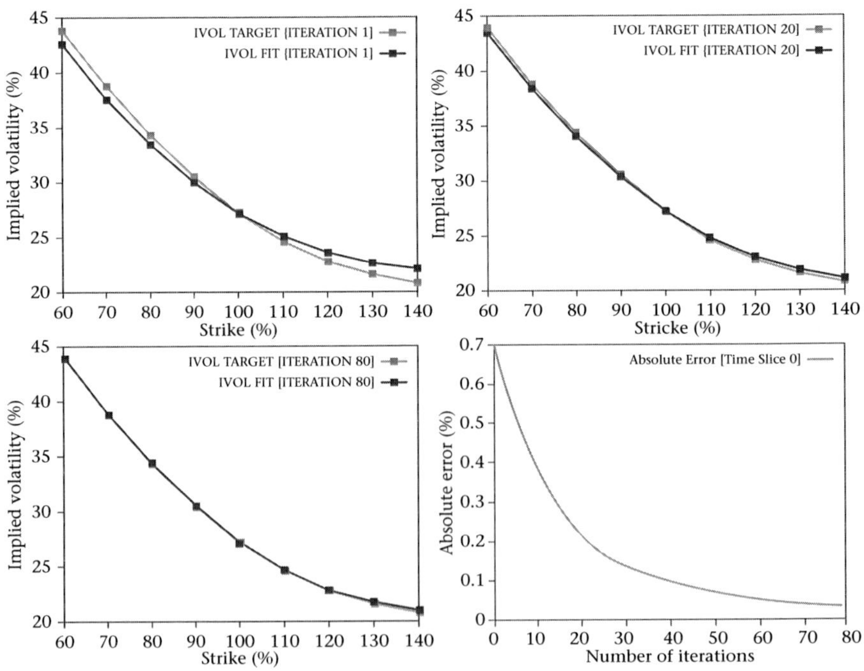

Figure 97 Fixed point algorithm calibration of the local volatility local

Once the model is obtained, that is calibrated, it has two main purposes

- Pricing and risk management.
- Stress tests, and most importantly the cega KT bucket.

For the pricing and the risk management, we compare valuation and greeks on a 10MUSD short position on 1Y best-of put options priced under the local correlation/volatility model (LVLC) calibrated on the red curve against the standard local volatility model with constant correlation matching ATM 1Y basket options (LV).

Results are expressed in KUSD:

Table 21 Valuation best of put

Model	PV	Delta cash	Gamma cash	Theta
LV	−487	2910	362	0,7
LVLC	−648	4802	709	2,2

We mentioned before that the local volatility model has met with a lot of success in the equity world. This is due to the fact it permits fine projection of the vega risk. It shows how to spend money using the different strikes and maturities of the volatility surface. This is what is commonly called the *super vega bucket.* The present model calibrates to the basket smile allowing a projection on the different strikes of calls on basket. This is what we can refer to as the *super cega bucket.* For example, in Figure 98, we show the super cega bucket for a call on worst of.

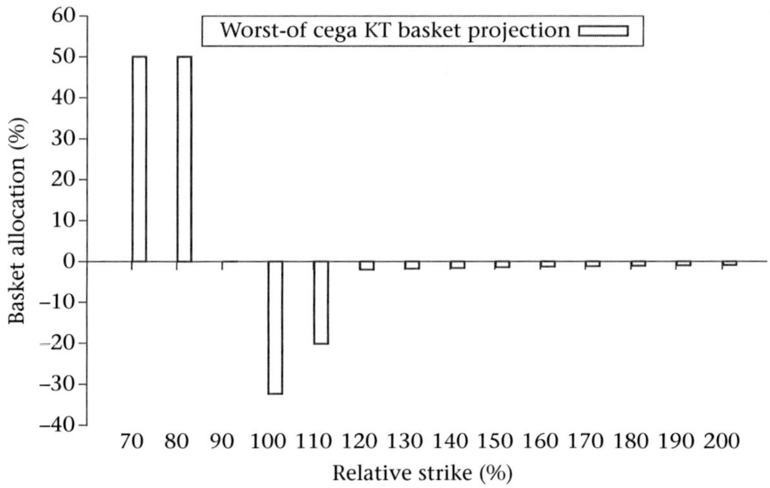

Figure 98 Super Cega KT for the call on worst of

Model estimation using an envelope approach

The spot values are not enough to describe the level of correlation. However, using two functions of the spot values we can envelop (have lower and upper bounds) the correlation level. So we produce a model that locally injects more or less correlation depending on the level of the spot.

The *Envelop modeling approach* models the upper (respectively the lower bound) bound of a random quantity Y with a function of the variable X.

In the stock world, the market does not provide sufficient information to calibrate basket skews – no or few basket option quotes are available. Besides, more exotic payoffs can be highly sensitive to twisted deformation of the correlation matrix. This 'Chewinggum' effect fully detailed in Langnau (2009) which occurs when spot dispersion is such that the average basket level barely changes whereas worst- and/or best-of performances are deeply altered cannot be well considered with correlation shifts λ only controlled by basket level B.

We therefore proceed with an empirical analysis depending on the multi-underlying option to evaluate. In this regard, we consider a payoff that pays at maturity T and a put on the best performance of a basket made up of n assets:

$$\left(K - \max\left(\frac{S_T^1}{S_0^1}, \ldots, \frac{S_T^n}{S_0^n}\right)\right)^+ \tag{7.31}$$

Where K stands for the option's strike expressed in %. It brings dependence on the best-performing asset so that it seems coherent to investigate a spot local correlation which singles out the best performance. Furthermore, the sensitivity with respect to correlation is positive so that these options are traded at the 'ask' implied correlation level of the seller.

Consider now the following parameterization – a standard Fisher transformation:

$$\lambda\left(S_t^1, \ldots, S_t^n\right) = \max\left(-\lambda_0 \times \tanh\left(\frac{s}{\lambda_0} L_t\right), \lambda_{\min}\right) \tag{7.32}$$

Where, $L_t = \max_{i=1,\cdots,n}\left[\log\left(\frac{S_t^i}{S_0^i}\right)\right]$

Toying with parameters λ_0, $\lambda_{\min}$ and s, we model λ from worst-case scenarios according to our risk-aversion by drawing more or less conservative correlation envelopes:

From the log-performance data (2008–2009), we compute λ_{Histo} and display its relation to the best performer. Best-of put options are sensitive to negative log-performances so that the analysis focuses on downside correlation.

Scenario 1. Conservative business level

Model correlation envelops historical realizations of λ_{Histo} in such a way that the empirical probability that realized correlation exceeds model correlation is null:

$$\lambda_0 = 81\%,\ \lambda_{\min} = 0\%,\ s = 16 \Rightarrow P\{\lambda_{Histo} < \lambda_{Model} | L_t < 0\} = 100\%$$

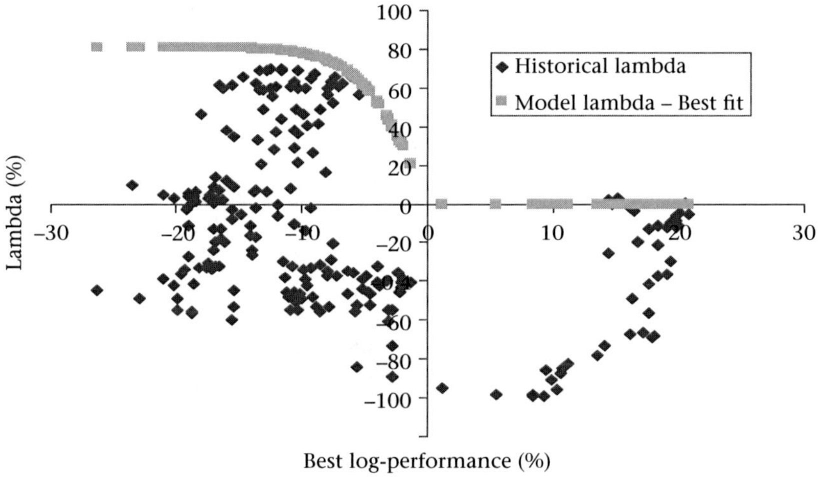

Figure 99 Lambda estimation for a conservative business level

Scenario 2. Moderate business level

Historical correlation outperforms model correlation for some rare events but it remains under most of the time:

$$\lambda_0 = 65\%,\ \lambda_{\min} = 0\%,\ s = 11 \Rightarrow P\{\lambda_{Histo} < \lambda_{Model} | L_t < 0\} = 90\%$$

Scenario 3. Acceptance business level

This scenario suits agents with a risk appetite such that model correlation underestimates realized correlation 20% of the time:

$$\lambda_0 = 50\%,\ \lambda_{\min} = 0\%,\ s = 8 \Rightarrow P\{\lambda_{Histo} < \lambda_{Model} | L_t < 0\} = 80\%$$

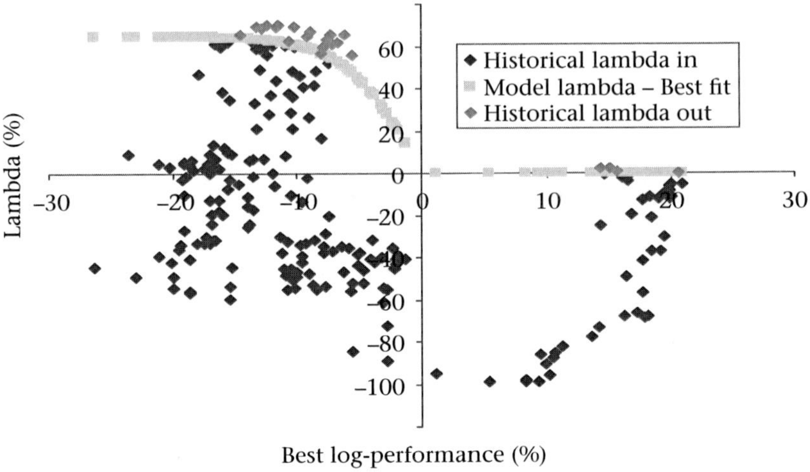

Figure 100 Lambda estimation for a moderate business level

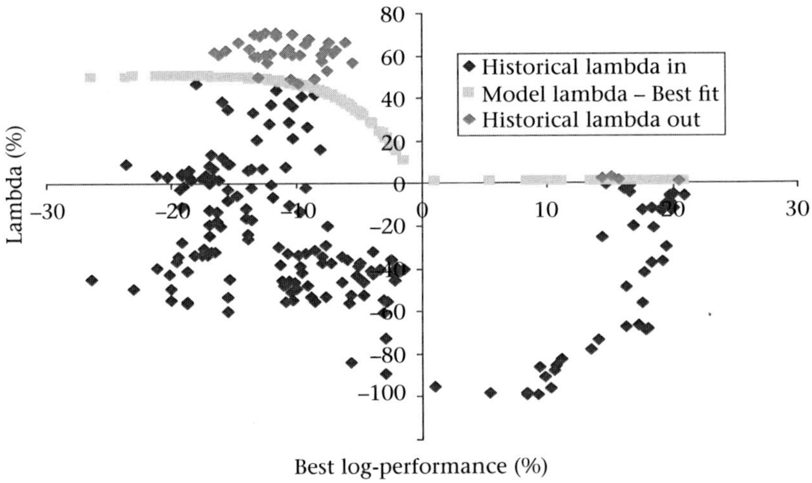

Figure 101 Lambda estimation for an acceptance business level

The functional form λ might not be appropriate to model the mean correlation level. However, it perfectly fits the envelope which is enough to conservatively hedge even in difficult times.

We focus on a 10MEur short position on best-of put. We compare the valuation impact with model choice between:

- Black & Scholes model (BS),
- Local volatility model (LV),
- Local correlation/volatility model (LVLC).

We stress the portfolio under three daily global spot shift scenarios at respectively −10%, 0% and +10% from strike levels keeping volatilities and correlations still. The 10% absolute daily shift is an extreme scenario that was encountered several times during the crisis from September 2008 until March 2009.

Suppose gamma PL is locked every 1%-spot shift by rebalancing the delta position by GAMMA_CASH(0), the gamma cash amount computed with 0%-spot shift. Then:

$$\text{PL\_HEDGE} = -\,\text{DELTA\_CASH}(0) * \text{SPOT\_SHIFT} - \text{SGN}(\text{SPOT\_SHIFT}) * \text{GAMMA\_CASH}(0) * \sum_{i=\text{SGN}(\text{SPOT\_SHIFT})*1\%}^{\text{SPOT\_SHIFT}} \text{SPOT\_SHIFT}-i$$

We compare this expression to PL_OPTION=PV(SPOT_SHIFT)−PV(0) to evaluate the robustness of the pricing models.

Results are displayed in KEur.

Table 22 PnL Option and its hedge during a large stress test similar to that observed during a crisis

Spot_shift	Model	PV	Delta_cash	Gamma_cash	Vega	Theta	PL_option	PL_hedge	PL
	BS	−881	4 363	−155	−11	0.6	−359	391	32
	LV	−765	4 020	−167	−9	0.3	−324	345	21
−10%	LVLC [Sc.1]	−1 099	5 857	−45	−13	1.1	−497	598	101
	LVLC [Sc.2]	−989	5 342	−107	−15	0.6	−437	464	27
	LVLC [Sc.3]	−912	4 889	−187	−13	0.6	−396	433	37
	BS	−522	3 144	−170	−15	0.9			
	LV	−440	2 695	−167	−15	0			
0	LVLC [Sc.1]	−603	4 117	−413	−22	0.3			
	LVLC [Sc.2]	−552	3 604	−231	−19	0.1			
	LVLC [Sc.3]	−516	3 275	−234	−19	0.1			
	BS	−281	1 946	−132	−15	0.9	241	−230	11
	LV	−240	1 522	−109	−12	0.7	200	−186	14
10%	LVLC [Sc.1]	−317	2 066	−239	−12	0.8	285	−205	80
	LVLC [Sc.2]	−295	1 906	−160	−12	0.8	257	−245	12
	LVLC [Sc.3]	−279	1 798	−164	−12	0.9	237	−210	27

The short best-of put position is long gamma so PL=PL_OPTION+PL_HEDGE is always positive. However, following a 10%-spot shift, we can expect some costly correlation remarking in BS and LV whereas LVLC has already anticipated the correlation change – it is all priced in!

As in the mono underlying case, we can finally ask ourselves what the price would be in the presence of the stochastic volatility dynamic. As before, we need to calibrate individual smiles and their dynamic. We also need to calibrate cross-terms as they appear frequently in the PnL explanation. The pricing is usually done under a super duper Monte Carlo. There are cases where closed form approximations exist. This concerns multi-European terminal payoffs where we have this proxy formula:

$$u_{SV} \cong u_{BS} + \frac{1}{6}T\sum_{i,j}^{n} \alpha_i\alpha_j\rho_{i,j}^{\sigma}\frac{\partial^2 u_{BS}}{\partial \ln\sigma_i \partial \ln\sigma_j} + \frac{1}{2}T\sum_{i,j}^{n}\alpha_j\sigma_i\rho_{i,j}^{\ln\sigma,\ln S}\frac{\partial^2 u_{BS}}{\partial \ln S_i \partial \ln\sigma_j} \tag{7.33}$$

Conclusion

Following the equity correlation debacle of 2008, from now on local correlation models need to be promoted and carried out in production to price and risk-manage multi-asset derivative products. Basket option prices allow robust calibration to be performed. Otherwise parametric estimation tailored to payoffs under consideration becomes relevant. A correlation envelope modeling in line with business risk appetite is then proposed. Smart implementation using dimension extension enables results to be obtained at no extra cost for a much richer model in information systems. In particular, greeks are adjusted to reflect part of the correlation risk reallocation from cega to delta while the gamma-theta ratio is substantially improved.

8 Discounting and General Value Adjustment Techniques

The collapse of Lehman has acted as a sharp reminder that financial modeling is about modeling PnL treasury shift. Indeed, holding financial products with Lehman as a counterparty can create a loss if our exposure is positive to Lehman at the time of default. This situation has created the need to follow the CVA (credit value adjustment – a measure of counterparty risk). How much should I adjust my price to reflect the possibility of my counterparty defaulting? There is also a symmetrical notion that is the DVA (debit value adjustment) which constitutes the answer to the damage my own default can create for my counterparties.

These notions have already long been taken into account for large financing transactions. The crisis, and ensuing regulation, has obliged financial players to make it available for all transactions and all banks.

In addition, when we are zooming in on the Lehman event we see that margin calls can generate a substantial treasury requirement at a given point in time. If this need is not met, it generates a filing under Chapter 11. This has pushed practitioners to follow marginal value adjustments in their models and also adapted their structures by creating a central desk that manages treasury needs. Bankers have understood that to survive they need to anticipate margin calls dependent on collateral agreements.

From survival in the short term to a profound revamping of the banking model, practitioners and bankers saw in these measures a route to allocating capital optimally. Nowadays, strategic decisions are based on capital consumption and only deep analysis of the generated cash flows and the general replication equation for the PnL evolution provide sounder insight into activities and their return on investment. Strategic and tactical capital allocation desks have been set up in the banking system to ensure agility and to adapt to the new financial paradigm.

Now consider another classical situation when your counterparty is a triple A (AAA) government institution. In this case, there is no margin call from this institution when it is indebted to the bank. But the bank posts collateral each time the institution owes some money to the bank. This asymmetry creates some modeling difficulties and breaks the nice linear paradigm of pricing and hedging.

More importantly, it generates a hedging cost, which implies different pricing and replication strategies.

Another case to mention and which is relatively common is how to value a multi-currency collateral agreement?

In other words how do you estimate the option of posting different types of collateral (different currencies/assets)?

This problem existed for a long time but had no consequences as the capital was in some sense cheap. Nowadays this is all different and it will remain so as it represents a real paradigm shift. Knowing this, it interesting to see how we materialize this optionality in the pricing and hedging of financial products?

In this chapter, we focus on these aspects in an incremental way. We provide an overview of all the techniques for price adjustments. These are sometimes quite simple and can be done just by changing the discounting curve.

This also needs to be accounted for and priced. We follow the overview presented in (Laurent, Amzelek, & Bonnaud, 2012).

Full and symmetric collateral agreement

As previously, we start with the simplest case. The bank is dealing with counterparty with no risk of default. Both the counterparty and the bank post collateral in a symmetrical way. We assume that the posted collateral is an asset with the following dynamic:

$$\frac{dA_t}{A_t} = r_A dt + \cdots$$

Let us consider C_t the amount at date t of the collateral account.

At time the, we post the asset A to compensate for the contract value Ct.

The number of securities posted at time t is $\frac{C_t}{A_t} \cdots$ The value of the posted collateral at time t+dt is equal to $\frac{C_t}{A_t} A_{t+dt}$. As a consequence, the variation margin of the time interval t and t+dt is equal to:

$$dVM(t) = C(t+dt) - \frac{C(t)}{A(t)} A(t+dt) \tag{8.1}$$

Which can be written as:

$$dVM(t) = dC(t) - C(t)\frac{dA(t)}{A(t)} \tag{8.2}$$

The **PnL contribution of the cash flows due to the collateral agreement** is given by:

$$\Delta PnL = \cdots + (1 - rdt)\left[h(t+dt) - C(t+dt) + dC(t) - C(t)\frac{dA(t)}{A(t)}\right] - (h(t) - C(t)) + \cdots \quad (8.3)$$

This amount is linked to the contract to be priced and hedged.

The exercise of figuring out the correct discounting articulates as follows:

- Make an assumption on the collateral level
- Find out the drift of the contract such that the expected PnL contribution is zero
- Use of the equivalence between the non-collateralized and the collateralized contracts in that case
- Derivation of a new pricing formula.

Now imagine that you are in the situation of a financial contract h which is dealt with a full collateralization agreement. This means that at any time C=h. The PnL contribution due to the collateral is given by:

$$\Delta PnL = \cdots + dh(t) - h(t)\frac{dA(t)}{A(t)} + \cdots \quad (8.4)$$

Now, if the contract h is priced and discounted with the drift of asset A, we know that$E(dh(t)) = h(t)\, r_A dt$, the average PnL contribution becomes zero and the pricing formula is the one for the non-collateralized contract. The pricing formula is given by:

Now let us consider a trade with a single maturity T

The contractual payoff at date T is h(T).

h(t) will denote the settlement price at time t of a collateralized trade with maturity T and the purpose is to compute such a settlement price.

At maturity T, the settlement price h(t) will converge to the contractual cash-flow.

Let us provide a contrast with the case of a default-free uncollateralized trade with the same terminal cash-flow h(T) as the collateralized trade. The time t price of such **uncollateralized** contract g(t) is provided by the discounted terminal and unique cash-flow at maturity g(T)=h(T):

$$g(t) = E^{Q}\left[h(T)\exp\left(-\int_t^T r(s)\,ds\right)\right] \quad (8.5)$$

The basic pricing rule is that the sum of the net expected discounted cash-flows, including the premium exchange at inception of the trade, equals zero:

$$0 = E^{Q}\left[-g(t) + g(T)\exp\left(-\int_t^T r(s)\,ds\right)\right] \tag{8.6}$$

Now let us turn back to the same payoff at maturity T, h(T), within a *collateralized* framework. At inception the net cash-flow is equal to $-h(t) + C(t)$. The net cash-flow at maturity is $h(T) - C(T)$. In between t and T, we need to account for the collateral cash-flows, most notably the variation margins:

$$\begin{aligned} 0 &= E^{Q} \Bigg[\underbrace{-h(t) + C(t)}_{\text{Inception}} + \underbrace{\int_t^T e^{-\int_t^s r(u)du}\, dVM(s)}_{\text{Variation margin}} \\ &\quad + \underbrace{(h(T) - C(T))\exp\left(-\int_t^T r(s)\,ds\right)}_{\text{Maturity}}\Bigg] \end{aligned}$$

The time t value of the collateral cash-flows is given by:

$$E^{Q}\left[C(t) + \int_t^T e^{-\int_t^s r(u)du}\, dVM(s) - C(T)\exp\left(-\int_t^T r(s)\,ds\right)\right] \tag{8.7}$$

If it is different from zero, then h(t) and g(t) are different.

Now let us turn to the first order PnL shift due to the posting of the collateral:

Perfect collateralization

Consider a contract which stops at timeτ, $\tau \le T$. We assume that at this stage the result of this end of contract is that the exiting party receives the settlement price $h(\tau)$ and returns the collateral amount $C(\tau)$

The pricing equation is now given by:

$$\begin{aligned} 0 = E^{Q}\Bigg[-h(t) + C(t) + \int_t^{\tau} e^{-\int_t^s r(u)du}\, dVM(s) + (h(\tau) \\ -C(\tau))\exp\left(-\int_t^{\tau} r(s)\,ds\right)\Bigg] \end{aligned} \tag{8.8}$$

Using that we are in perfect collateralization scheme $h(t) = C(t); h(\tau) = C(\tau)$ which leads to:

$$0 = E^Q\left[\int_t^\tau e^{-\int_t^s r(u)du} dVM(s)\right] \tag{8.9}$$

This means that the expected discounted value of the variation margins paid while the position is held equals zero.

We exploit Equation (8.19) by taking the limit $\tau = t + dt$ and we obtain from the following equation$0 = E^Q[dVM(t)]$.

Since

$$dVM(t) = dC(t) - C(t)\frac{dA(t)}{A(t)} = dh(t) - h(t)\frac{dA(t)}{A(t)} \tag{8.10}$$

We obtain: $E^Q[dh(t)] = h(t)E^Q\left[\frac{dA(t)}{A(t)}\right]$.

The pricing equation becomes:

$$0 = E^Q\left[-h(t) + h(T)\exp\left(-\int_t^T r_A(s)\,ds\right)\right] \tag{8.11}$$

In the perfect collateralization case, we discount using the forecast rate for the posted asset.

A simple way to obtain this result is to note that in the case of the perfect collateralization scheme, the impact on the expected PnL is given by:

$$\Delta PnL = \cdots + C(t)\left(rdt - E\left(\frac{dA_t}{A_t}\right)\right)\ldots \tag{8.12}$$

So choosing a discount factor such that $r = r_A$ ensures an average contribution equal to zero just like the uncollateralized contract. Therefore the pricing is unchanged.

In particular, in the case of posting cash we obtain the so-called OIS discounting with the pricing formula:

$$0 = E^Q\left[-h(t) + h(T)\exp\left(-\int_t^T r_{OIS}(s)\,ds\right)\right] \tag{8.13}$$

Applications

In the next section we consider different classical situations:

- Repo market.

- Optimal collateral posting.
- Partial collateral posting.

On each occasion, we consider the integral formulation and the local formulation for the PnL explanation in order to find the right discounting factor.

Repo market

In the repo market, a large set of securities can be posted, quite often bonds.

The PnL impact due to the collateralization is given by:

$$\Delta PnL = \cdots + C(t)\left(rdt - repo(t)dt\right)\cdots. \tag{8.14}$$

Choosing the discounting for the repo factor annihilates the extra PnL contribution and we obtain the following pricing formula:

$$0 = E^{Q}\left[-h(t) + h(T)\exp\left(-\int_t^T repo(s)\,ds\right)\right] \tag{8.15}$$

Optimal posting of collateral

In some cases, a set of I instruments are posted and this is a matter of choice in the process of posting collateral. Being optimal in this case means posting the asset with the maximum return at any time.

The PnL impact due to the collateralization is given by:

$$\Delta PnL = \cdots + C(t)\left(rdt - \max_{i\in\{1,\ldots,I\}} r_{A_i}(t)\,dt\right)\ldots \tag{8.16}$$

If we choose the discount factor in order to cancel this extra PnL induced by the optimal choice of collateral, we obtain the following pricing formula:

$$0 = E^{Q}\left[-h(t) + h(T)\exp\left(-\int_t^T \max_{i\in\{1,\ldots,I\}} r_{A_i}(s)\,ds\right)\right] \tag{8.17}$$

Partial collateralization

The case of partial collateralization is quite common. We assume that the collateral is equal to $C(t) = \alpha(t)\, h(t)$. The margin variation is equal to:

$$dVM(t) = d(\alpha(t)\, h(t)) - \alpha(t)\, h(t)\, \frac{dA(t)}{A(t)} \tag{8.18}$$

The pricing equation between t and $t + dt$ is equal to:

$$\begin{aligned} 0 = E^Q [&-h(t) + \alpha(t)\, h(t) + (1 - r(t)\, dt)\, (dVM(t) + h(t + dt) \\ &-\alpha(t + dt)\, h(t + dt))] \end{aligned}$$

This gives the following local pricing equation:

$$E^Q [dh(t)] = [(1 - \alpha(t))\, r(t) + \alpha(t)\, r_A(t)]\, dt \tag{8.19}$$

The pricing formula in this case is given by:

$$0 = E^Q \left[-h(t) + h(T) \exp\left(-\int_t^T (1 - \alpha(s))\, r(s) + \alpha(s)\, r_A(s)\, ds \right) \right] \tag{8.20}$$

Using this result, we can now turn to the case of asymmetric collateralization.

Asymmetric collateralization

This formula can also be used in the case of asymmetric collateral with a haircut defined as follows:

$$\begin{aligned} \alpha(t) &= 0 \qquad \text{if } h(t) > 0 \\ \alpha(t) &= 1 \qquad \text{if } h(t) \leq 0 \end{aligned}$$

The pricing formula in the case of asymmetric collateral becomes:

$$0 = E^Q \left[-h(t) + h(T) \exp\left(-\int_t^T r(s)\, 1_{\{h(s)>0\}} + r_A(s)\, 1_{\{h(s)\leq 0\}}\, ds \right) \right] \tag{8.21}$$

We can also extend the previous formula in the case of possible default of the counterparty (CVA problem)

$$0 = E^Q\left[-h(t) + h(T)\exp\left(-\int_t^T ((r(s) + \lambda(1-R))\, 1_{\{h(s)>0\}} + r_A(s)\, 1_{\{h(s)\le 0\}})\, ds\right)\right] \tag{8.22}$$

Where, the loss in case of default is given by $(1-R)\,h(t)\,1_{\{h(t)>0\}}$ with probability λdt.

In the case of asymmetrical funding in the presence of default risk for the counterparty, we obtain similar pricing formulae:

$$0 = E^Q\left[-h(t) + h(T)\exp\left(-\int_t^T ((r_b(s) + \lambda(1-R))\, 1_{\{h(s)>0\}} + r_l(s)\, 1_{\{h(s)\le 0\}})\, ds\right)\right] \tag{8.23}$$

Where, r_b is the borrowing rate and r_l is the lending rate.

Although the derivation of these formulae is simple, they are quite difficult to solve numerically. Indeed, in the asymmetric case the discounting rate is dependent on the future valuation of the contract and its sign. This is what we call a Backward Stochastic Differential Equation (BSDE). This type of issue is classical for optimal stopping time problems (such as American options, callables, early exercise problems). In a PDE framework, it is quite easy to solve but, typically, this is limited to few dimensions (not exceeding 3). In Monte Carlo, solutions like the Longstaff and Schwartz Method (LSM) technique are possible. This is beyond the scope of this book.

Once again, when trying to explain the PnL evolution new terms appear and models need to be adapted. In previous sections, complex convexity terms had to be taken into account. In this section, we adjusted the discount factor according to collateral agreements. At this stage we have explored pricing and hedging algorithms and we turn to investment strategies. We leverage the statistical methods that form the core of the algorithms and combine martingale processes to reveal added value within these strategies.

9 Investment Algorithms

An algorithm comprises a finite number of steps to accomplish a task. Algorithms are found everywhere nowadays, and thanks to the internet, Google and Amazon for example, they have simplified our lives.

In the investment world, there are two classes of algorithms, discretionary and quantitative.

An investor who uses a discretionary algorithm will use it without knowing. He will, for example, choose his/her investment universe based on fundamental analysis. Imagine that he believes that the telecom sector in Europe will perform well with the advent of a new technology. He will narrow his search to find a telecom company in a European country which could benefit from this technology.

A quantitative investor might make the same investment using a set of data-driven algorithms.

Programmatically, he will look for a signal that singles out one sector from another, one region from another. This belongs to a signal detection type of technique. Then an assumption on the prediction is made. The quantitative investor will then allocate his capital based on risk. Execution and slippage are also a concern and need to be taken into account to obtain the final performance for the investment strategy.

In this part of the book, we would like to provide an answer to the simple question of how to design a scientific methodology to analyze quantitative strategies.

A quantitative strategy is a strange beast. It takes a universe of data, computes indicators (signals), computes predictors, allocates capital and observes the output results. It may be viewed as a huge mathematical function of all its inputs. Once this function is up and ready to produce orders in the market, we want to know if what has been detected in the past is useful for the future. We have found that in pricing derivatives the key problem is model risk. We have designed a special vehicle, a toxicity index, to incrementally pick the right modeling technique. What is the right methodology to deal with this huge beast that is the quantitative investment strategy?

What is a good strategy?

After a process of computation with past data, a strategy generates the following orders: hold a number of shares Δ_t at time t.

We insist on the fact that the previous computation of the number of shares can only be done with information available before t. So Δ_t uses information $\{S_{-\infty} \ldots S_{t-2}, S_{t-1}\}$.

S_{t-1} is the spot value at a previous timestamp. This could be one tick before for high frequency traders, one day before for medium frequency trader and so on. The point here is to rely on past data strictly speaking. Many strategies show extremely high returns just because they rely on future information. Beware of this common bug. Our purpose is to analyze well-implemented strategies with no bug and we recommend doing two independent implementations to make sure such bugs do not exist. Once this is done, we are ready to analyze how good the strategy is. We would like to design a set of measures which give us enough information to decide on implementing a strategy for real.

The wealth evolution for such a strategy is given by:

$$C_{t+1} - C_t = \Delta_t (S_{t+1} - S_t) \tag{9.1}$$

We have ignored transaction costs and other slippage effects. The final wealth after n steps is then given by:

$$C_n = C_0 + \sum_{t=0}^{n-1} \Delta_t (S_{t+1} - S_t) \tag{9.2}$$

What is interesting in this formula is that it looks like the replicating portfolio for options. Here, as we want to maximize the final wealth we need to have the strategy Δ_t *parallel* to the future spot return $(S_{t+1} - S_t)$. Then, the final wealth is positive $C_n = C_0 + \sum_{t=0}^{n-1} \alpha_t (S_{t+1} - S_t)^2$ with $\alpha_t \geq 0$.

We can record the number of times where the strategy is aligned to future spot realization, that is when we get the right decision or, in other words, when we hit right. We denote p the probability of hitting right, we call it the hit ratio This represents the proportion of right decision of the strategy.

$$p = \frac{\sum_{t=0}^{n-1} 1\{\Delta_t (S_{t+1} - S_t) > 0\}}{n} \tag{9.3}$$

This measure is certainly important to follow to quantify the proportion of time where our decisions are right.

If p is close to 100% then we gain at all times. If p is close to 0% then we lose at all times. This case is interesting because we just need to reverse the order to obtain 100% right decisions. What makes a strategy uncertain in outcome is when the hit ratio is around 50%. But does it suffice just to know p to decide whether to make an investment or not?

Is this measure (hit ratio) enough? Is a strategy with a very high p (or a very low p) a good one?

Not necessarily! Imagine you have a strategy with a hit ratio of 90%. This means that 9 decisions out of 10 are correct. Now, if we earn on average 10 when we have the right decision and lose on average 100 when we have the wrong decision, our expected wealth would be equal to $9/10*(+10)+(1/10)(-100)=(-1)<0$. So the strategy on average ends up negative.

The hit ratio is therefore a good measure but not a sufficient one to characterize successful strategies. We need to record two more measures when qualifying a strategy: the expected loss that is the average loss when we make a wrong decision leading to unsuccessful trade and the expected gain that is the average gain when make a right decision leading to a successful trade.

Let us denote L ($L<0$) the loss if the trade is unsuccessful and G the gain if the trade is successful. The profit on average of the strategy is given by:

$$\text{Profit} = pG + (1-p)L \tag{9.4}$$

We can now define the breakeven probability q as the probability that makes the previous Profit on average equal to zero. This greatly the breakeven volatility which makes the average PnL in the option hedging equal to zero. In the investment case, the breakeven probability is given by the following equation:

$$q = \frac{-L}{G-L} \tag{9.5}$$

We are now ready to define an important measure that calculates how more often we are right compared to the breakeven probability. In other words, we would like to measure if our hit ratio is greater than the breakeven probability or not.

We call this measure the strategy edge and it is calculated as the difference between p, the hit ratio and q the breakeven probability.

$$\text{edge} = p - q \tag{9.6}$$

When the edge is zero, it means that our expected profit from this strategy is zero. When the edge is negative it means that strategy finishes on average below zero. When the edge is positive, it means that the strategy gives correct answers more often than what is needed to breakeven.

Typically, good strategies will have an edge above 10%. Sometimes they can reach 30% or 40%.

With these measures are we done? Can we invest safely in such a strategy?

The answer is no. Because even with all these favorable indicators we can still start investing at a bad time and lose all our money in one market path. How can we assess bad start risk for a strategy that is sound overall?

When we return come back to the definition of the final wealth we see dependence on the initial date 0 and the final one n. We can assess this risk by computing the minimum sum on contiguous subset of the incremental wealth. In mathematical terms, this means finding the following minimum:

$$\min_{i<j} \sum_{k=i}^{j} \Delta_k \left(S_{k+1} - S_k\right) \tag{9.7}$$

This is also known as the *maximum drawdown*. In plain English, this means the maximum loss from peak (wealth maximum) to valley (wealth minimum).

An unlucky investor may invest at a peak and take his/her wealth all the way down to a trough. He/she will then be sensitive to this bad starting point.

Algorithmically, the previous measure needs to calculate over all couples $i<j$ (their number is $n\,(n-1)/2$) the sum of the subset starting from i and finishing at j (on average n/2 operations). Naïvely, we then need $n^2(n-1)/4$ operations to compute such a measure. If the back test is done on 10 years of daily data, this represents 10^{10} operations: an extremely high computational cost.

However, there is a very fast implementation which relies on an algorithm using only n operations.

A low drawdown means that you are less sensitive to the starting point of the strategy. This also means that you can probably leverage the strategy to benefit from higher returns.

There are also other measures that need to be included to have complete qualification of the strategy. Indeed, we note the classical ones such as average rate of return, standard deviation, negative standard deviation, Sharpe ratio and Sortino ratio.

The average rate of return for an investment can be calculated on any time unit from minutes to days and years. We define the Compound Annual Growth Rate CAGR as follows: If T is the total return of Q years the total the CAGR is given by:

$$CAGR = (1+T)^{\frac{1}{Q}} - 1 \tag{9.8}$$

The *Sharpe ratio* is a risk adjusted performance measure. The higher this measure, the better. Typically, strategies will have a Sharpe ratio around 1.

$$Sharpe = \frac{R - R_b}{Std} \tag{9.9}$$

R is the average return, Rb is the benchmark return (typically the risk-free rate) and Std is the standard deviation of the R−Rb.

The Sharpe ratio is an exceptional indicator that needs to be followed. However, it will penalize strategies that perform well with volatility. To remedy this known drawback, we introduce the Sortino ratio which takes into account only the 'negative' volatility Stdn

$$Sortino = \frac{R - R_b}{Stdn} \tag{9.10}$$

Stdn is the standard deviation of the negative returns only.

With all these measures, we have a useful dashboard with which to analyze a strategy.

An interesting measure that combines drawdown and return is the *Sterling* measure; it is given by the following formula:

$$Sterling = \frac{R}{\text{maximum drawdown} + 10\%} \tag{9.11}$$

Let us summarize the measures defined so far:

Table 23 Classical measures of performance

Average return	Measure of performance
Sharpe	Risk adjusted performance
Sortino	Risk adjusted performance corrected for positive volatility
Hit ratio	Percentage of right decision
L	Average loss if unsuccessful trade
G	Average gain if successful trade
Edge	Hit ratio adjusted by the breakeven probability
Sterling	Risk adjusted performance

With this dashboard we can compare strategies.

Is this dashboard sufficient to characterize the quality of a strategy?

It is reasonable to answer yes. However, there are limits to this comparison exercise. Indeed, we need to compare them for a sufficiently long period enough or more importantly, under various market conditions and market regimes.

Here are some results of this type of dashboard for the simplest strategy which consists of a buy and hold on the SX5E from Jan 2007 to Jan 2013.

Table 24 Buy and hold SX5E from Jan 2007 to Jan 2013

Hit ratio	**50.00%**
Average gain	0.78%
Average loss	−0.80%
Sharpe ratio	−30.91%
Drawdown	−17.52%
Edge	−0.56%
Sterling	0.29%
CAGR	−6.56%

We observe that the hit ratio is 50% with a negative edge. Overall, this strategy lost at a rate of 6.56% annually compounded. The sensitivity to the initial point is measured with the maximum drawdown which is a negative 17.52%. The Sharp ratio is negative. The conclusion is that the buy and hold strategy on the SX5E for the period 2007 to 2013 is not a good performing strategy. This is in line with the graph of the spot chart below:

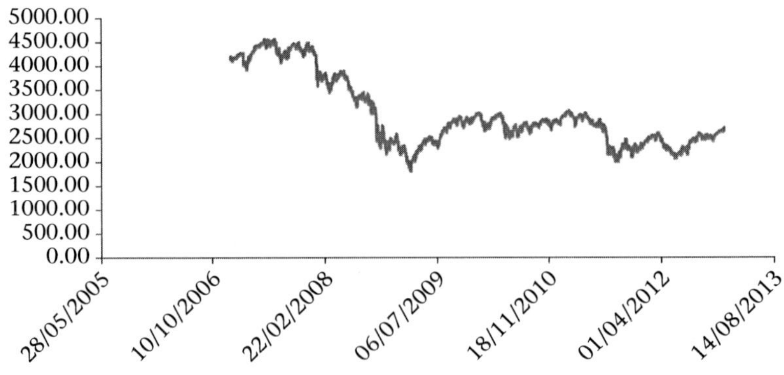

Figure 102 SX5E spot chart for the period 2007–2013

A simple strategy

Imagine that we know the price process and want to design a trading strategy to exploit its movements.

We suppose that the process is given by:

$$dS_t = \mu(S_t)\,dt + \sigma(S_t)\,dW_t$$

Let $\Delta_t$be the allocation at time t. It is designed to maximize the total utility from now to infinity$\int_0^\infty e^{-rs} U(\Delta_t dS_t)$. A second order definition is enough to define the utility function $U(0) = 0, U'(0) = 1, U''(0) = -\frac{1}{G}$ where G is a measure of risk appetite. It can be proven (see Martin & Schöneborn, 2011) that the optimal allocation is given by:

$$\Delta_t = \frac{\mu(S_t)}{\sigma^2(S_t)} G \tag{9.12}$$

This result is well known since the work of Kelly (see Martin & Schöneborn, 2011, Kelly).

We can rewrite this result using the process as follows:

$$\Delta_t = \frac{E\left(X_{t+dt} - X_t \,|\text{information till t}\right)}{E\left((X_{t+dt} - X_t)^2 \,|\text{information till t}\right)} G \tag{9.13}$$

This representation explicitly shows that the optimal allocation relies on the prediction of the future return and volatility.

If the volatility approaches zero, the investor will put an infinite amount of money in the asset. This could be a long position if the drift is positive or short position in the opposite case. This could create a ruinous situation. It is therefore reasonable to ensure a cap, to avoid unnecessary numerical and investment 'explosions'.

Typically, we usually cap the Kelly-type of allocation to 2. So let us define the following Kelly strategy on SX5E defined as follows:

Estimate the parameters

We estimate the parameters of the process using a classical EWMA (Exponential Weighting Moving Average). We put a learning rate λ and estimate the local drift and variance using the recursion equations:

$$\mu_{i+1} = (1-\lambda)\,\mu_i + \lambda \ln\left(\frac{S_{i+1}}{S_i}\right)$$
$$\sigma_{i+1}^2 = (1-\lambda)\,\sigma_i^2 + \lambda \ln^2\left(\frac{S_{i+1}}{S_i}\right) \tag{9.14}$$

Set up the prediction

Prediction of the volatility is equal to its estimate, however, we assume that the SX5E is somewhat *mean reverting* and the best prediction of the future return is equal *minus* the estimated return:

$$E\left(X_{t+dt} - X_t\,|t\right) = -\mu_t\,dt$$

Set up the back test

With this formulation we can generate the back test for such a strategy. In the figure we show the back test for this Kelly mean reverting strategy and compare it with the buy and hold strategy:

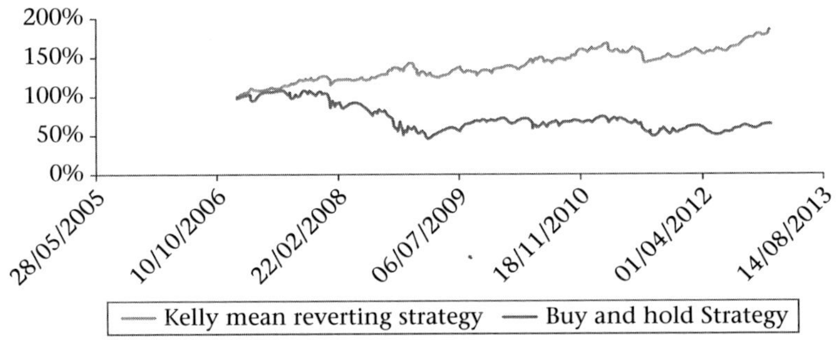

Figure 103 Kelly mean reverting strategy chart compared with the buy and hold strategy

Now we obtain better results and we can run our set of indicators to analyze the quality of the strategy:

In the previous strategy, we use few parameters to run the strategy. We must then answer the important question of over-fitting. Do we memorize too much from the past and basically not learn? We are just long the past. If the past repeats itself we can do well. On the contrary, if the future differs from the past, our premises won't be satisfied and this will imply future underperformance.

Table 25 Table 25 Kelly mean reverting strategy on SX5E from Jan 2007 to Jan 2013

Hit ratio	53.61%
Average gain	0.58%
Average loss	−0.54%
Sharpe ratio	97.90%
Sortino	106.09%
Drawdown	−7.96%
Edge	5.61%
Sterling	2.65%
CAGR	10.37%

Reverse the time

Another easy test to perform to see if the strategy is not too much based on the past is to play the strategy on the spot times series taken in *reverse time*. If a strategy works in practice, it is due to its power of prediction and its asset allocation. If we reverse the time, we break a key element of the strategy. So if the strategy works even in reverse time this is a bad sign.

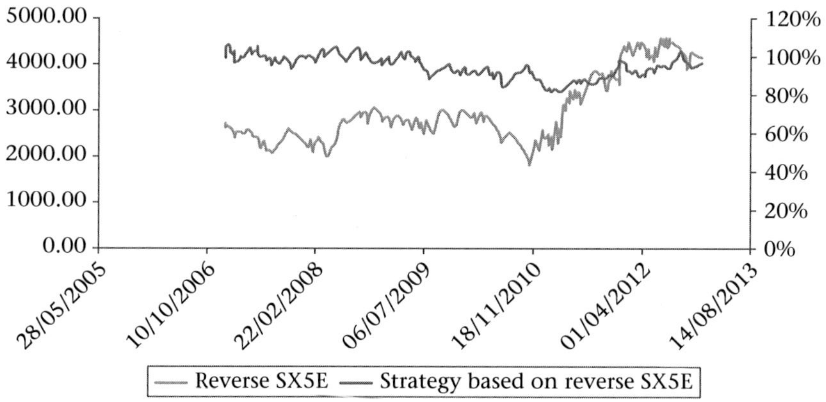

Figure 104 Kelly strategy performance on reverse SX5E

In Figure 104, we observe the reverse SX5E spot path as well as the Kelly strategy. The strategy is not performing well. It remains flat. This result is reassuring. It shows that the real Kelly strategy on the real SX5E path is probably based on a real signals within the data and not on noise.

All these elements give us confidence that the identified strategy is not memorizing too much from the past and is seemingly extracting a real signal from the data.

Before giving a mathematical measure for the over-fitting problem, a warning on data to be avoided in terms of learning:

Two types of data should be avoided when learning the adequate parameters of a strategy: monotonous data, presence of a big jump in the data. Learning from data of this type is biased. We will capture the obvious and not detect rich patterns in the future.

This technique of reversing time is very useful at present. Since the subprime crisis, the American Federal Reserve has poured billions into the markets. This is known as the quantitative easing (QE). The effects have been beneficial for the US and global economies. One issue, however, is to understand (December 2013) what will happen when this process comes to a halt. An easy way to generate scenarios in preparation for this event is to play the major indices in reverse time. In addition, as time operators learn fast and adapt more quickly, it is interesting to speed up the reversing operation to simulate possible scenarios.

Avoid this data when learning

These are typical graphs that illustrate this type of data:

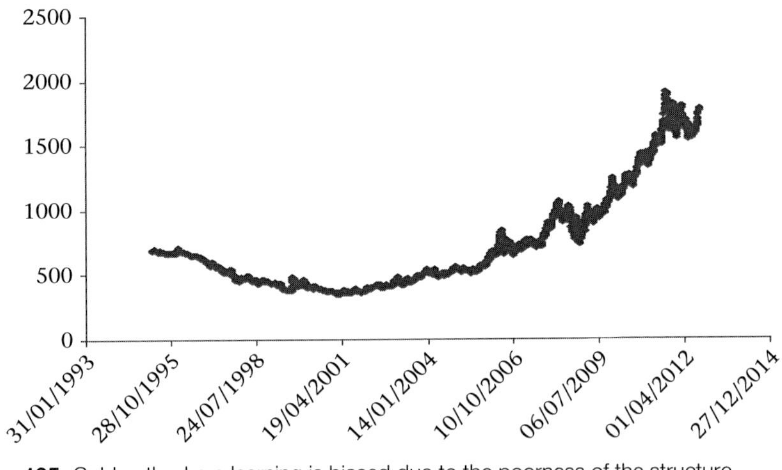

Figure 105 Gold path where learning is biased due to the poorness of the structure

As before, however, we need to have a measure of over-fitting that can be compared between strategies. A good way to estimate the possible over-fitting is to calculate the probability of obtaining such a performance by chance.

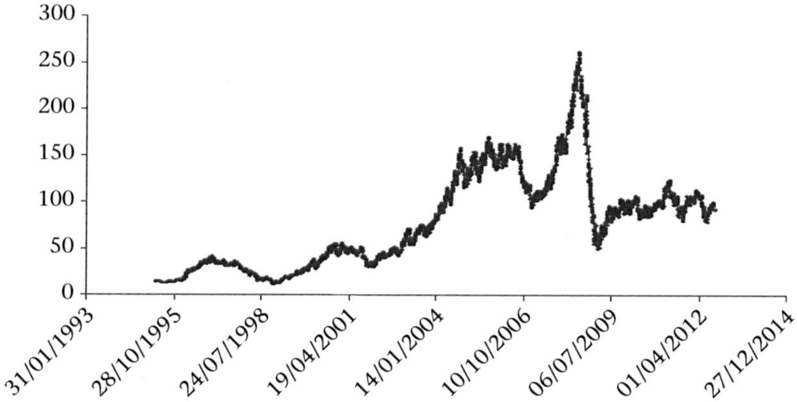

Figure 106 Crude oil where learning is biased due to the presence of a jump

To do so we consider a mathematical process for which the asset is a martingale. The statistical properties of this martingale match the ones from the historical data of the process. Basically, the linear autocorrelation is set to zero and we put a high autocorrelation on the volatility as observed in practice.

A potential process is given by:

$$\begin{cases} dS_t = S_t\sigma_t dW_t \\ d\sigma_t = -\lambda_\sigma \sigma_t dt + \alpha\sigma_t d\tilde{W}_t \\ < d\tilde{W}_t, dW_t >= \rho dt \end{cases} \quad (9.15)$$
$$S_0, \sigma_0$$

For such a martingale process it is impossible to designate a strategy that generates PnL for sure. The best estimator of tomorrow's spot is today's spot. We won't be able to have a buy or sell signal based on the future return. Any strategy Δ_t as defined previously (i.e. which depends only on past data) cannot generate profit for sure.

Yet, when we perform a Monte Carlo simulation with dozens of thousands of random paths, there exist paths for which the Kelly strategy as defined above generates good profit. In

The measures of performance for this particular path are the following:

In Figure 107, we observe a good performance on a particular path of a martingale process. We used the following reasonable parameters for the process $\sigma_0 = 20\%$; $\lambda_\sigma = 30\%$; $\alpha = 40\%$. We know that we cannot generate any signal with such a process. It is then important to assess how often such strategies occur randomly. If they happen too often our strategy can just be qualified as the result of chance or noise and there is certainly some over-fitting. If the results of such a strategy happen very rarely, we can be confident that the combination of our universe

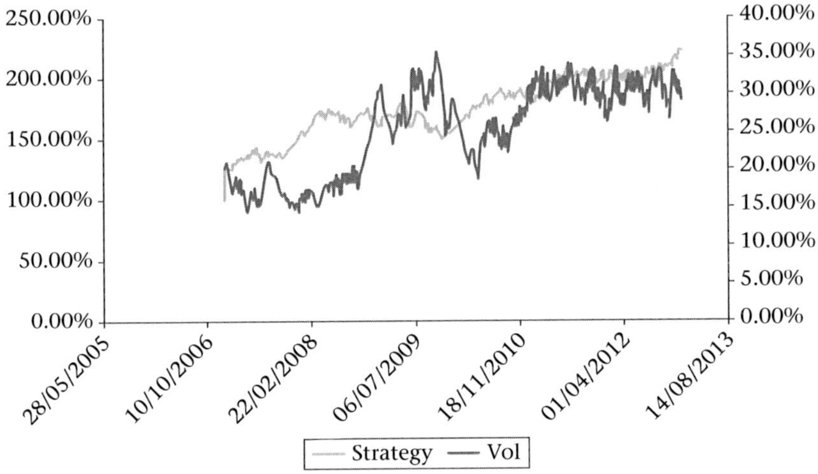

Figure 107 A good performance obtained randomly

Table 26 Good performance obtained on a random path

Hit ratio	**50.80%**
Average gain	0.85%
Average loss	−0.72%
Sharpe ratio	91.08%
Sortino	106.93%
Drawdown	−5.92%
Edge	4.98%
Sterling	1.92%
CAGR	13.75%

of allocation and the strategy applied is not a matter of chance. We can say that we have captured a good signal and there is alpha to be taken with some confidence.

In Figure 108, we present the cumulative distribution of Sharpe ratio performance obtained by simulating the stochastic volatility martingale process. The bold point represents the location of the Kelly strategy on real data. Following the lines of Langnau (Langnau, Quantitative aspects of investments, 2013), we are now ready to propose a toxicity index to measure the **toxicity of over-fitting.**

$$\gamma_{\text{investment}} = \text{Prob}\left(\text{Random Sharpe} \geq \text{Sharpe Investment}\right) \tag{9.16}$$

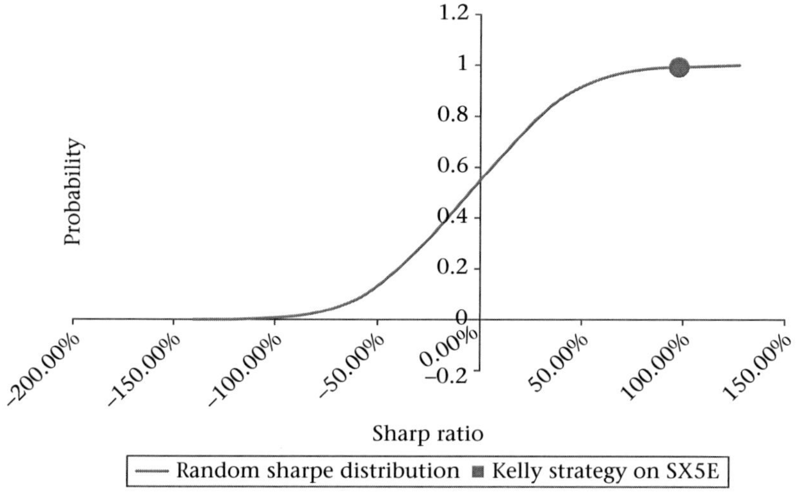

Figure 108 Random Sharpe distribution versus Kelly mean reverting SX5E strategy

In our case, we obtain the value of$\gamma_{\text{investment}} = 0.70\%$. This means that we have less than 1% or more precisely 0.70% chance that the observed Sharpe is the result of pure chance. It is then reasonable to think that our Kelly strategy applied on the SX5E data is good and is not suffering from over-fitting syndrome.

When we obtain an over-fitting toxicity above 5%, we believe that we enter a dangerous region where our strategy fits the data too much and could underperform when implemented for real.

With this stochastic model we can also calculate greeks, like vega vegavolvol and vegalambda. This is essential to investors. They implement a strategy and within their systems they can only report delta sensitivity. At any point in time they are either long or short delta. We know that strategies perform differently within different market regimes, therefore a strategy needs to report something extra such as volatility sensitivity or even volvol sensitivity and lambda sensitivity. This can be done thanks to the process. For similar paths which generate similar performances, we can freeze the random numbers and perturb the parameters to figure out the sensitivity to these parameters.

The previous simulation was obtained with the following parameters $\sigma_0 = 20\%$; $\lambda_\sigma = 30\%$; $\alpha = 40\%$. We perturb each of the parameters and see the impact on the performance. We choose to report the Sharpe measure. For the volatility we simulate a path with the same random numbers and keep all parameters of the process fixed except for the volatility. We do the same for the rest of the parameters. We record the results in the following tables:

These results presented in Tables 27, 28 and 29 mean that the strategy is short volatility, long lambda and long volatility of volatility.

Table 27 Volatility scenario and impact of the strategy on the Sharpe

Volatility	Sharpe
19%	93,34%
20%	91.08%
21%	89.26%

Table 28 Lambda scenario and impact of the strategy on the Sharpe

Lambda	Sharpe
20%	90.25%
30%	91.08%
40%	92.03%

Table 29 Volatility of volatility scenario and impact of the strategy on the Sharpe

Volvol	Sharpe
20%	88.17%
40%	91.08%
60%	94.74%

So far, we have shown how to undertake the 'price discovery' of financial instruments, which can be complex. We have also established measures of toxicity, for pricing hedging or investment exercises. This gives real insight into the derivatives world and the investment world.

We need one last building block to complete our arsenal for quantitative investment. This concerns *risk management*. This particular block should be adaptive and highly reactive, in view of the rapid changes that can occur in financial markets. This comes with a deep understanding of risk. The volatility thermometer is a measure that needs to be followed. In the next chapter, we present a new risk monitoring technique that helps follow the market dynamic and protects hedging strategies and investment strategies from paradigm shift.

Strategies are assets

This is a simple and yet important remark. When you develop a strategy, you develop an algorithm and you try to use it for different assets. You select the assets for which it seems to work. You do all the back tests with simulation to have a clear view of the validity domain for the strategy. One simple idea that should always be borne in mind is that a strategy in itself can be viewed as an asset. You can therefore try your investment algorithm on an existing strategy.

In Figure 109, we represent a typical situation, where we have a strategy that seemed to work well during the crisis and then fade away after May 2009.

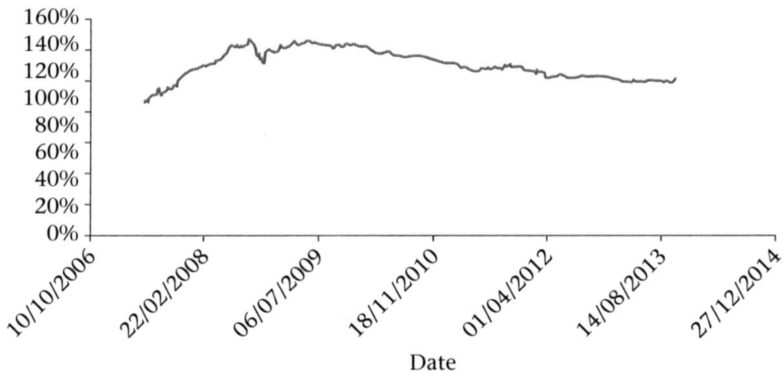

Figure 109 Typical strategy with a region of performance and a region of underperformance

This is very common. One explanation of this phenomenon is that many players spotted the anomaly and traded it away. Another plausible explanation is that the market has adapted and entered a new regime.

The performance measures for this particular VIX Future strategy are the following:

Looking at the graph in Figure 109, we immediately notice that the strategy is not working anymore. Interpreting the numbers only, this is not easy. How can we reuse this index and adapt to this low moving performance change?

This is where it is very useful to see the strategy as a specific asset. We apply the simple Kelly strategy to this index and here are the results in Figure 110.

The measures of performance for the Kelly strategy applied to a volatility strategy are the following:

This technique is powerful to transform good strategies into better ones. We call it the alpha booster technique.

Table 30 Performance for a volatility index strategy based on VIX futures

Hit ratio	**48.79%**
Average gain	0.28%
Average loss	−0.24%
Sharpe ratio	32.95%
Sortino	50.68%
Drawdown	−5.83%
Edge	1.80%
Sterling	0.22%
CAGR	2.22%

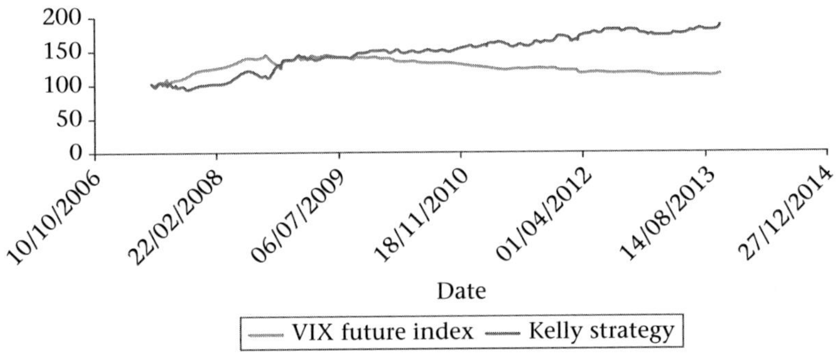

Figure 110 Kelly Strategy applied to a given VIX future strategy

Multi-asset strategy construction

In this section, we present a general framework for building multi-asset strategies.

Our methodology for strategy construction is based on the following steps:

1. Signal detection.
2. Prediction model.
3. Risk minimization (portfolio allocation).
4. Best execution.
5. Back testing and results summarization.

Signal detection

Let $p_t^1, \ldots, p_t^n$ be n tradable assets. Let $x_t^i = p_t^i - p_{t-1}^i$ the change in price of these assets. Assessing arithmetic performances means that the purpose of the strategy

Table 31 Performance of a Kelly Strategy applied on a volatility index strategy

Hit ratio	**53.18%**
Average gain	0.51%
Average loss	−0.46%
Sharpe ratio	102.93%
Sortino	157.85%
Drawdown	−4.73%
Edge	5.46%
Sterling	101.09%
CAGR	10.18%

is to calculate the number of shares associated with each asset in order to extract alpha.

The classical approach in signal theory is to normalize the data.

In the case of the mono underlying asset, this is a division by the standard deviation. In the multi-asset case, we compute the variance covariance of additive returns and consider the following signal:

$$Cov^{-\frac{1}{2}} x_t \tag{9.17}$$

We build a mean reversion indicator which is the associated autocorrelation calculated as follows:

$$\frac{< x_t Cov^{-1} x_{t+lag} >}{< x_t Cov^{-1} x_t >} \tag{9.18}$$

Where x_t represents the multi-dimensional signal. We apply this methodology to the increments for the variance swaps 1m, 3m, 6m, 9m, 1y for the universe of indices {SPX, SX5E, UKX and DAX}.

The choice of this universe of options is based on the fact that all these options are very liquid and can be traded with a good size.

Cov is the filtered matrix of variance covariance of the volatility returns. It can be seen as a squared volatility of volatility.

The filtering is based on random matrix theory. (see Bouchaud & Potters, 2005) for financial applications.

More precisely, we can write the following decomposition into principal components applied to the correlation matrix

$$Cor = diag\,(1/\sigma_1,\ldots,1/\sigma_m)\,X^T X\; diag\,(1/\sigma_1,\ldots,1/\sigma_m)$$

$$Cor = PDP^T \tag{9.19}$$

$$\text{D is a diagonal matrix } D = diag\,(\lambda_1,\ldots,\lambda_m)\,.$$

The eigenvalues of this correlation matrix are sorted in ascending order $\lambda_1 < \cdots < \lambda_m$. Random matrix theory tells us then that only a small portion of this spectrum represents information and the rest of it is pure noise. This is illustrated in Figure 111.

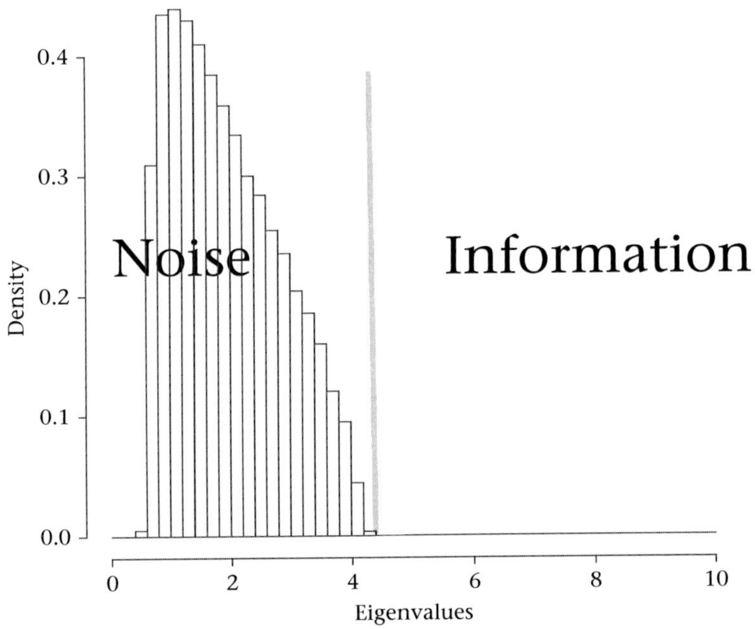

Figure 111 Illustration of random matrix theory

In Figure 111, we illustrate the spectrum of a random matrix. On the left of the vertical bar the spectrum is purely random and should not be taken into account. The theorem behind this shape is the Marcenko–Pastur theorem and exists for Gaussian returns.

In the case of non-Gaussian returns as will be explained in the next chapter, we have recourse to the simulation approach. We indeed simulate independent fat-tailed distribution (in fact we simulate q Gaussian variables) and calculate the spectrum of the matrix of variance covariance which should theoretically be the identity. We identify the part of the spectrum that differs from the identity, such as the noise. This approach is experimental and yet very efficient. The noise part in the fat-tail case compared to the Gaussian case where the theorem applies is wider. Fat tails create dependence between variables with a bigger part of noise.

In order to take this information into account we use one method among others, the clipping approach. It consists in averaging all the eigenvalues that belong to the noise area.

If we note i* the index below which the spectrum is pure noise, we construct the new correlation matrix by performing the two steps:

1. Clipping

$$\tilde{\lambda}_1 = \lambda_1, \ldots, \tilde{\lambda}_{i*} = \lambda_{i*} \textbf{ and } \tilde{\lambda}_{j=i*,\ldots,m} = \frac{1}{m - i^*} \sum_{j=i^*+1}^{m} \lambda_j$$

$$\tilde{Cor} = diag\,(1/\sigma_1, \ldots, 1/\sigma_m)\, P\; diag\left(\tilde{\lambda}_1, \ldots, \tilde{\lambda}_m\right) P^T\; diag\,(1/\sigma_1, \ldots, 1/\sigma_m)$$

2. Normalization

$$\tilde{Cor}_{i,j} \leftarrow \frac{\tilde{Cor}_{i,j}}{\sqrt{\tilde{Cor}_{i,i}\tilde{Cor}_{j,j}}}$$

This last equation insures that the obtained matrix is an admissible correlation matrix with a diagonal 1.

From this newly obtained correlation matrix, we build the filtered covariance matrix given by the following equation:

$$\tilde{Cov} = diag\,(\sigma_1, \ldots, \sigma_m) * \tilde{Cor} * diag\,(\sigma_1, \ldots, \sigma_m)$$

This process builds a filtered correlation matrix. This is similar to a factorial approach where we project all the assets on a few factors and calculate the resulting correlation matrix.

Autocorrelation results

Lag typically ranges from 1 day to a couple of weeks.

In Figure 112, the autocorrelation for one day is around −15%. If we calculate the same measure for the stocks universe it is just −2%. This level of autocorrelation observed on the volatility space is strong and exploitable for alpha generation.

We take this signal into account to build a prediction model and exploit it for strategies.

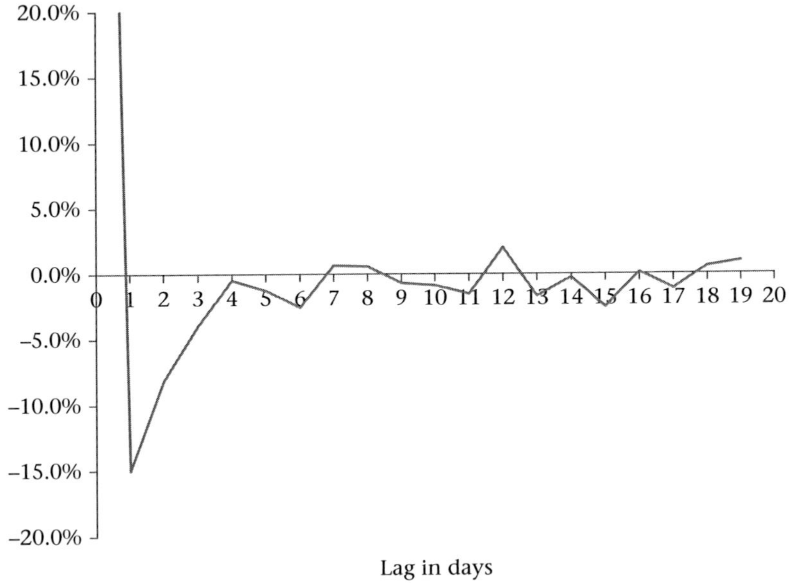

Figure 112 Autocorrelation results

Prediction model

At this stage, we construct a model that is consistent with the observed signal. We shall not build a structural model that is. showing the right structure of the different interactions of the volatilities. Instead, we build a predictive model which calibrates (in a sort of moment-matching) the previous strong signal. If the signal was purely Gaussian, then moment-matching the autocorrelation is enough to exactly identify the process. In our case, the signal is non-Gaussian and this moment-matching technique is inspired from the pricing techniques that appear for Asian and basket options. In this case we consider a sum of log normal variables and approximate them with a particular log normal variable which shares the first two moments with the real process.

The simplest prediction model has the following form. The predicted value of the volatility return over the day i is given by

$$\hat{x}_i^{\sigma} = x_i^{*,\sigma} \tag{9.20}$$

Where

$$x_i^{*,\sigma} = -x_{i-1}^{\sigma} \tag{9.21}$$

We can predict the volatility return from close (i−1) to close(i), $\hat{r}_i^{\sigma}$, using an auto regressive model of order p: this will enable us to capture more of the identified signal for lags ranging from 1 to p. In this case, we will have the following equation:

$$x_i^{*,\sigma} = \sum_{k=1}^{p} a_k x_{i-k}^{\sigma} \tag{9.22}$$

In the sequel, we restrict ourselves to the simplest model, that is AR(1) as described by Equations (9.19) and (9.20).

Another simple way to construct the prediction returns is to build an exponentially weighted moving average (EWMA). Typically, $\lambda = 90\%$: this represents a half-life time of 10 days.

The formula is then given by:

$$x_i^{*,\sigma} \cong \frac{\sum_{k=0}^{N-1} \lambda^k x_{i-k}^{\sigma}}{\sum_{k=0}^{N-1} \lambda^k} \tag{9.23}$$

Risk minimization

At this stage, we have identified a signal that is strong enough to build a model that matches the essential characteristics and properties of the signal. This model is also called the predictive model, allowing us to predict returns. Now, we are ready to apply the portfolio approach defined by Markowitz. We build a long/short portfolio that minimizes risk and captures the mean reversion feature on the volatility of returns. The long part is equal to the short part in cash.

The optimal weights n_i (i.e. the number of assets) are computed in such a way as to minimize the following function:

$$F_t = \underbrace{\frac{1}{2}\sum_{i,j} n_i^* \tilde{C}ov^* n_j}_{A} - \underbrace{\sum_i n_i x_i^{*,\sigma}}_{B} + \underbrace{\lambda \sum_i w_i p_i(t)}_{C} \tag{9.24}$$

A: represents the risk of the position,

B: represents the expected return,

C: represents the cash neutrality equation.

The weights are then given by the following formula:

$$n_i = \sum_j \tilde{C}ov_{i,j}^{-1} x_j^{*,\sigma} - \frac{\sum_{j,k} p_j(t)\, \tilde{C}ov_{j,k}^{-1} x_k^{*,\sigma}}{\sum_{j,k} p_j(t)\, \tilde{C}ov_{j,k}^{-1} p_k(t)} \sum_j \tilde{C}ov_{i,j}^{-1} p_j(t) \tag{9.25}$$

The algebraic nominal engaged in this strategy is zero, as $\sum_i n_i p_i(t) = 0$ by construction.

As previously mentioned, this approach follows the lines of the Markowitz construction. It is also a generalization of the Kelly approach in one dimension.

This optimization makes the weights align on the prediction, just like the Kelly approach through the term B. At the same time we take volatility into account just like Kelly through the term A. Here, we also take into account the correlation matrix in its inverse and it is then important to perform the Random Matric Theory filtering beforehand. The term C is simply a normalization term.

We perform the theoretical back test with strategies that use the previous weights with constant nominal.

We perform the same entry strategy based on the previous weights and consider exit strategies after twenty days.

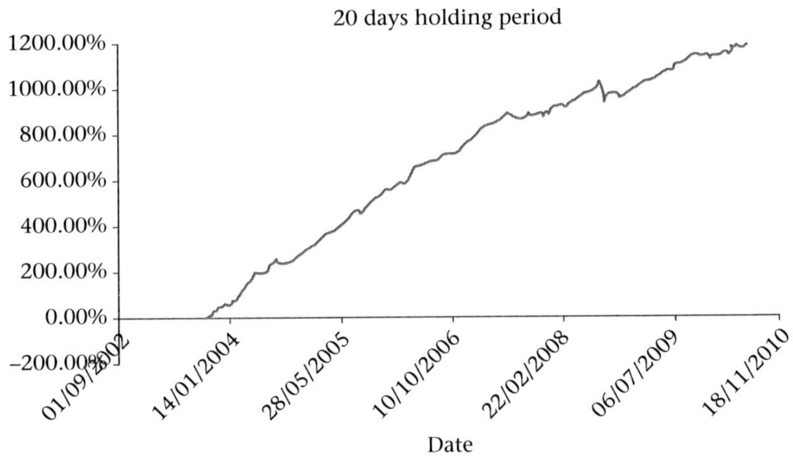

Figure 113 Volatility strategy equity line

In Figure 113, we observe an impressive equity line. Indeed, we obtain a yearly return of approximately 19.53% and a Sharpe ratio of 3.17.

This theoretical back-test is very important to spot if there is any alpha to be extracted from a given universe of tradeables. In practice, there is an extra cost associated with every transaction. We therefore need to adjust our trading policy to trade less often taking into consideration our current position. The next section highlights this point and proposes a proxy solution.

The optimal weights n_i in the presence of transaction costs must solve a different optimization problem. If we note n_i^0 our current position then we compute the optimal weights in such a way to optimize both the alignment with the predictions (generate alpha) and the initial position (reduce cost of transactions). We introduce a blending factor between these two effects: γ_c

We just change the prediction model to take into account the blending factor and keep the same optimization problem.

$$x_i^{*,\sigma} \leftarrow (1-\gamma_c)\, x_i^{*,\sigma} + \gamma_c n_i^0 \tag{9.26}$$

If the blend factor is equal to one, this means that the prediction is replaced by the current holding. In this particular optimization, we do not care about the signal and the future prediction. We just want to build a portfolio with minimum risk knowing our current holding. This makes sense when the signal is not so strong and the cost of rebalancing quite high. On the contrary, when the blend factor is equal to zero, we are back to the previous problem where the cost of transactions is considered negligible. This is the case in the presence of strong signal.

10 Building Monitoring Signals

A Fat-tail toxicity index

In the pricing section, we have seen the importance of fat tail for the forward skew modeling and especially for Crash put options. The alpha process can be very useful to design a very good indicator to detect the beginning of large movements or alternatively to detect large movements.

The construction of the alpha-stock process is done as presented in Chapter 5, Equation (5.18):

$$\frac{dS_t}{S_t} = \sigma_\alpha \, dL_\alpha (t) \tag{10.1}$$

The volatility σ_α is lower than the volatility estimated from a Brownian motion σ_2 (alpha equal to two corresponds to the Gaussian case).

As previously presented in Chapter 5, σ_α is estimated using the Koutrouvelis estimator, whereas, the normal volatility is estimated using the classical volatility estimator:

$$\sigma_2 = \sqrt{\frac{252}{\mathrm{N}} \sum_{t=1}^{N} \ln^2 \left(\frac{S_t}{S_{t-1}} \right)} \tag{10.2}$$

In Figure 114, we observe that the alpha volatility estimation is lower than the normal volatility estimator. This is expected as the alpha volatility does not absorb large returns. Also, it is noticeable that this new estimator has a **diffusive behavior** offering better forecast and hedging facilities.

From these two volatility definitions, it is possible to detect non-diffusive assets with a normalized indicator – the fat-tail toxicity indicator:

$$I = 1 - \frac{\sigma_\alpha}{\sigma} \tag{10.3}$$

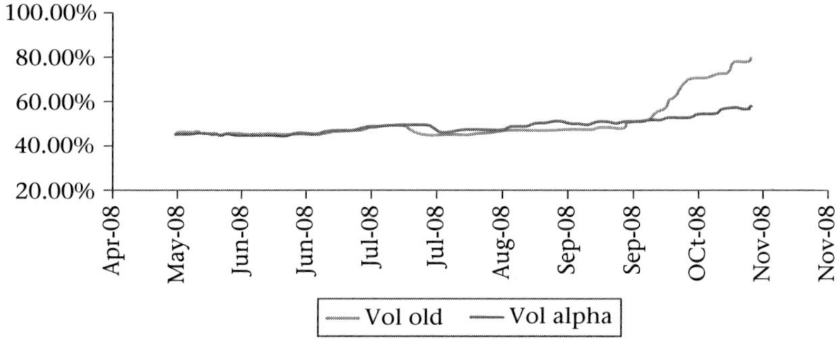

Figure 114 Comparison of normal volatility and alpha volatility

This indicator remains always between 0 and 1. When it is 0 the asset can be classified as a diffusive asset. When it is close to 1, the asset shows fat tails and must be looked at with caution.

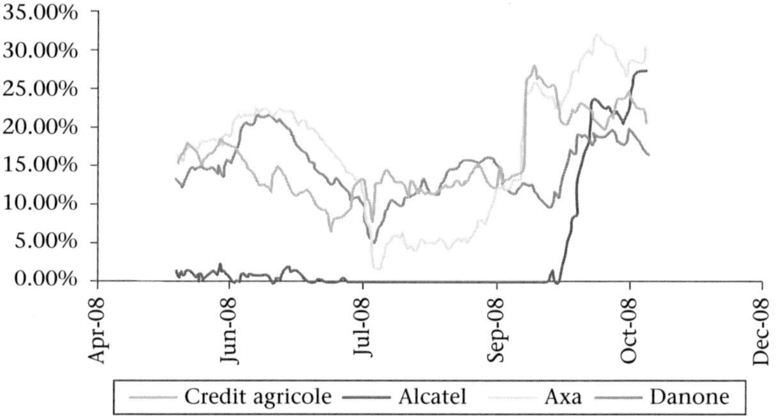

Figure 115 Fat tail toxicity indicator for several stocks

In Figure 115, we calculate the fat-tail toxicity index for several stocks during the beginning of the subprime crisis. Financial and insurance stocks showed fat-tail toxicity before the subprime bubble exploded with the fall of Lehman Brothers. Alcatel radically altered its behavior owing to the spread of the crisis to the whole economy.

The fat-tail indicator is useful for asset allocation. Indeed, this number gives us a useful measure of risk perception. It tells us when some assets change behavior and to what extent events in the market spread to all assets.

However, the main drawback of this new indicator is that it is the result of a complex algorithm and cannot be tailor-made to describe a payoff.

Returning to the Koutrouvelis algorithm in Chapter 5, we can note how it functions. Indeed, to detect the fat-tail shape, the algorithm uses all the sample, overweighting tail returns and underweighting the sample within the distribution mode. Thereafter, to estimate the alpha volatility, it does the opposite. Specifically, it underweights outliers. We can therefore propose an alpha volatility estimator that mimics the exact algorithm. This is represented by the harmonic average of log returns square.

$$\sigma_\alpha \cong \sqrt{252 \frac{\sum_{t=1}^{N} 1\left\{\left|\ln\left(\frac{S_t}{S_{t-1}}\right)\right| > B\right\}}{\sum_{t=1}^{N} 1\left\{\left|\ln\left(\frac{S_t}{S_{t-1}}\right)\right| > B\right\} \frac{1}{\ln^2\left(\frac{S_t}{S_{t-1}}\right)} + 1\left\{\left|\ln\left(\frac{S_t}{S_{t-1}}\right)\right| \leq B\right\} \frac{1}{B^2}}} \tag{10.4}$$

There are two elements in this formula:

1. The expression is a harmonic average instead of the arithmetic average of squared returns.
2. A selection of returns that is high enough to avoid a division by zero.

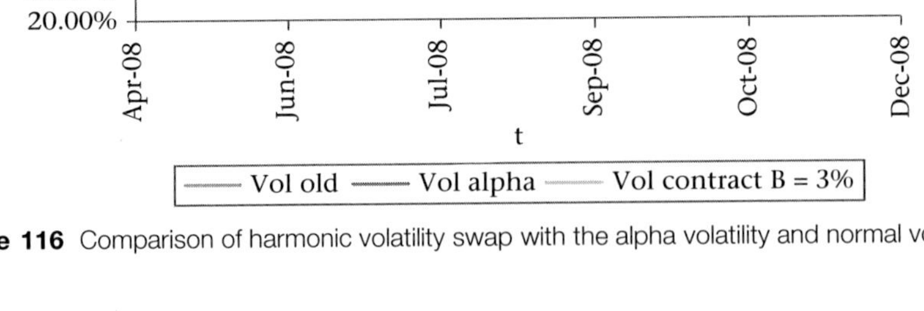

Figure 116 Comparison of harmonic volatility swap with the alpha volatility and normal volatility

In Figure 116, we observe that the alpha volatility is close to the harmonic estimation with a Barrier B = 3%.

In the next section, we propose volatility signals and algorithms to follow the variations for volatilities and detect market regimes.

B Volatility signals

We have seen in previous chapters that volatility modeling (smile and its dynamic) is essential to price and hedge derivative products correctly.

We have seen that we use the same methodologies as in the exact sciences to build the pricing methodology and the associated hedging it. During this journey, two types of knowledge have to concur to create the fair valuation. On the one hand, we built model knowledge of a mathematical nature, on the other hand, data confrontation which highlighted invariants belonging to the quasi Newtonian-type of modeling.

In the quantitative investment area, we have defined a set of measures and indicators to help assess the sanity of the proposed strategies. We observed that simulation techniques of martingale processes can be helpful in quantifying the over-fitting toxicity for a given strategy.

Yet we know that we live in a non-Newtonian world, where the constants governing the observed equilibrium can change at any time.

In this chapter, we go further in data modeling and design a key market indicator that highlights the market regime. This information is critical for traders who hedge positions, as well as for investors. It quickly provides them with the new constants that govern the market and allows them to adapt their positions accordingly. Before we go further, we raise a 'philosophical' issue.

Can mathematical models provide added value to investing?

An esteemed investor, Simmons, described his job as 'testing, testing and testing'. Basically, he proposes systematic exploration of all markets in a search for alpha. This work, as mentioned in the introduction, to some degree resembles astronomy.

To maintain consistency, we focus on volatility and question its role in asset manager decision making.

Indeed, volatility is a key indicator for asset managers. We present a robust methodology for improving asset management performance. More specifically, we offer new tools to cope with the new paradigm and to meet one of the most important criteria in asset management that is capital preservation.

The world has changed dramatically and what have been called 'Black Swans',that is to say rare, extraneous events, are becoming increasingly common and risk undermining performances in the asset management world.

We present a quasi-Newtonian data modeling methodology. We build models that have some rationale and, as in gravitational modeling, we establish some invariants that help us structure stock returns. This is quasi-Newtonian as we believe that these invariants may change over time due to profound changes in market structure (operators, liquidity, regulatory constraints). The model remains one of interest as it offers a clear description of what is now familiar to the financial community and even the general public, the notion of market regime.

Market regime identification is essential in our investment process. It allows a simple signal to be built enabling the operator to adapt. The operator then acts as a 'good father', moving away from crisis regime so as to shield his/her capital from downside risk, that is tail risk.

There is no need to optimize one's position and indeed it is better not to optimize so as to avoid the classic over-fitting problem.

The purpose of the operator is to implement the following overlay strategy consisting of the disposal of risky assets in times of crisis. We give a few examples that indicate that our approach is robust and generically applicable to all asset classes.

Since the Lehman Brothers collapse in September 2008 and interest-rates wake of the subprime crisis, there has been a string of crises (debt crisis, liquidity crisis, and sovereign debt crisis).

The frequency of these crises has increased and many asset managers have suffered deep, sometimes unrecoverable, losses.

Crises are clearly becoming more commonplace. This points to the limitations in modeling and it is not reasonable to aspire to a model of a pure Newtonian type. However, the tail structure has been fairly stable despite the crisis and the radical paradigm shift.

We can draw a comparison with an earthquake, in that we cannot predict when it will occur (although there are often prior tremors) but once it does happen (and after appropriate 'classification') we know precisely what rescue resources to provide to cope with the ensuing damage.

We do not doubt the skill or alpha capacity of asset managers. However, this alpha generally just means a performance beating a specific benchmark. Many of them have incurred heavy capital losses resulting in bankruptcy and massive capital withdrawals.

As a consequence of this paradigm shift, investors are now in the hunt for absolute returns.

To achieve these goals, asset managers and allocators need to combine alpha generation (which can be based on stock picking, technical analysis, fundamental analysis and strategic thinking) with rigorous risk management.

Our work forms part of generic risk management that can complement an existing alpha generation approach.

It is therefore less optimal than methods that detect precisely what is included in the alpha generation process. This may appear to be a deficiency but, in fact, when dealing with historical data we can easily fall into the over-fitting trap. It turns out that our approach is robust and boasts a strong, generic track record.

This section follows the same logic as in the article (Metane, 2009). Indeed, it is a simple quantitative approach that provides asset managers with tactical and effective signals.

The sequel will detail the **nature of returns** (marginal distribution and their dynamic). We also propose a simple statistical model. Afterwards, we suggest different ways to build **relevant signals** to follow up **market regimes.** Finally, we use the corresponding market regime segmentation to **analyze the performance of different asset classes and strategies.** Finally, we offer a tactical allocation technique based on market regimes to protect alpha and shield capital from tail risk.

Nature of the returns

There is a huge literature that studies the distribution of financial returns. We can make a modest contribution by showing the limits of any approach that identifies the nature of the returns. Indeed, as we are dealing with the social sciences, we lack general laws of conservation from which we can derive a unique mathematical formulation. However, there are some statistics which can help us identify the likely type of distribution.

Before going on to deal with what we believe to be the precise law of returns, we need to recall one of the most important theorems in statistics. The Central Limit Theorem (CLT) stipulates that if one repeats a finite variance experiment in an independent manner, whatever the experiment, the estimates error will be distributed with a standard normal distribution. This distribution is known as a Gaussian distribution, as it was Gauss who first derived the CLT and gave a reason for the appearance of this distribution.[1]

In the financial context, there was a generalization of the CLT assuming infinite variance experiments with independence which generates Levy type of distributions. These give heavy tails as observed in the data, but claiming independence for returns is incorrect. Indeed, it is well known that there is major autocorrelation for absolute values returns.

To understand the *marginal distribution* for financial returns, we can rely on recent mathematical results that show that we can obtain fat tails as a result of a CLT with finite variance returns, but with a global correlation between the returns. This theorem is due to Tsallis and co-authors (Umarov, 2008).

Table 32 Central limit theorems under different assumptions

(Independent) $q = 1$	**(Globally correlated)** $q \neq 1$	
$\sigma < \infty$	Gaussian density	Q Gaussian density
$\alpha = 2$	Classic central limit theorem CLT	$p(v) \propto \frac{1}{v^{\frac{2}{(q-1)}}}$
$\sigma = \infty$	Levy distribution	Q Levy density
$0 < \alpha < 2$	Levy-Gnedeko CLT	$p(v) \propto \frac{1}{v^{\frac{(1+\alpha)}{(1+\alpha q-\alpha)}}}$
	$p(v) \propto \frac{1}{v^{\alpha+1}}$	

[1] It was Laplace and Demoivre, before Gauss, who first introduced the normal distribution. However, Gauss's name has been issued owing to the central limit theorem.

The Tsallis theorem offers a *new attractor* which justifies the financial returns being distributed following a q-Gaussian, which is a particular form of student distribution with a number of degree of freedom μ linked to the value of q in the following equation:

$$q = 1 + \frac{2}{\mu + 1} \tag{10.5}$$

The positive aspect of this modeling is that q is almost invariant and is equal to *1.44*. This value did not change for a long time and describes the nature of fat tail risk. In the wake of the subprime crisis, the value changed a little because markets price this extreme risk differently. For example, for the *financial sector* we observe that the value rose from 1.4 before the subprime crisis to 1.57 after. It has since remained around this value despite the repetition of crisis.

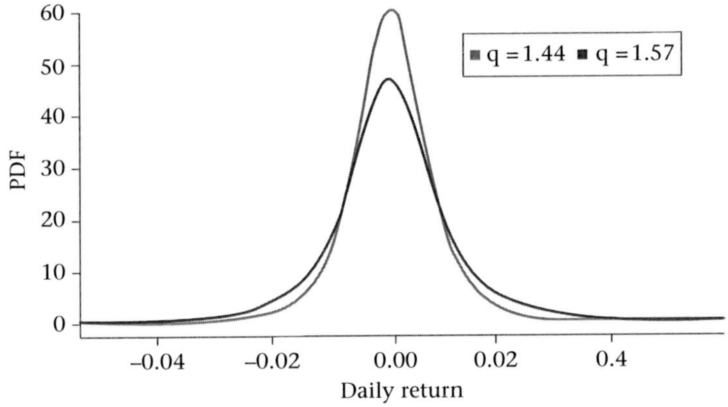

Figure 117 q-Gaussian distribution

In Figure 117, we graph the q Gaussian distribution for two different values, 1.44 pre-crisis value and 1.57 post-crisis value for the financial sector. For 1.57 the distribution is fatter in the tails and has stronger peak in the middle.

We can repeat the analysis of q estimation before and after the crisis for the different sectors and we observe in Figure 118, the same phenomenon. The value of q has increased post subprime crisis. Tail risk is more since after the subprime crisis.

The Tsallis theorem (central limit theorem) and the statistical estimation of the parameters suggests that the true nature of financial returns is a q Gaussian. This is in line with the tail estimation in Chapter 5, as it generates fat tail with a similar tail index.

To extract a good signal from this knowledge, we need to model the dynamic of the returns.

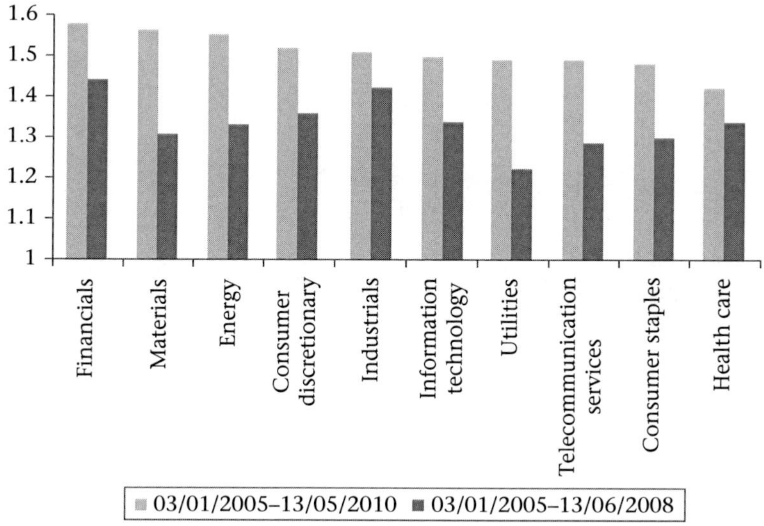

Figure 118 q Estimation for different sectors before and after the crisis

A first step to unveil the dynamic nature of the returns is to look at data. We observe in Figure 119, that the returns form clusters over periods of time. Qualitatively, we claim that SPX returns occur as a succession of Gaussian regimes.

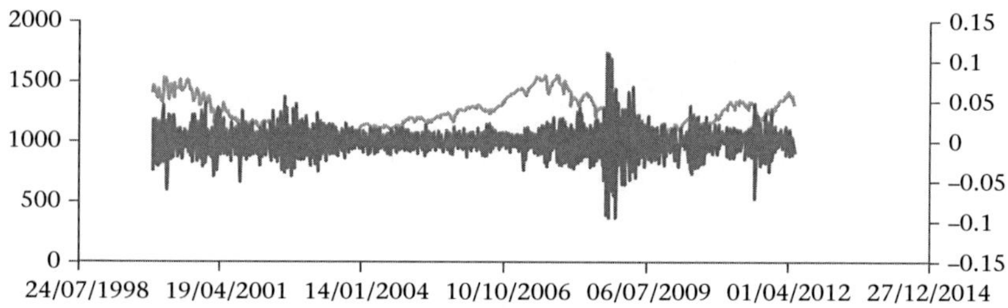

Figure 119 SPX Prices and returns. Clusters are clearly identified

This is consistent with a mathematical theorem which stipulates that q Gaussian distribution is a mixture of Gaussian distributions.

$$p(v|\beta) \propto e^{-\frac{1}{2}\beta v^2}$$

$$f(\beta) \propto |\beta^{\frac{n}{2}-1} e^{-\frac{n\beta}{2\beta_0}}$$

$$p(v) = \int_0^{\infty} f(\beta)\,p(v|\beta)\,d|\beta \quad \text{(gamma mixture of Gaussian density)}$$

$$\Rightarrow p(v) \propto \frac{1}{\left(1+\frac{1}{2}\beta\left(q-1\right)v^2\right)^{\frac{1}{q-1}}} \quad \text{(q Gaussian Density)} \qquad (10.6)$$

The value at risk is a good example of application and verification of this distribution. If we fit the q parameter on the SX5E, we can compute the value at risk within this process and check, for example, the number of exceptions that are observed.

$$\begin{aligned} \text{VaR}(99\%) \text{ in Gaussian world} &= 2.33\,\sigma\sqrt{dt} \\ \text{VaR}(99\%) \text{ in a q Gaussian world} &= \text{adjustment} \times 2.33\sigma\sqrt{dt} \end{aligned} \tag{10.7}$$

The adjustment term in Equation (10.7) is the ratio of the 99% quantile of the q Gaussian and the Gaussian one. In the typical case of 1.44, it represents 1.4.

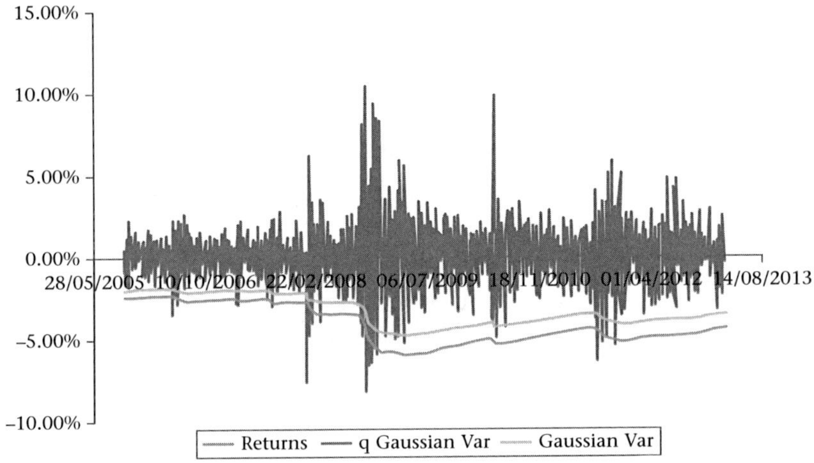

Figure 120 SX5E daily returns and Value at Risk under the Gaussian and q Gaussian models

In Figure 120, we examine the SX5E daily returns and compute the Value At Risk (VaR) under two different models, the Gaussian model and the q Gaussian Model. For a 99% percentile, we expect to have two exceptions per year. With the Gaussian VaR, we obtain an average of 5 exceptions a year. With the q Gaussian approach, we obtain 1.76 exceptions per year. This is very close to what we expect. At this stage, we can make the following remark by computing the trend for the number of exceptions per year in the Gaussian VaR.

In Figure 121, we see that even with an inferior model and a robust estimator we can detect the emergence of crisis very early on. The beginning of August 2008 is an early marker of the turbulent times ahead. Once again it argues for an incremental implementation of models.

So far, we have characterized the nature of the returns with a decent level of confidence, and exploited it to extrapolate the distribution and provide a fairly good calculation of the Value at Risk. In the next section, we continue the modeling

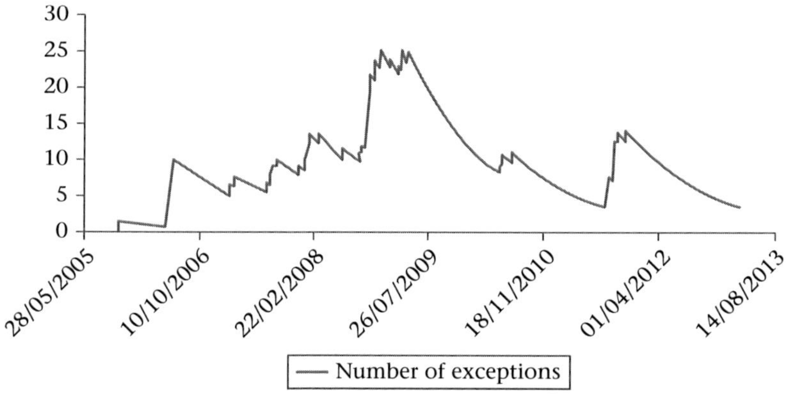

Figure 121 Trend for the number of Gaussian VaR exceptions for SX5E index

effort to design a dynamic model for the returns. This is an essential block for global market risk monitoring.

The dynamic of the returns

The simplest way to model this succession of Gaussian regimes (states) is to assume a model with different levels of Gaussian parameters (mean and standard deviation) complemented with a transition matrix between the different states.

We consider a system with the state described by a Markov Chain X not observed directly but rather visible via a continued observation process which we call the signal.

The system dynamic is then given by the following equation:

$$X_{k+1} = AX_k + B_{k+1}$$
$$y_{k+1} = m(X_k) + \sigma(X_k)\, w_{k+1}$$

A is the transition matrix from one state to the other.

The parameters m, σ represent respectively the mean and standard deviation for each state.

This model is called Hidden Markov Model (HMM).

A full presentation of the model and estimation of its parameters can be found in the PhD thesis (Loulidi, Modélisation stochastique en finance, application à la construction d'un modèle à changement de régime avec des sauts, 2008). An application to the VIX signal is presented in (Loulidi, Reghaï, & Treulet, How to predict volatility quantitatively, 2008).

To conclude this section, we can provide a reminder of the main results. There is a strong evidence (both data and the emergence of new mathematical theorems) that returns follow a q Gaussian distribution (a special student distribution).

HMM model is the simplest dynamic model that is consistent with the marginal distribution.

Signal definition

The construction of a financial signal that can serve as an input for screening markets is a key step in the process of alpha protection for a given investment.

There is not one generic signal for all risk management purposes. Key properties need to be well understood in the design of such a signal:

- Geographical region
- Sector exposure
- Market observables and liquidity
- Market interconnection
- Nature of the underlying.

Let us see via a few examples how these properties determine the relevant choice of signal.

Example 1: Signal associated with the US or EUR market equity universe

Table 33 US and EUR equity market

Property	Remark
Geographical region	Matters.
Sectorial exposure	Not relevant unless the investment is too concentrated.
Market observables and their liquidity	VIX, VSTOXX, Volatility indices US interest rate curve ITRAXX.
Market interconnection	High – markets are too optimized and therefore too fragile when hit by crises.
Nature of the underlying	Linear.

For such a universe, the VIX or the VSTOXX is well suited in general. However, it can miss some interconnections between the credit market and the equity market. Besides, the fixed income market is also a key determinant of overhaul financial market health. The fact that these markets are highly interconnected in times of crisis makes the choice of a good crisis indicator less problematic.

In practice, we propose using the Advanced Risk Perception Index (ARPI), designed in 2001 by Patrick Artus, chief economist at NATIXIS.

The idea behind this signal is to combine on an equal footing the VIX level, the slope of the yield curve (preferably the US yield curve) and ITRAXX level (credit spread indicator).

VIX represents heat in equity markets. The ITRAXX represents heat in the credit market, and the interest rate slope represents heat in the fixed income market.

These indicators are liquid and represent different markets with different types of values. To make this indicator possible, we normalize each indicator to make their values comparable to the unity. Once this is done, a simple average is performed between the three indicators.

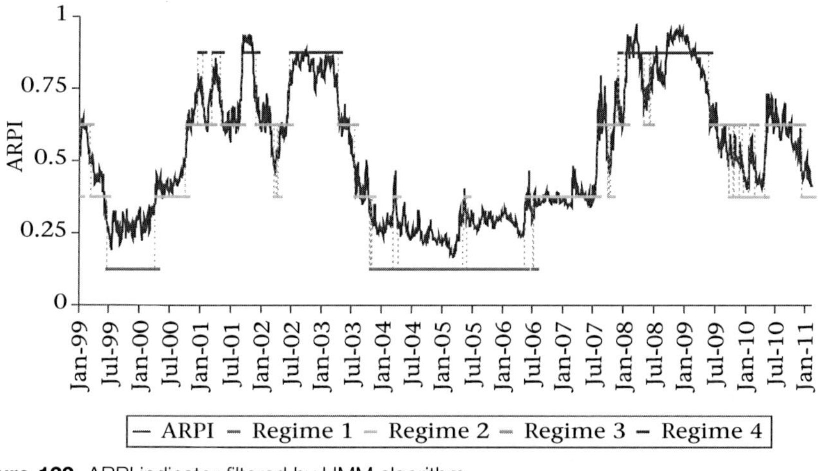

Figure 122 ARPI indicator filtered by HMM algorithm

In Figure 122, we observe that the ARPI lies between zero and one. So the normalization technique is then effective. When the indicator is close to one, the markets are in crisis. When the indicator is close to zero, the markets are calm. Around 2000 and 2001, the ARPI level is close to one. This represents the dot com crisis. In 2008, the ARPI is close to one and this is the subprime crisis.

The ARPI needs to be monitored as it expresses the health of financial markets. However, this indicator needs to be smoothed slightly to give a simple and clear indication. HMM will figure out the hidden state of this signal. In particular, we note that thanks to this filtering we detect crisis states in advance.

It is a kind of collaborative filtering approach, as from the different markets and index calculation plus its filtering we could already detect that something was going awry prior to the subprime crisis. We would not be able to predict the Lehman collapse but a market with high risk was clearly identified thanks to this monitoring.

Example 2: Signal associated with the Chinese equity universe

Chinese assets under management now amount to over $5 trillion. China displays fundamentally positive growth and in addition current regulations forbid Chinese investors from investing more than 5% of their assets outside China. So to obtain long term returns Chinese asset managers plough their money into Chinese stocks.

Table 34 A signal for the Chinese equity market

Property	Remark
Geographical region	Matters.
Sector exposure	Not relevant unless the investment is too concentrated.
Market observables and liquidity	No VIX-like index.
	No liquid interest rate curve.
	Stocks are liquid.
Market interconnection	Moderate.
Nature of the underlying	Linear.

In this situation, we can compute the Cross-Sectional Volatility (CSV) for Chinese market equity returns. This technique is described in (Martellini, July 2011). The basic formula is given by the following equation:

$$CSV_t = \sqrt{\sum_{i=1}^{N_t} w_{it}\left(r_{it} - \bar{r}_t^{(w_t)}\right)^2}$$

$$\bar{r}_t^{(w_t)} = \sum_{i=1}^{N_t} w_{it} r_{it} \tag{10.8}$$

Where w_{it} is the normalized market capitalization of the asset i at time t.

This approach is very interesting. It replaces the implied volatility index when not available or not sufficiently liquid. It is also a powerful means by which to tailor signals. Within their own portfolio composition, asset managers can build this signal easily and spot difficult times. This vital information will ensure right timing in terms of investment protection.

Example 3: Signal associated with a derivative portfolio

What is interesting here is to derive a signal adapted to non-linear portfolio. Asset managers and derivative desks alike have non-linear exposures. They need to build a signal that captures their portfolio regimes. It is vital for hedging and especially for implementing stress test portfolio hedging.

We use the following notations:

$$\Delta_i^{cash}(t) = \text{ delta cash expressed in euros of the i underlying}$$

$$S_i(t) = \text{ value of the i underlying}$$

$$CSV_\Delta(t) = \frac{1}{\sqrt{dt}}\sqrt{\sum_{i=1}^{N} w_{it}\left(r_{it} - \bar{r}_t^{(w_t)}\right)^2}$$

$$w_{it} = \frac{\left|\Delta_i^{cash}(t-1)\right|}{\sum_j \left|\Delta_j^{cash}(t-1)\right|}$$

$$r_{it} = \ln\left(\frac{S_i(t)}{S_i(t-1)}\right)$$

$$\bar{r}_t^{(w_t)} = \sum_{i=1}^{N_t} w_{it} r_{it} \quad (10.9)$$

In Equation (10.9), we show the cross sectional weighted volatility index (weights based on the deltas).

If we apply this methodology to a typical derivative desk we obtain the following result.

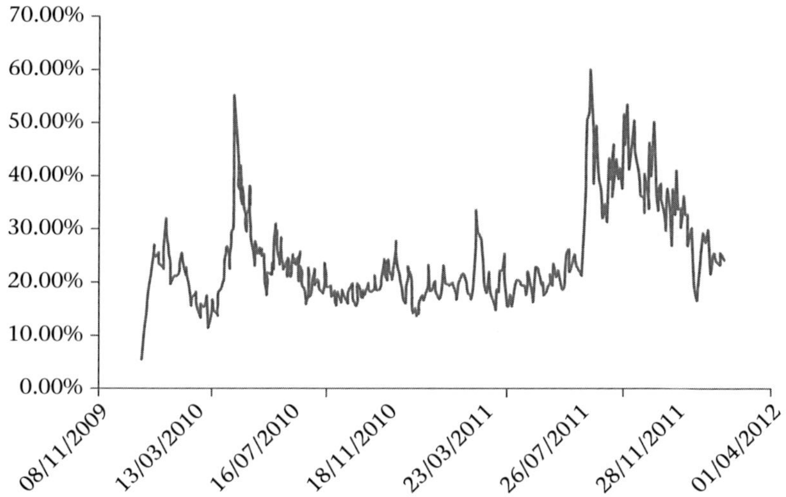

Figure 123 CSV for a non-linear portfolio

In Figure 123, we show the value of the CSV for a nonlinear portfolio. Peaks in the portfolio coincide with volatility peaks in the market.

This data can be filtered with three regimes in the HMM model which give the following reasonable results:

In Figure 124, we calculate the different regimes for the nonlinear portfolio. This information could guide derivatives risk managers to engage with trading when they feel that the derivative book is under pressure.

The choice of the signal combined with the HMM model gives an objective segmentation of the data. To a certain extent, we can colour the different periods of time and group them into clusters which belong to the same market state or regime.

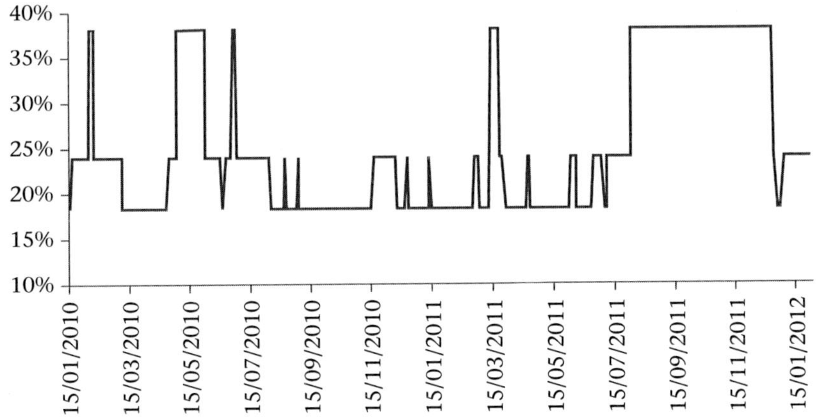

Figure 124 HMM model applied to cross sectional volatility

This segmentation is essential to understanding the behavior of assets, strategies and derivative books at different periods of time. Successful segmentation brings some color on the performance of assets and shows that if the market is globally efficient (no arbitrage opportunity) this is not true for a given regime.

In the next section, we analyze the key statistical properties of assets and investment strategies per market regime. This information can be seen as the dynamic cartography of the universe of instruments.

Asset and strategies cartography

In this section, we study the performance for different asset classes under different regimes. We use the ARPI index regimes segmented according to the HMM model.

We can take all types of asset classes (equities, real estate, commodities, Bonds MLT, Bond ST) and observe their returns and volatility according to regime. Here are the results:

Table 35 Returns by asset class and regime

Regime/Asset	Equity	Real estate	Commodity	Bond mlt	Bond st
1	17.39%	13.86%	27.92%	3.83%	3.05%
2	16.73%	15.83%	16.95%	1.24%	1.59%
3	4.66%	17.54%	13.93%	10.52%	7.97%
4	−5.01%	−12.30%	−23.34%	8.82%	6.72%
Total	9.01%	9.93%	10.76%	6.06%	4.80%

Table 36 Volatilities by asset class and regime

Regime/Asset	Equity	Real estate	Commodity	Bond mlt	Bond st
1	13.06%	11.31%	23.62%	6.50%	5.32%
2	15.42%	13.42%	19.82%	6.16%	4.97%
3	20.05%	19.37%	22.58%	7.07%	5.92%
4	38.13%	38.33%	34.89%	8.67%	6.87%
Total	22.72%	22.05%	25.31%	7.07%	5.72%

As expected, in Tables 35 and 36, we observe that market regimes discriminate between different assets. Equity for example, shows an annual return of 17.39% (Table 35: Returns) and a volatility of 13.06% (Table 37) under regime 1 (calm). It represents the best asset class in terms of Sharpe ratio (return on volatility). Under crisis regime, that is regime 4, equity performs very badly with a negative annual return −5.01% and a very high volatility of 38.13%. In such a regime, (Bonds MLT and Bonds ST provide good annual returns with moderate volatility.

Given these observations, it very natural to build alpha protection processes. Indeed, it is as simple as exiting risky assets when we are in crisis regime. Let us apply this approach with some simple examples. In Figure 125, we apply this mechanism on both the SX5E index and the Gold index. We observe that the rapid monitoring of crisis allows the investor to go out from risky assets at the right time.

Strategies are assets of a particular type. We can therefore study the conditional statistical properties per regime. In particular, we focus on value and growth funds. Here are the results for this list of funds:

Table 37 Cartography of value and growth strategies

Fund	Type	Calm	Volatile	Uncertain	Crisis
VTV US	Value	4.40%	16.46%	−26.93%	14.57%
RVT US	Growth	1.98%	13.35%	−10.78%	13.85%
CDCOGVI LX	Value	1.26%	13.37%	3.12%	0.52%
BMCIX US	Growth	7.05%	14.35%	−12.88%	25.92%

In Table 37, we observe that there are clear differences in performance by regime. What is remarkable is that in regime 3, fund performance is negative. This regime should thus be avoided! Under the other regimes, these funds perform reasonably well and we can include these funds in our portfolio allocation with clear control of risk.

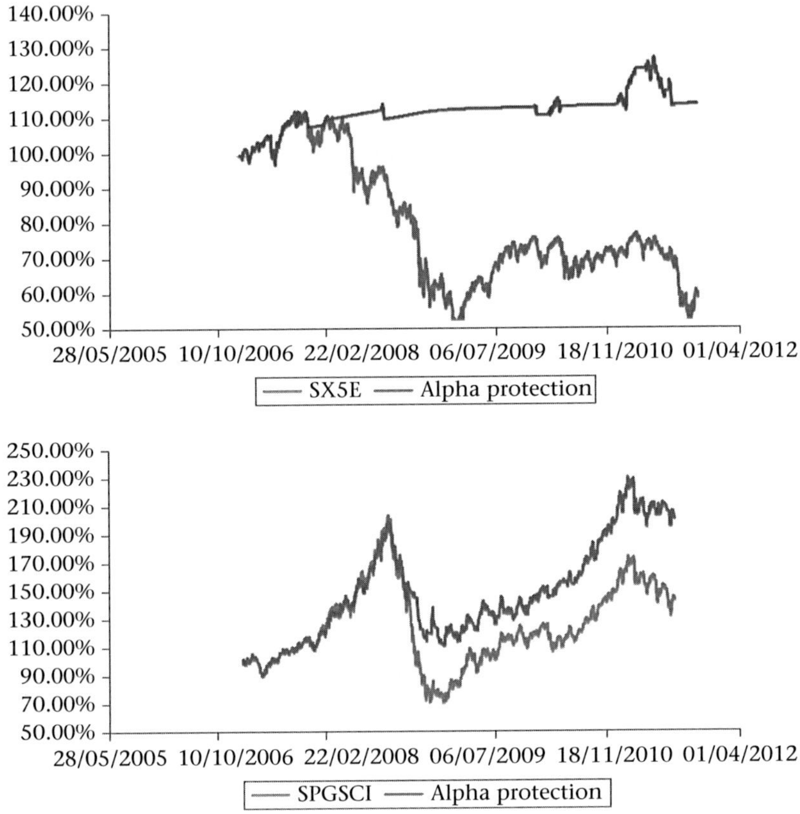

Figure 125 Strategies based on the HMM algorithm

Asset management

Let us now summarize our generic risk management technique. We start by looking at the investment universe. After this, a good signal is used to monitor market regimes. This signal is fed to the HMM algorithm to extract the market state or regime. Risk management then requires application of common sense with a fine estimate of the statistical properties of the assets concerned. This asset management technique tends to replace non-working correlation diversification (correlation breaks when most needed) by time diversification. This last identifies the different behaviors of assets per equivalent segments of times (regimes). Then when the assets show very negative returns in a given regime, asset allocation tends to remove them from the allocation universe. The timing of such a move is dictated by a sound market-monitoring tool. In the previous chapter, we concentrated on volatility signals. These are very reactive when the crisis displays the first signs of overheating. In practice, this mechanism of crisis detection allows extreme risk to be efficiently avoided. When the spike is detected the investor has plenty of time to hedge its positions in a systematic way and efficient way. It is a myth to believe that crisis has an immediate impact on all the markets. Once it is there it will last for some time and one should not bet and not risk manage at these crucial moments.

However, when the market rallies, the volatility signal is a lagging indicator and we need to complement it with a rapid calculation of drift, as in the Kelly strategy, or undertake change with the correlation signal, which shows a rapid return to equilibrium, as will be shown in the next section.

C Correlation signals

The future realized correlation is an important element in the pricing of many multi-asset derivatives. It is also a key component in the asset allocation problem and strategy optimization. In this chapter, we shall present a new methodology to infer the future correlation. It relies on another successful combination of statistics (CAPM model) and stochastic techniques (model-free skew asymptotic methods).

We propose a forward-looking correlation estimation which enables the estimation of a correlation risk premium.

We generalize the Pat Hagan formula for a basket of options which allows computation of the implied correlation skew. This measure is important in detecting crisis regimes.

There is the market of options on stocks and the market of options on the corresponding index. Thanks to our newly developed basket-implied smile calculation, we create a link between the basket skew calculated from the component and the one computed directly from indices. So we can follow up a correlation skew between these two markets. When the market is nervous, operators start hedging – mainly via options on indices (typically put options or crash puts). This distorts the correlation skew and gives a very clear signal of imminent crisis.

Simple basket model

To extract the future correlation we shall use options on stocks and options on indices. More precisely, we consider that the market trades at the same time the following set of options: stock options $\left(S_T^i - K\right)^+$and basket option$(B_T - K)^+$. The basket is defined as follows. $B_T = \sum_{i=1}^{N} w_i S_T^i$.

We will calculate the correlation between the asset i and the basket using the CAPM model combined with asymptotic calculation.

J.P. Fouque (2005) (see Fouque & Kollman, 2010) obtain similar results using perturbation theory. Their calculation is based on the partial differential equation pricing. They obtain a forward-looking estimation of the beta.

Estimating correlation level

In the CAPM model, returns of the basket are linked to the return of a given stock by the following simple relationship:

$$\frac{dS_t^i}{S_t^i} = \beta_i \frac{dB_t}{B_t} + \varepsilon_t^i \tag{10.10}$$

Where, ε_t^i represents the specific risk associated to the asset i. We note that:

$$\mathrm{E}\left(\frac{dB_t}{B_t}\varepsilon_t^i\right) = 0 \tag{10.11}$$

Using previous equations we note that volatilities are linked by the following equation:

$$\sigma_t^i = \sqrt{\beta_i^2 \sigma_B^2 + \sigma_\varepsilon^{i2}} \tag{10.12}$$

Therefore, we can compute the following:

$$d\sigma_t^{i2} = \beta_i^2 d\sigma_B^2 + d\sigma_\varepsilon^{i2} \tag{10.13}$$

From which we deduce the following simple result:

$$\mathrm{E}\left(\frac{dS_t^i}{S_t^i}\frac{d\sigma_t^{i2}}{\sigma_t^{i2}}\right) = \beta_i^3 \frac{\sigma_B^2}{\sigma_t^{i2}} \mathrm{E}\left(\frac{dB_t}{B_t}\frac{d\sigma_B^2}{\sigma_B^2}\right) \tag{10.14}$$

Now let us recall the model-free result of (Durreleman, 2005), where he shows that for any model one can infer the link between the dynamic and the implied volatility surface. Indeed, he shows that:

$$< \frac{dS_t}{S_t}, \frac{d\sigma_t^2}{\sigma_t^2} >= \lim_{T\to 0} 8\Sigma(K,T)\frac{\partial \Sigma(K,T)}{\partial \ln K} dt \tag{10.15}$$

By combining Equations (11.5) and (11.6), we obtain:

$$\sigma_t^i \frac{\partial \Sigma_i(K,T)}{\partial \ln K} = \beta_i^3 \frac{\sigma_B^2}{\sigma_t^{i2}} \sigma_B \frac{\partial \Sigma_B(K,T)}{\partial \ln K} \tag{10.16}$$

We finally obtain the beta estimation just like (Fouque & Kollman, 2010):

$$\beta_i = \frac{\sigma_t^i}{\sigma_B} \sqrt[1/3]{\frac{\frac{\partial \Sigma_i(K,T)}{\partial \ln K}}{\frac{\partial \Sigma_B(K,T)}{\partial \ln K}}} \tag{10.17}$$

This formula calculates the beta of the asset i using an expansion calculation.

The beta can also be expressed as a function of the correlation:

$$\beta_i = \frac{\sigma_t^i}{\sigma_B} \rho_{i,B} \tag{10.18}$$

Therefore, we have the following forward-looking correlation estimation:

$$\rho_{i,B} = \sqrt[1/3]{\frac{\frac{\partial \Sigma_i(K,T)}{\partial \ln K}}{\frac{\partial \Sigma_B(K,T)}{\partial \ln K}}} \tag{10.19}$$

This formula can be extended to two assets pertaining to the same index.[2].

With this formula, we can define implied correlation estimation from the skews, calculated as an average over all couples belonging to the index. We obtain the following forward-looking estimator of the correlation from the skews:

$$\rho_{\text{implied}}^{\text{skew}} = \frac{1}{\frac{n(n-1)}{2}} \frac{1}{\left(\frac{\partial \Sigma_B(K,T)}{\partial \ln K}\right)^{\frac{2}{3}}} \sum_{i<j} \sqrt[1/3]{\frac{\partial \Sigma_i(K,T)}{\partial \ln K} \frac{\partial \Sigma_j(K,T)}{\partial \ln K}} \tag{10.20}$$

This equation tells us that a correlation position is similar to a spread of skew positions.[3]

This equation is forward looking and can be compared with the historical correlation. This difference can be used to calculate the correlation risk premium.

We make the analysis as of the end of 2010.

In Figure **126**, we observe that the 3m historical correlation at the end of 2010 is starting to decline. This phenomenon was identified as some kind of correlation burst. Less correlation between assets is a positive sign for the equity markets.

---

[2] The same methodology applied to two assets belonging to the same index gives the simple and elegant formula: $\rho_{i,j} = \sqrt[1/3]{\frac{\frac{\partial \Sigma_i(K,T)}{\partial \ln K} \frac{\partial \Sigma_j(K,T)}{\partial \ln K}}{\left(\frac{\partial \Sigma_B(K,T)}{\partial \ln K}\right)^2}}$.

[3] $\rho_{i,j}++ \quad \Leftrightarrow \quad \frac{\partial \Sigma_i(K,T)}{\partial \ln K}++\& \frac{\partial \Sigma_j(K,T)}{\partial \ln K}++\& \frac{\partial \Sigma_B(K,T)}{\partial \ln K}--$

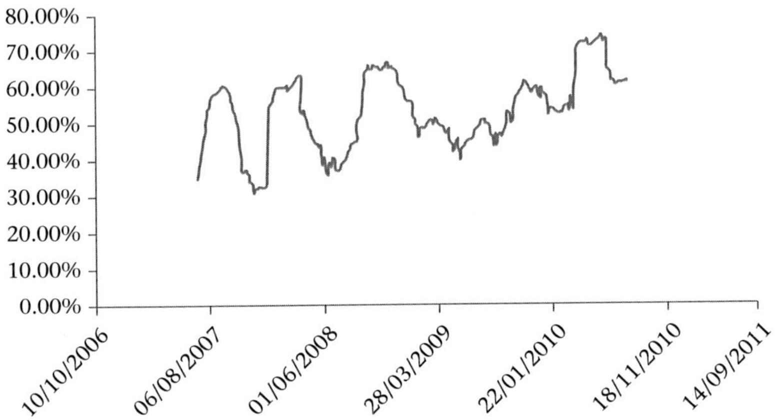

Figure 126 Average historical correlation for the SX5E universe

In practice, traders use another implied correlation measure. It is based solely on at the money implied volatilities. Indeed, in 2004, several papers (Bossu & Gu, 2004; Tierens & Anadu, 2004; Statman & Scheid, 2004) have addressed the implied calculation of the correlation based on at the money basket options or through dispersion trades (variance swap on a basket versus a basket of variance swaps). We retain the Bossu approximation that is given by the following equation:

$$\rho_{\text{implied}}^{\text{atm}} = \frac{\Sigma_B(ATM,T)^2}{\frac{1}{n}\sum_{i=1}^{n}\Sigma_i(ATM,T)^2} \tag{10.21}$$

In Figure 127, we observe that the implied correlation calculated from the skews is stable at a relatively high level from March 2009 until November 2010.

From basket at the money volatilities and using a moment matching approach we can also calculate forward implied correlation estimation.

In Figure 128, a comparison is made between the difference correlation estimators: correlation from historical data, correlation from implied volatilities and correlation from implied skews.

The historical correlation produces a smooth curve, as expected. This is due to the fact it is a lagging indicator and there is a small change in the data set between one day and the next. The implied correlation from the volatilities uses the SX5E at the money volatility seen as an index and seen as a basket (we take capitalization factors into account). The correlation implied from this technique is quite commonly followed and is forward looking. It is volatile due to its usage of a massive amount of volatile volatilities. The last indicator based on the skews is less volatile

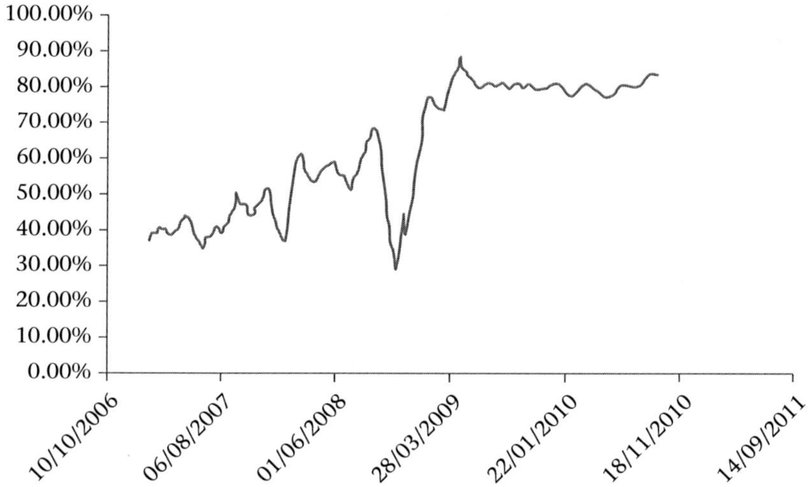

Figure 127 Average Implied correlation using the skew calculation

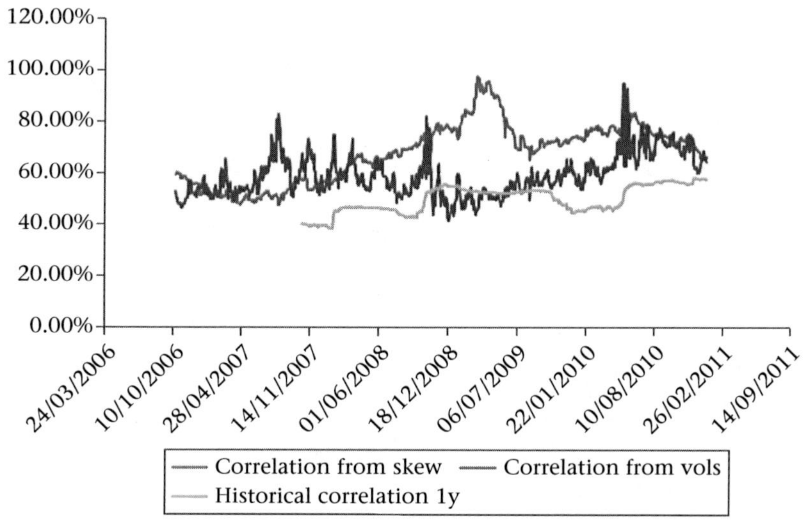

Figure 128 Comparison of three different correlation estimators (historical, implied from volatilities and implied from skews)

even if forward looking. The key feature of the correlation skew estimator stems from the following observations:

We observe that a non-linear estimator can detect something new for this forward-looking estimator. When we compare the forward correlation skew based on the historical one (we study the ratio in Figure **129**) we observe many interesting properties:

1. The ratio between the forward-looking skew estimator and the future correlation realization series is highly mean reverting.
2. The minimum of this series is 1, meaning that this new estimator gives an estimate of the correlation-risk premium.
3. The times where the ratio is close to 1 (no risk premium is always followed by an explosion in risk premium). This new risk indicator provides excellent timing for dispersion trades.

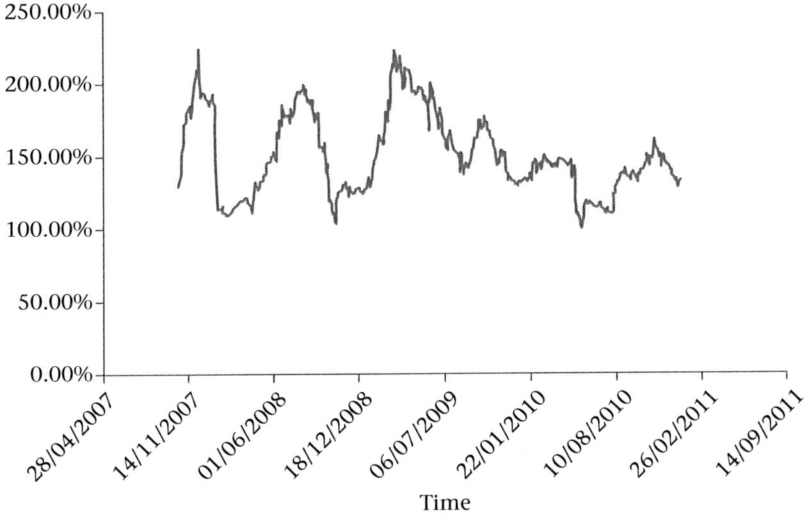

Figure 129 Ratio of the implied correlations from the skew and the historical correlation

Implied correlation skew

Let us work under the general diffusive dynamic:

$$\begin{aligned} \frac{dS_{i,t}}{S_{i,t}} &= \sigma_i dW^S_{i,t}, \quad i=1,\ldots,n \\ \frac{d\sigma_i}{\sigma_i} &= \alpha_i dW^\sigma_{i,t} \\ &< dW^u_{i,t}, dW^v_{j,t} >= \rho^{u,v}_{i,j}\left(S_{1,t},\ldots,S_{n,t},Z_{i,j,t}\right)dt,\ldots,u,v\in\{S,\sigma\} \end{aligned} \tag{10.22}$$

This dynamic includes stochastic volatility and local correlation. The correlation can be a function of asset prices and some extra diffusive factor $Z_{i,j,t}$. The reason for this choice is to match the PnL explanation equation for a particular hedger (delta and vega). We are interested in deriving the basket skew implied from the previous dynamic.

We introduce some notations for the sequel. These appear naturally during the calculation.

$$\omega_i = \frac{p_i S_i}{\sum_{j=1}^{n} p_j S_j}$$

$$\sigma_B^2 = \sum_{i,j=1}^{n} \rho_{i,j}^{SS} \sigma_i \sigma_j \omega_i \omega_j$$

$$\beta_{i,j} = \frac{\rho_{i,j}^{SS} \sigma_i \sigma_j \omega_i \omega_j}{\sum_{i,j=1}^{n} \rho_{i,j}^{SS} \sigma_i \sigma_j \omega_i \omega_j}$$

$$\beta_i = \sum_{j=1}^{n} \beta_{i,j} = \sum_{j=1}^{n} \beta_{j,i} \tag{10.23}$$

These parameters appear naturally in the description of the basket option:

- w_i Proportion of the asset i in the total basket.
- σ_B Basket normal volatility.
- $\beta_{i,j}$ Proportion of the covariance of the asset i with the asset j within the total basket variance.
- β_i Contribution of the asset i within the total basket variance.

If you consider the following variable:

$$X_t = B_T^{\frac{1}{\sigma_B}}$$

This choice is made in such a manner as to make the variable X as close as possible to a Brownian motion. We obtain the following result:

$$dX_t = \frac{\sum_{i=1}^{n} \sigma_i \omega_i dW_{i,t}^S}{\sigma_B} - \frac{1}{2} \ln X_t \frac{d\sigma_B^2}{\sigma_B^2} + \theta_t dt$$

$$\frac{d\sigma_B^2}{\sigma_B^2} = \sum_{i,j=1}^{n} \beta_{i,j} \frac{d\rho_{i,j}^{SS}}{\rho_{i,j}^{SS}} + 2 \sum_{i=1}^{n} \beta_i \frac{d\sigma_i}{\sigma_i} + 2 \sum_{i=1}^{n} \beta_i \frac{d\omega_i}{\omega_i} \tag{10.24}$$

With θ_t a drift that vanishes at time zero.

With this formulation, we see that X behaves like a local volatility model with a local volatility of the form:

$$\sigma^2(X_t) = Var\left(\frac{\sum_{i=1}^{n}\sigma_i\omega_i dW_{i,t}}{\sigma_B} - \frac{1}{2}\ln X_t \frac{d\sigma_B^2}{\sigma_B^2}\middle| X_t\right) \tag{10.25}$$

We obtain the classical Pat Hagan formula in the one-dimensional case, as mentioned in the Chapter 3. This means that if we estimate the previous local volatility, we are able to price vanilla options and therefore deduce the skew. The term θ_t is quite complex and difficult to handle. However, as noted, this term vanishes when the time to maturity goes to zero. With this property, we are able to obtain exact smile results close to today.

To be able to make this calculation, we shall relax a few assumptions. We start by considering a sub-model, the multi-stochastic volatility model.

Multi-dimensional stochastic volatility

In the case of no local correlation, we can use the previous approach combined with a moment matching approach. More precisely, we have the following equation:

$$\begin{aligned}
X_t &= B_T^{\frac{1}{\sigma_B}} \\
\frac{dX_t}{X_t} &= \sigma(X_t)\, dZ_t \\
\sigma^2(X_t) &= 1 - 2\ln(X_t)\sum_{i,j=1}^{n}\frac{\sigma_i}{\sigma_B} w_i\beta_j\alpha_j\rho_{i,j}^{S,\sigma} + \ln^2(X_t)\sum_{i,j=1}^{n}\beta_i\alpha_i\beta_j\alpha_j\rho_{i,j}^{\sigma,\sigma}
\end{aligned} \tag{10.26}$$

We moment match the coefficients for the terms $\ln(X_t)$ and$\ln^2(X_t)$. It gives a new formula à la Pat Hagan with equivalent correlation $\tilde{\rho}$and volatility of volatility $\tilde{\alpha}$:

$$\begin{aligned}
\tilde{\alpha}^2 &= \sum_{i,j=1}^{n}\beta_i\alpha_i\beta_j\alpha_j\rho_{i,j}^{\sigma,\sigma} \\
\tilde{\rho}\tilde{\alpha} &= \sum_{i,j=1}^{n}\frac{\sigma_i}{\sigma_B} w_i\beta_j\alpha_j\rho_{i,j}^{S,\sigma}
\end{aligned} \tag{10.27}$$

Basically, we have created an equivalent local volatility model with simplified parameters.

In the multi-dimensional case, the skew is generated from the term $\tilde{\rho}\tilde{\alpha}$and the curvature from the term$\tilde{\alpha}^2$. Their formulation in the multi-dimensional case calls for some remarks:

Multi-dimensional skew has many sources:

- Mono underlying skew through the diagonal term$\tilde{\rho}\tilde{\alpha}$. This is represented by the sum$\sum_{i=1}^{n} \frac{\sigma_i}{\sigma_B} w_i \beta_i \alpha_i \rho_{i,i}^{S,\sigma}$. Hedging-wise, the trader sees in his PnL a contribution of the diagonal vanna of the asset i in his PnL $\Delta PnL = \cdots + w_i \frac{\beta_i}{\sigma_B} \frac{\partial^2 \pi}{\partial S_i \partial \sigma_i} \Delta S_i \Delta \sigma_i$. This accounts for the change in the vega of the asset i when the spot of the asset i moves.
- Cross contribution: This represents the change of the vega of the asset j when the trader hedges the delta of the asset i. More precisely, it is calculated using the off diagonal terms of$\tilde{\rho}\tilde{\alpha}$i.e. $\sum_{i \neq j}^{n} w_i \frac{\beta_j}{\sigma_B} \alpha_j \sigma_i \rho_{i,j}^{S,\sigma}$. Hedging wise the trader sees in his PnL a contribution of the cross vanna of the asset i in his PnL

$$\Delta PnL = \cdots + w_i \frac{\beta_j}{\sigma_B} \frac{\partial^2 \pi}{\partial S_i \partial \sigma_j} \Delta S_i \Delta \sigma_j.$$

Homogeneous case

Applying the previous formula to a homogeneous basket case, we obtain general rules that are useful for rapid assessment.

We simplify the model by stating that all stocks have the same volatility, there is a uniform correlation between two different stocksρ^S, a uniform correlation between volatilities ρ^σ and all stocks have the same volatility and volatility of volatility.

We also assume that all stocks have the same skew generated by unique correlation number $\rho^{S,\sigma}$.

$$\frac{dS_{i,t}}{S_{i,t}} = \sigma \, dW_{i,t}^S, i = 1, \ldots, n$$
$$\frac{d\sigma_i}{\sigma_i} = \alpha \, dW_{i,t}^\sigma$$
$$< dW_{i,t}^S, dW_{j,t}^S >= \rho^S dt,$$
$$< dW_{i,t}^\sigma, dW_{j,t}^\sigma >= \rho^\sigma \, dt$$

We assume that the skew for each underlying is the same:

$$< dW_{i,t}^S, dW_{i,t}^\sigma >= \rho^{S,\sigma} \, dt$$

With this specification, we lack some necessary information. This concerns the correlation of a stock with the volatility of another stock. We saw previously that this number entered in the basket skew calculation via the cross vanna sensitivity.

We therefore complete the correlation matrix by assuming a constant correlation for the cross vanna terms:

$$\rho_{i,j}^{S,\sigma} = \rho^{\sigma} \rho^{S,\sigma} \quad i \neq j$$

The resulting equivalent parameters satisfy:

$$\sigma_B^2 = \sigma_S^2 \left(\rho^S \left(1 - \frac{1}{n} \right) + \frac{1}{n} \right)$$

$$\tilde{\alpha}^2 = \alpha^2 \left(\rho^{\sigma} \left(1 - \frac{1}{n} \right) + \frac{1}{n} \right)$$

$$\tilde{\rho}\tilde{\alpha} = \frac{\alpha \sigma_S}{\sigma_B} \left(\rho^{\sigma} \rho^{S,\sigma} \left(1 - \frac{1}{n} \right) + \frac{1}{n} \right)$$

Taking the limit for a large basket, we obtain the following results:

Stock representation	Baske representation	Description	Comment
σ_S	$\sigma_B = \sigma_S \sqrt{\rho^S}$	Basket is less volatile. However, in case of crisis, the correlation increases.	Correlation breaks when most needed.
$\rho^{S,\sigma}$ ρ^{σ} ρ^S	$\tilde{\rho} = \sqrt{\frac{\rho^{\sigma}}{\rho^S}} \rho^{S,\sigma}$	$\rho^{S,\sigma}$ explains the skew of the stock. ρ^{σ} describes the average correlation between the different volatilities. ρ^S describes the average correlation between the stocks.	Typically, volatilities are less correlated than the stocks themselves. We obtain a lower correlation between the basket and its volatility. And this implies a lower skew. This effect worsens because of the next row.
α	$\tilde{\alpha} = \alpha \sqrt{\rho^{\sigma}}$	α Describes the volatility of the volatility.	The basket volatility of the volatility is lower. It uses a similar formula than the basket volatility.

Typical values for $\rho^S = 80\%, \rho^\sigma = 60\%$, so we have the following order of magnitude:

$$\frac{\sigma_B}{\sigma_S} \approx 90\%, \frac{\tilde{\alpha}}{\alpha} = 75\%, \frac{\tilde{\rho}}{\rho^{S,\sigma}} = 85\%$$

With this numerical application, we observe that the basket skew is lower than its counterpart for each stock. This is in contradiction with what is observed in data. In order to fit the observed data, we need to add some skew to the basket based on a local correlation model.

The homogeneous approximation does not explain the difference between the skew for the index seen as a basket and seen as a mono underlying index.

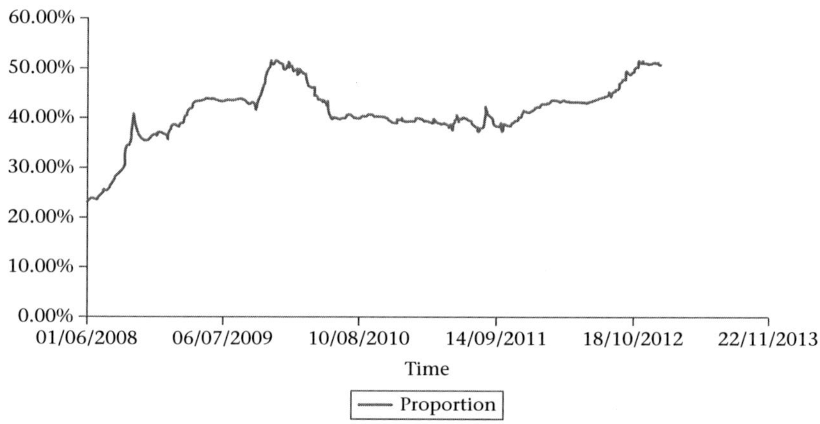

Figure 130 Proportion of the index skew from the individual skews

In Figure 130, we perform the real calculation taking into account all assets with their own volatility, volatility of volatility, their own skew and calculating all the correlations. We observe that only a fraction of the index skew is explained by the multi-stochastic volatility model. We represent the proportion of the explained skew and see that it is statistically less than 50% of the index skew.

In Figure 130 we illustrate the proportion of the index skew that is explained by the individual skews (vanna terms) and the cross skews (coss vanna terms).

Hence there is a missing ingredient without which we cannot explain the observed skew. This is known as the correlation skew. We achieve this modeling in the next section introducing the local correlation model.

Local correlation model

We assume that the correlation is diffusive.

More precisely, we set the following correlation dynamic:

$$\frac{d\rho_{i,j}^{SS}}{\rho_{i,j}^{SS}} = \alpha_{i,j} dZ_t^{\rho}$$

We assume that the Brownian driving the correlation is correlated both to spot and volatility drivers.

$$< dZ_t^{\rho} dW_{i,t}^{S} >= \rho_{i\rho}^{S} dt \quad \text{And} \quad < dZ_t^{\rho} dW_{i,t}^{\sigma} >= \rho_{i\rho}^{\sigma} dt$$

Based on these assumptions, we can obtain the following equivalent local volatility for the modified process:

$$\begin{aligned}\sigma^2(X_t) = \quad & 1 \quad \textbf{No Correl} \qquad \textbf{Extra term with Correl} \\ & -2\ln(X_t)\left\{\sum_{i,j=1}^{n} \frac{\sigma_i}{\sigma_B} w_i \beta_j \alpha_j \rho_{i,j}^{S,\sigma} + \frac{1}{2} \sum_{i,i_1,j_1}^{n} \frac{\sigma_i}{\sigma_B} w_i \beta_{i_1 j_1} \alpha_{i_1 j_1}^{\rho} \rho_{i,\rho}^{S}\right\} \\ & + \ln^2(X_t)\left\{\sum_{i,j=1}^{n} \beta_i \alpha_i \beta_j \alpha_j \rho_{i,j}^{\sigma,\sigma} + \frac{1}{4} \sum_{i_1,j_1,i_2,j_2}^{n} \beta_{i_1 j_1} \beta_{i_1 j_1} \alpha_{i_2 j_2}^{\rho} \alpha_{i_1 j_1}^{\rho} + \sum_{i,i_1,j_1}^{n} \beta_i \beta_{i_1 j_1} \alpha_{i_1 j_1}^{\rho} \rho_{i,\rho}^{\sigma}\right\}\end{aligned}$$

For a local correlation model, the extra terms look like:

$$\begin{aligned}\sigma^2(X_t) \quad = \quad & 1 \qquad \textbf{No Correl} \qquad \textbf{Extra term with Correl} \\ - \quad & 2\ln(X_t) \left\{\sum_{i,j=1}^{n} \frac{\sigma_i}{\sigma_B} w_i \beta_j \alpha_j \rho_{i,j}^{S,\sigma} + \frac{1}{2} \sigma_B \frac{d\lambda}{dB} \sum_{i_1,j_1}^{n} \beta_{i_1 j_1} \frac{1-\rho_{i_1 j_1}}{\rho_{i_1 j_1}(1-\lambda)+\lambda}\right\} \\ + \quad & \ln^2(X_t) \left\{\sum_{i,j=1}^{n} \beta_i \alpha_i \beta_j \alpha_j \rho_{i,j}^{\sigma,\sigma} + \ldots\right\}\end{aligned}$$

The previous equation states how the skew and the curvature of the basket smile is affected when introducing the local correlation.

In particular, the skew is magnified through the introduction of the negative correlation between the spots and the correlation level. We introduce the magnifying factor as follows:

$$1 + \frac{\sum_{i,j \neq k}^{n} \sigma_i w_i \rho_{i,\rho}^{S} \beta_{j,k} \alpha_{j,k}^{\rho}}{\sum_{i,j=1}^{n} \sigma_i w_i \beta_j \alpha_j \rho_{i,j}^{S,\sigma}}$$

In the homogeneous case, where we have the individual skew and all parameters of correlation between volatility, correlation and asset, we can back out at the level of volatility of correlation, a unique number that summarizes the correlation skew measure.

More precisely, we calibrate the volatility of volatility for the index and its implied correlation and compute the implied volatility of correlation using the following formula:

$$\alpha^{\rho} = \frac{\rho_I \alpha_I \Sigma_I - \sum_{i,j=1}^{n} \sigma_i w_i \beta_j \alpha_j \rho_{i,j}^{S,\sigma}}{\sum_{i,j \neq k}^{n} \sigma_i w_i \rho_{i,\rho}^{S} \beta_{j,k}}$$

This number is not very common. It represents the volatility of the correlation process. It is the level to be input in a basket stochastic correlation model to fit the index skew.

To remain in the usual pricing format, we can visualize the impact of such a newly implied parameter on the extra skew that is generated within the local correlation model.

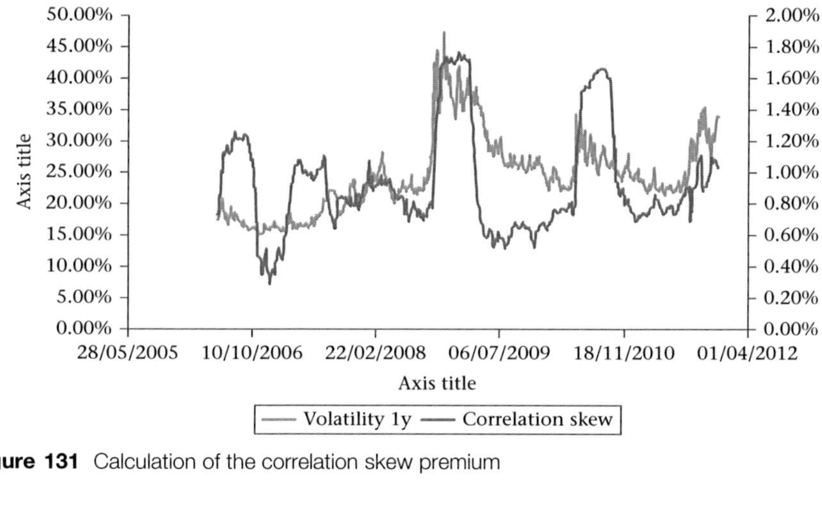

Figure 131 Calculation of the correlation skew premium

We observe in Figure 131, that the correlation risk premium expressed as the difference of volatilities between 90% strike and the 100% strike is normally around 0.60%–0.80% for one year options. We also observe that when the volatility explodes (change of regime) this spread jumps to a level of 1.60%. We also see that correlation reverts to its original level faster than the volatility. The probable reason why the correlation skew jumps when the regime changes is that the index skew jumps (market buys protection) whereas the individual stock skew (less liquid) does not immediately follow.

These observations have several implications:

- Just like volatility, the correlation skew indicator gives the market timing for regime changes (detects a crisis).
- It reverts to normal equilibrium faster than volatility does (this gives a faster signal for the market recovery).
- In case of change of regime, market makers can continue pricing dispersion spreads by accurately adjusting the spread between the individual components and the index skew.

Once again, we observe the importance of increasing the interactions between the stochastic calculus and the statistics. It is of utmost importance to have risk-monitoring tools that allow you to detect the changes in regime (market crisis and reveries). For each regime, a special pricing policy is implemented following its own invariants. We therefore move from one Newtonian model with special parameters to another special Newtonian model. The constants (invariants) used in pricing are extracted in Kelplerian fashion and need to be monitored and adjusted. They are not universal but they seem to be stable over time.

General Conclusion

Quantitative pricing and investment are art forms which can profit from the exact sciences. These sciences are more than two hundred years old and show us the path to take as well as differences with the financial world. Financial equations can evolve with regulation and social behavior. However, central limit theorems establish some statistical attractors which are important invariants that should be captured. We present a methodology that combines statistical invariants with classical pricing models. We also show how martingale models, usually designed for pricing, can be used to assess the quality of an investment strategy. We define measurable quantities, that we call toxicity indices, which allow us to rank financial products and investment strategies.

We complement modeling tools by proposing risk-monitoring mechanisms to follow up on market regimes. We establish some essential properties needed to design the right signals to follow. We also present some powerful algorithms to filter these signals and extract a simple actionable output.

This book seeks to aid the general reader by offering an overall methodology to play with models and which take advantage of hindsight. The stance here is practical and provides techniques to build sound quantitative investment strategies and to test them properly. One main takeaway is that models are approximations of shifting reality. Contrary to the situation in physics, the relevance of financial models must be persistently monitored to ensure that they fit their end purpose. In pricing, they are designed to account for the cost of hedge while in investment they are designed to help predict the future and control risk.

Solutions

Exercise 1

1. The main purpose of a financial model is to provide a means to explain the PnL evolution. Financial models differ from physical models in that they do not have universal laws on which we can base modeling. Therefore their objective is more modest.
2. Financial models are not universal. They are not based on immutable principles such as the principle of conservation of energy, for example. They depend on the prevailing market regime. One should remain cautious as to the validity of models and keep measuring their performances.
3. The shape of the skew of the form a+b/sqrt (T) is purely descriptive. This is not predictive. It is a representation that simplifies the world but does not predict where it goes. This is a Keplerian model. The trouble with this approach is that even if at any time this type of representation is sufficient to describe the observed data, it remains dependent on the prevailing equilibrium. We will not be able to predict the equilibrium but we can take it into account, once established, to model something else. With models of this type, we are not market makers but market followers.

Exercise 2

1. We perform a second order expansion of the function f around the expected value of the process X and then take the average. We obtain:

$$E\big(f(X)\big) \cong f(E(X)) + \frac{1}{2} Var(X) f''(E(X))$$

In the multi-dimensional case, we do the same:

$$f(x_1,\dots,x_n) = f(x_1(0),\dots,x_n(0)) + \sum_{i=1}^{n} (x_i - x_i(0))\, \partial_{x_i} f(x_1(0),\dots,x_n(0))$$
$$+ \frac{1}{2} \sum_{i,j=1}^{n} (x_i - x_i(0)) \big(x_j - x_j(0)\big)\, \partial_{x_i x_j} f(x_1(0),\dots,x_n(0))$$

We apply the expectations and obtain the result:

$$E\left(f\left(X_1,\ldots,X_n\right)\right) \cong f\left(E\left(X_1\right),\ldots,E\left(X_n\right)\right) + \frac{1}{2}\sum_{i,j=1}^{n} CoVar\left(X_i,X_j\right)\frac{\partial^2 f}{\partial x_i \partial x_j}\left(E\left(X_1\right),\ldots,E\left(X_n\right)\right)$$

Exercise 3

	Payoff	General rule	Numerical application
Call	$(S_T - S_0)^+$	$\pi_C \cong \sigma S_0 \sqrt{\frac{T}{2\pi}}$	$\pi_C \cong 16$
Asian	$\left(\frac{1}{T}\int_0^T S_t dt - S_0\right)^+$	$\pi_A \cong \frac{1}{\sqrt{3}}\sigma S_0 \sqrt{\frac{T}{2\pi}}$	$\pi_A \cong 9.22$
Lookback Max	$(M_T - S_0)$ with $M_t = \max_{s\in[0,t]} S_s$,	$\pi_L \cong 2\sigma S_0 \sqrt{\frac{T}{2\pi}}$	$\pi_L \cong 32$

It is of great importance to know the order of magnitude for prices. This is a classic approach for physicists. Indeed, thanks to this the modeller has a first inkling into priorities and knows where he needs to go to fetch hedging cost and knows how to extend his model if needed.

Exercise 4

1. In the case of a stationary local volatility (does not depend on time) we can use the BBF formula (Beresticky-Busca-Florent), which states that the implied volatility is equal to the harmonic mean of the local volatility

$$\sigma_{imp}(K) \cong \frac{\ln(K/S_0)}{\int_{S_0}^{F} \frac{1}{s\sigma(s)} ds}$$

Applying this formula to our form of local volatility gives:

$$\sigma_{imp}(K) \cong \frac{\ln(K/S_0)}{\int_{S_0}^{F} \frac{1}{s+\lambda} ds} = \sigma \frac{\ln(K/S_0)}{\ln\left((K+\lambda)/(S_0+\lambda)\right)}$$

2. We apply Ito formula:

$$df(S_t) = f'(S_t)\,dS_t + \frac{1}{2}f''(S_t)\,\sigma^2 S_t^2\,dt,$$

For the function $\left(\sqrt{S_t} - \lambda\right)$. We obtain $=: d\left(\sqrt{S_t} - \lambda\right) = \sigma\left(\sqrt{S_t} - \lambda\right) dW_t$. Therefore $\sqrt{S_t} - \lambda$ is a shifted lognormal

$$\sqrt{S_t} - \lambda = \left(\sqrt{S_0} - \lambda\right) \exp\left(\sigma W_t - \frac{1}{2}\sigma^2 t\right)$$

3. Assume that the local volatility $\sigma^2(s) = \alpha^2 \ln^2\left(\frac{s}{S_0}\right) + 2\rho\alpha\sigma_0 \ln\left(\frac{s}{S_0}\right) + \sigma_0^2$. We then use the BBF formula $\sigma_{imp}(K) \cong \frac{\ln(K/S_0)}{\int_{S_0}^{F} \frac{1}{s\sigma(s)} ds}$. It gives the following implied volatility function

$$\sigma_{imp}(K) = \sigma_0 f\left(\frac{\ln\left(\frac{S_0}{K}\right)}{\sigma_0}\right), \text{ with } f(x) = \frac{\alpha x}{\ln\left(\frac{\sqrt{\alpha^2 x^2 - 2\alpha x\rho + 1} - \rho + \alpha x}{1-\rho}\right)}$$

This is the classical Pat Hagan formula for short-term maturity (cf. Hagan, Kumar, Lesniewski, & Woodward, 2002).

4. For a given diffusion $d\log(S_t) = \sigma_t dW_t - \frac{1}{2}\sigma_t^2 dt$. When we integrate from 0 to t, we obtain: $\log\left(\frac{S_t}{S_0}\right) = \int_0^t \sigma_s dW_s - \frac{1}{2}\int_0^t \sigma_s^2 ds$. Taking the expectation: $E\frac{1}{T}\int_0^T \sigma_s^2 ds = -2E\left(\log\left(\frac{S_T}{S_0}\right)\right)$. Applying Peter Carr's formula, we obtain the following decomposition:

$$\begin{aligned} E\frac{1}{T}\int_0^T \sigma_s^2 ds &= \sigma_{BS}^2 \\ &-2\left(\int_0^{S_0} \frac{1}{K^2}\left(\mathrm{Put}_{BS}(K,T,\Sigma(K,T)) - \mathrm{Put}_{BS}(K,T,\sigma_{BS})\right) dK \right. \\ &\left. + \int_{S_0}^{\infty} \frac{1}{K^2}\left(Call_{BS}(K,T,\Sigma(K,T)) - \mathrm{Call}_{BS}(K,T,\sigma_{BS})\right) dK\right) \end{aligned}$$

Exercise 5

The toxicity dividend index is built using two assumptions, the constant dividend amount and the dividend yield.

Under the proportional dividend model, the price of the cliquelet is given by:

$$\pi_{pd} = 1 - \frac{D_{12}}{S_0}$$

Under the constant dividend amount, the price of the cliquelet is given by:

$$\pi_{pd} = 1 - \frac{D_{12}}{S_0} \exp\left(\sigma^2 T_1\right)$$

The dividend toxicity index is equal to:

$$\phi_{div} = \frac{D_{12}}{S_0} \frac{\left|\exp\left(\sigma^2 T_1\right) - 1\right|}{2 - \frac{D_{12}}{S_0}\left(1 + \exp\left(\sigma^2 T_1\right)\right)}$$

A proxy for small dividend yield and volatility is then given by:

$$\phi_{div} \approx \frac{1}{2} \frac{D_{12}}{S_0} \sigma^2 T_1$$

We observe that the toxicity index for the cliquelet is dependent on the volatility level and the yield level. The higher the volatility, the higher the toxicity index.

Bibliography

Abergel, & Tachet. (2009). On a non-linear partial integro-differential equation.

Albanese. (2007). Operator methods, Abelian processes and dynamic conditioning.

Avellaneda. (2002). Reconstructing the volatility surface. *Risk Magazine.*

Berestycki, Busca, & Florent. (2001). Asymptotics and calibration of local volatility models.

Buehler. (2010). Dividends modelling.

Burtschell, Gregory, & Laurent. (2005). Beyond the Gaussian Copula: stochastic and local correlation.

Chibane, & Law. (October 2012). A volatilite interest in local volatility: a hybrid model for long dated equity structures.

Dupire. (1994). Pricing with a smile. *Risk Magazine.*

Dupire. (2004). Basket skew. *Working Paper.*

Durreleman. (2005). *From spot to implied volatilitites.*

Fouque, & Kollman. (2010). Calibration of stock Betas from skews of implied volatilities.

Gatheral. (2006). *The volatilty surface, a Practitioner's guide.* Wiley.

Gatheral, & Wang. (2011). The variational most-likely-path.

Gatheral, W. (2010). The Heat-Kernel most-likely-path approximation.

Guyon, & Henry-Labordère. (2010). From spot volatilites to implied volatilities.

Hagan, Kumar, Lesniewski, & Woodward. (2002). Managing smile risk. *Wilmott Magazine,* 84–108.

Karoui, E., & Durreleman. (2007). *Basket skew.*

Kelly. (s.d.). A new interpretation of information rate. *Bell System Technical Journal, 35,* 917–926.

Langnau. (2009). *Introduction into local correlation modelling.*

Loulidi. (2008). *Modélisation stochastique en finance, application à la construction d'un modèle à changement de régime avec des sauts.* Bordeaux: Ecole doctorale de Mathématiques et Informatique.

Loulidi, Reghaï, & Treulet. (2008). *How to predict volatility quantitatively.* Paris: Natixis Securities.

Mandelbrot, B. (Juin 4, 1962). Extraits des comptes rendus des séances de l'Académie des sciences, 3968–3970.

Martellini. (July 2011). *Introducing a new form of volatility index: the cross sectional volatility index.* Paris: Institut Louis Bachelier, EDHEC Risk Institute.

Martin, & Schöneborn. (2011). Mean Reversion pays, but costs. *Risk Magazine.*

Martini, C. (2009). Calibrating SVI model - Zeliade white paper.

Metane. (2009, February 17). Récupéré sur SSRN: http://ssrn.com/abstract=962461

Piterbarg. (2006). Markovian projection for volatility. *Risk Magazine.*

Reghaï. (April 2006). The hybrid most likely path. *Risk Magazine.*

Reghaï. (Février 2008). Relax and smile: calibration du modèle de volatilité locale et extensions. *Conférence TAM TAM.*
Reghaï, Boya, & Vong. (2012). Quantum local volatility. *SSRN.*
Reghaï, Klaeyle, & Boukhaffa. (2012). LSV with a mixing weight. *SSRN.*
Reghai, Vong. Boya. (2012). Quantum local volatility.
Thorp. (1966). The Kelly criterion in Black Jack Sports Betting and the stock market.
Umarov, T. S. (2008). *Journal of Maths.* Milan.
Umarov, Tsallis, & Steinberg. (2008). q Gaussian. *Milan Journal Math,* 307.
Vehel, & Walter. (2001). Les Marchés fractals.

Index